FILM STUDIES
An Introduction

Ed Sikov

COLUMBIA UNIVERSITY PRESS   NEW YORK

COLUMBIA UNIVERSITY PRESS

Publishers Since 1893

NEW YORK   CHICHESTER, WEST SUSSEX

Library of Congress Cataloging-in-Publication Data
Sikov, Ed.
    Film studies : an introduction / Ed Sikov.
        p. cm. — (Film and culture)
    Includes index.
    ISBN 978-0-231-14292-2 (cloth : alk. paper) — ISBN 978-0-231-14293-9 (pbk. : alk.
paper) — ISBN 978-0-231-51989-2 (ebook)
    1. Motion pictures.   I. Title.   II. Series.
    PN1994.S535 2010   2009033082

Columbia University Press books are printed on permanent and durable acid-free paper.

This book is printed on paper with recycled content.
Printed in the United States of America

References to Internet Web sites (URLs) were accurate at the time of writing. Neither the author nor Columbia University Press is responsible for URLs that may have expired or changed since the manuscript was prepared.

The author and Columbia University Press gratefully acknowledge permission to quote material from John Belton, *American Cinema/American Culture*, 3d ed. (New York: McGraw-Hill, 2008); copyright © 2008 The McGraw-Hill Companies, Inc.

for **Adam Orman**
and the other great students in my life

for **John Belton**
and the other great teachers in my life

CONTENTS

PREFACE: WHAT THIS BOOK IS—AND WHAT IT'S NOT   XI

INTRODUCTION: 1

REPRESENTATION AND REALITY

ONE **MISE-EN-SCENE: WITHIN THE IMAGE**   **5**

What Is Mise-en-Scene?   5

The Shot   7

Subject-Camera Distance—Why It Matters   9

Camera Angle   12

Space and Time on Film   16

Composition   18

STUDY GUIDE: ANALYZING THE SHOT   **21**

WRITING ABOUT THE IMAGE

TWO **MISE-EN-SCENE: CAMERA MOVEMENT**   **24**

Mobile Framing   24

Types of Camera Movement   25

Editing within the Shot   28

Space and Movement   30

STUDY GUIDE: ANALYZING CAMERA MOVEMENT   **34**

WRITING ABOUT CAMERA MOVEMENT

THREE **MISE-EN-SCENE: CINEMATOGRAPHY**   **38**

Motion Picture Photography   38

Aspect Ratio: From 1:33 to Widescreen   39

Aspect Ratio: Form and Meaning   42

Lighting   44

Three-Point Lighting   45

Film Stocks: Super 8 to 70mm to Video   48

Black, White, Gray, and Color   49

A Word or Two about Lenses   50

STUDY GUIDE: ANALYZING CINEMATOGRAPHY   **53**

WRITING ABOUT CINEMATOGRAPHY

FOUR **EDITING: FROM SHOT TO SHOT**   **55**

   Transitions   55

   Montage   57

   The Kuleshov Experiment   60

   Continuity Editing   61

   The 180° System   67

   Shot/Reverse-Shot Pattern   68

STUDY GUIDE: ANALYZING SHOT-TO-SHOT EDITING   **70**

WRITING ABOUT EDITING

FIVE **SOUND**   **74**

   A Very Short History of Film Sound   74

   Recording, Rerecording, Editing, and Mixing   76

   Analytical Categories of Film Sound   78

   Sound and Space   81

STUDY GUIDE: HEARING SOUND, ANALYZING SOUND   **84**

WRITING ABOUT SOUND AND SOUNDTRACKS

SIX **NARRATIVE: FROM SCENE TO SCENE**   **89**

   Narrative Structure   89

   Story and Plot   90

   Scenes and Sequences   91

   Transitions from Scene to Scene   95

   Character, Desire, and Conflict   97

   Analyzing Conflict   98

STUDY GUIDE: ANALYZING SCENE-TO-SCENE EDITING   **101**

WRITING ABOUT NARRATIVE STRUCTURE

SEVEN **FROM SCREENPLAY TO FILM**   **103**

   Deeper into Narrative Structure   103

   Screenwriting: The Three-Act Structure   104

   Segmentation: Form   105

   Segmentation: Meaning   107

     A Segmentation of *Inside Man*   108

STUDY GUIDE: STORY ANALYSIS AND SEGMENTATION   **113**

WRITING ABOUT WRITING

EIGHT **FILMMAKERS**   **116**

   Film—A Director's Art?   116

   Authorship   117

   The Auteur Theory   119

   The Producer's Role   121

   Teamwork   123

STUDY GUIDE: THE PROBLEM OF ATTRIBUTION   **126**

WRITING ABOUT DIRECTORS

NINE **PERFORMANCE**   **129**

    Performance as an Element of Mise-en-Scene   129

    Acting Styles   130

    Stars and Character Actors   131

    Type and Stereotype   132

    Women as Types   133

    Acting in—and on—Film   134

    Publicity: Extra-Filmic Meaning   136

STUDY GUIDE: ANALYZING ACTING   **138**

WRITING ABOUT ACTING

TEN **GENRE**   **143**

    What Is a Genre?   143

    Conventions, Repetitions, and Variations   145

    A Brief Taxonomy of Two Film Genres—the Western   146

    and the Horror Film

    Genre: The Semantic/Syntactic Approach   148

    Film Noir: A Case Study   150

        Film Noir: A Brief History   152

        Film Noir's Conventions   153

STUDY GUIDE: GENRE ANALYSIS FOR THE INTRODUCTORY STUDENT   **155**

WRITING ABOUT GENRES

ELEVEN **SPECIAL EFFECTS**   **158**

    Beyond the Ordinary   158

    Optical and Mechanical Special Effects   162

    Computer-Generated Imagery (CGI)   164

STUDY GUIDE: EFFECTS AND MEANING   **166**

WRITING ABOUT SPECIAL EFFECTS

TWELVE **PUTTING IT TOGETHER: A MODEL 8- TO 10-PAGE PAPER**   **169**

    How This Chapter Works   169

    "Introducing Tyler," by Robert Paulson   170

GLOSSARY   187

ACKNOWLEDGMENTS   199

INDEX   201

This book is designed to provide a basic introduction to the academic discipline known as film studies. It covers, in the first eleven chapters, the fundamental elements of formal film analysis, from the expressive content of individual images to the ways in which images link with one another; from the structures of narrative screenplays to the basics of cinematography, special effects, and sound. The book's final chapter is a step-by-step guide to writing a final paper for the kind of course for which this textbook has been written.

Film Studies is a primer—a pared-down introduction to the field. It is aimed at beginners. It simplifies things, which is to say that the information it contains is straightforward and aimed at every student who is willing to learn it. It's complicated material, but only to a point. The goal here is not to ask and answer every question, cover every issue and term, and point out the exceptions that accompany every rule. Instead, *Film Studies* tries to cover the subject of narrative cinema accurately but broadly, precisely but not comprehensively. It is a relatively short book, not a doorstop or makeshift dumbbell. It isn't meant to cover anything more than the basic elements of formal film studies.

This book is about feature-length narrative cinema—movies that tell fictional stories that last from about ninety minutes to three or three and a half hours. It does not cover documentaries, which are about real people and events. It's not that documentary filmmaking is not worth studying; on the contrary. It's just that *Film Studies* is strictly an introduction to narrative cinema. Similarly, there is nothing in *Film Studies* about avant-garde films—those motion pictures that are radically experimental and noncommercial in nature. Film history is full of great avant-garde works, but that mode of filmmaking is not what *this* book is about.

People who study movies think about them in different and divergent ways. Scholars have explored sociological issues (race, ethnicity, religion, and class as depicted in films) and psychological issues (how movies express otherwise hidden ideas about gender and sexuality, for instance, or how audiences respond to comedies as opposed to horror films), to cite only a few of the various lenses through which we can view films. Researchers can devote themselves entirely to the study of film history—the nuts-and-bolts names, dates, and ideas of technological and aesthetic innovation that occurred on a global level. Similarly, the study of individual national cinemas has provided critical audiences with a broad range of cinematic styles to pursue, pinpoint, and enjoy.

Film Studies is not about any of these subjects. It is, to repeat, a primer, not an exhaustive examination of film interpretation, though the book has been expressly designed to accompany as wide a variety of film courses as possible.

This book centers on aspects of film form. You will learn the critical and technical language of the cinema and the ways in which formal devices work to create expressive meaning. Hopefully, if you go on to study film from a psychological or sociological perspective, or explore a particular national cinema, or take an upper-level film course of any kind, you will use the knowledge you gain here to go that much deeper into the films you see and study. This book serves as a first step. If this turns out to be your only exposure to film studies, you will still be able to bring to bear what you learn here to any film you ever see in the future.

Most film textbooks are awash in titles, names, and dates, and *Film Studies* is in certain ways no different—except in degree. In order to illustrate various points with examples, *Film Studies* does refer to a number of real movies that were made by important filmmakers at specific times in the course of film history. But in my experience, introductory students, when faced with the title and even the briefest description of a film they have never seen (and most likely will never see), tend to tune out. As a result, I draw a number of examples in *Film Studies* from hypothetical films; I will ask you to use your own imagination rather than draw impossibly on knowledge you don't already have about films you haven't seen. Moreover, each individual film class has its own screening list. Indeed, from a professor's perspective, one of the great pleasures of teaching cinema studies classes lies in picking the films to show and discuss. *Film Studies* tries not to get in the way of individual professors' tastes. In short, this book does not come with its own prearranged list of films you must see.

Some film studies textbooks contain hundreds of illustrations—film stills, drawings, graphs, and frame enlargements, many of which are in color. *Film Studies* does offer illustrations when necessary, but in order to keep the book affordable, they are not a prominent feature.

In fact, *Film Studies* tries to be as practical and useful as possible in many ways. It aims for the widest readership and is pitched accordingly. It draws most of its examples from American films because they are the films that most American students have seen in the past and are likely to see in the future. It is designed to accompany a wide spectrum of film courses but is focused most clearly on the type of mainstream "Introduction to Film" class that is taught in practically every college and university in the United States and Canada.

I hope it works for you.

Film Studies

REPRESENTATION AND REALITY

Consider the word REPRESENTATION (see glossary). What does it mean—and what technology does it take—to represent real people or physical objects on film? These are two of the basic questions in film studies. The dictionary defines the verb *to represent* as "to stand for; to symbolize; to indicate or communicate by signs or symbols." That's all well and good as far as it goes. But in the first one hundred years of motion pictures, the signs and symbols onscreen were almost always *real* before they ended up as signs and symbols on movie screens.

We take for granted certain things about painting and literature, chief among them that the objects and people depicted in paint or described in words do not necessarily have a physical reality. You can paint a picture of a woman without using a model or even without having a specific real woman in your mind. You can paint landscapes you've never actually seen, and in fact you don't have to paint any real objects at all. Your painting can be entirely nonrepresentational—just splashes of color or streaks of black paint. And bear in mind that all works of art, in addition to being representations, are also real things themselves. The woman Leonardo da Vinci painted against a mysterious landscape may or may not have existed, but the painting commonly known as the *Mona Lisa* is certainly a real, material object.

In literature, too, writers describe cities that never existed and people who never lived. But on film—at least narrative films like the ones you're going to learn about in this book—directors have to have something real to photograph. Now, with the increased use of digital and computer-generated imagery (CGI), of course, things are changing in that regard, but that's a subject for a later chapter. For the time being, consider the fact that in classical world cinema, in all but a few very rare cases, directors had to have something real to photograph with a film camera. A filmmaker could conceivably take a strip of CELLULOID—the plastic material that film is made of—and draw on it or paint it or dig scratches into its surface; experimental filmmakers have been known to use celluloid as a kind of canvas for nonrepresentational art. But otherwise a filmmaker must photograph real people and things. They may be actors wearing makeup and costumes, but they're still real human beings. These actors may be walking through constructed **sets**, but these sets have a physical reality; walls that look like stone may actually be made of painted wood, but *they are still real, material walls.*

Even animated films are photographed: artists paint a series of ANIMATION CELS, and then each cel is photographed. The physical reality of *The Hunchback of Notre Dame*—the Walt Disney movie, not the Victor Hugo novel—is not the character of Quasimodo, nor is it an actor playing Quasimodo, but rather the elaborate, colorful, stylized drawings that had to be photographed, processed, and run through a projector to make them move. Those drawings have a physical reality, and Disney animators are masters at making them seem doubly real through shading, layering, and other means of creating a sense of depth.

Let's approach this issue another way. If Picasso, Warhol, and Rembrandt each painted a portrait of the same person, most educated people would immediately understand that the result would be three very different-looking paintings. We recognize that a painting's meaning is at least partly a matter of its FORM—the shape and structure of the art work. Even if three painters from the same general culture in the same general period painted the same person—say, Rembrandt, Hals, and Vermeer—we would see three different views of that person—three very different paintings.

The same holds true in literature. If, say, Ernest Hemingway, James Joyce, and Chuck Palahniuk all described the same person, we would end up reading three diverse pieces of prose. They'd all be written in English, and they'd be describing the same individual, but they simply wouldn't *read* the same. Some details may be similar, but each writer would describe those details differently using different words and sentence structures. And because the form would be different in each case, we would take away from the writing three different impressions—three ways of thinking and expressing and feeling.

But photography, particularly motion picture photography, appears on the surface to be of a different order. You take a real thing, and you photograph it. You take an event and you film it. And unless you monkey with the camera or the film processing and do all kinds of things to deliberately call attention to your presence as the filmmaker, if you and your friend and her friend and her friend's friend all filmed the same event, you would all come up with similar looking films—or so you might assume.

This book will show you how and why each of your films would be different and why those differences matter to the art form. You will learn to see the ways in which filmmakers express ideas and emotions with their cameras.

For example, let's say that three aspiring directors—all from the University of Pittsburgh—decide to film what they each consider to be a characteristic scene at a major league baseball game. The three film students head over to PNC Park with nothing but small video cameras, and they don't leave their seats in the right field grandstand. Ethan is planning to use his footage in the ROMANTIC COMEDY he's making based on a guy he knows who is obsessed with one of the Pirates' infielders. Ethan's friend, Shin Lae, is making a drama about a little boy with autism who loves baseball. And Shin Lae's friend, Sanjana, hasn't yet figured out what her story will be let alone how she will develop it, but she already knows that she wants to include random shots taken at a baseball game.

When the Pirates' Luis Cruz hits a foul ball into the stands, the three filmmakers each have their cameras running. It's the same moment in time, the same foul ball, but the three young directors see the event from three different perspectives. Ethan wants to show the whole action from beginning to end in a continuous shot, so just before the windup he frames the pitcher, batter, and catcher in the same image so he can show the ball move from mound to plate to air and, eventually, thanks to his ability to move the camera he's holding, the ball finds its way into a fan's bare fist. His built-in microphone picks up the sharp crack of the bat connecting with the ball, the crowd's initial roar of expectation, the collective groan of disappointment when the ball crosses the foul line, and finally a quick burst of distant applause at the fan's catch.

Shin Lae, on the other hand, cares more about the boisterous reaction of a group of Cub Scouts nearby than she does about the particular batter or the events of the game itself. When she notices that the pitcher is about to wind up, she points her camera not at either the pitcher or the batter but instead at the scouts, who are a few rows above her. She simply records the boys' shouts and facial expressions, which range from eagerness to glee to disappointment and finally to envy as the fan successfully nabs the ball. Sanjana, meanwhile, has not been paying attention to the baseball game at all. (She hates sports and has only agreed to come along in order to film things.) While Ethan and Shin Lae get increasingly wrapped up by the game, Sanjana has become fascinated by a group of shirtless, heavily tattooed, and increasingly drunk bikers to her right. She has already filmed a security guard telling them to quiet down, but something about this group of urban outlaws appeals to her—particularly the fattest, hairiest one. She aims her camera on him and him alone and just films him sitting there, yelling, drinking, swearing, and—eventually—raising his hairy paw and nabbing Luis Cruz's foul ball to the cheers of the crowd. She tilts her camera up slightly to keep his head from leaving the image, and tilts it back down when the crowd stops cheering and the biker takes his seat again.

Same game + same scene + same action = three different films. Why? Because each filmmaker has made a series of choices, and each of those choices has artistic, expressive consequences.

This is one of the key aesthetic issues of cinema studies—learning to see that an apparently unmediated event is in fact a mediated work of art. At first glance, we tend not to see the mediation involved in the cinema; we don't see the *art*. All we see—at first—is a representation of the physical reality of what has been photographed. And in a strange paradox, classical American filmmaking is saddled with the notion that it's purely artificial. The lighting tends to be idealized, the actors' faces are idealized by makeup, the settings are sometimes idealized. . . . Just to describe something as "a Hollywood vision of life" is to say that it's phony. The objects and people in Hollywood films are thus too real and too fake, all at the same time. How can we make sense of this?

CHAPTER 1
MISE-EN-SCENE: WITHIN THE IMAGE

WHAT IS MISE-EN-SCENE?

Film studies deals with the problems of reality and representation by making an initial assumption and proceeding logically from it. This assumption is that all representations have meaning. The term MISE-EN-SCENE (*also* mise-en-scène) describes the primary feature of cinematic representation. Mise-en-scene is the first step in understanding how films produce and reflect meaning. It's a term taken from the French, and it means *that which has been put into the scene* or *put onstage*. Everything—literally everything—in the filmed image is described by the term *mise-en-scene*: it's the expressive totality of what you see in a single film image. Mise-en-scene consists of *all of the elements placed in front of the camera to be photographed: settings, props, lighting, costumes, makeup, and figure behavior (meaning actors, their gestures, and their facial expressions).* In addition, *mise-en-scene includes the camera's actions and angles and the cinematography*, which simply means photography for motion pictures. Since *everything* in the filmed image comes under the heading of mise-en-scene, the term's definition is a mouthful, so a shorter definition is this: *Mise-en-scene is the totality of expressive content within the image.* Film studies assumes that everything within the image has expressive meanings. By analyzing mise-en-scene, we begin to see what those meanings might be.

The term *mise-en-scene* was first used in the theater to describe the staging of an action. A theater director takes a script, written and printed on the page, and makes each scene come alive on a stage with a particular set of actors, a unique set design, a certain style of lighting, and so on. The script says that a scene is set in, say, a suburban living room. Okay, you're the director, and your task is to create a suburban living room scene on stage and make it work not as an interchangeable, indistinguishable suburban living room, but as the specific living room of the particular suburban characters the playwright has described on the page—characters you are trying to bring to life onstage. The same holds true in the cinema: the director starts from scratch and stages the scene for the camera, and every element of the resulting image has expressive meaning. Even when a film is shot on LOCATION—at a preexisting, real place—the director has chosen that location for its expressive value.

It's important to note that mise-en-scene *does not* have anything to do with whether a given scene is "realistic" or not. As in the theater, film studies doesn't judge mise-en-scene by how closely it mimics the world we live in. Just as a theater director might want to create a thoroughly warped suburban living room set with oversized furniture and distorted walls and bizarrely shaped doors in order to express her feeling that the characters who live in this house are crazy, so a film director creates mise-en-scene according to the impression he or she wishes to create. Sometimes mise-en-scene is relatively realistic looking, and sometimes it isn't.

Here's the first shot of a hypothetical film we're making: we see a man standing up against a wall. The wall is made of . . . what? Wood? Concrete? Bricks? Let's say bricks. Some of the bricks are chipped. The wall is . . . what color? White? No, let's say it's red. It's a new wall. No, it's an old wall, and some graffiti has been painted on it, but even the graffiti is old and faded. Is it indoors or outdoors? Day or night? We'll go with outdoors in the afternoon. The man is . . . what? Short? No, he's tall. And he's wearing . . . what? A uniform—a blue uniform. With a badge.

Bear in mind, nothing has happened yet in our film—we just have a policeman standing against a wall. But the more mise-en-scene details we add, the more visual information we give to our audience, and the more precise our audience's emotional response will be to the image we are showing them. But also bear in mind the difference between written prose and filmed image. As readers, you have just been presented with all of these details in verbal form, so necessarily you've gotten the information sequentially. With a film image, we seem to see it all at once. Nothing is isolated the way things are in this written description. With film, we take in all the visual information quickly, *and we do so without being aware that we're taking it in.* As it happens, studies of human perception have proven that we actually take in visual information sequentially as well, though a great deal more speedily than we do written information. Moreover, filmmakers find ways of directing our gaze to specific areas in the image by manipulating compositions, colors, areas of focus, and so on. By examining each of these aspects of cinema, film studies attempts to wake us up to what's in front of us onscreen—to make us all more conscious of what we're seeing and why.

To continue with our example of mise-en-scene: the man is handsome in a Brad Pitt sort of way. He's a white guy. In his late thirties. But he's got a black eye. And there's a trace of blood on his lower lip.

So we've got a cop and a wall and some stage blood, and we film him with a motion picture or video camera. Nothing has happened by chance here; we, the filmmakers, have made a series of artistic decisions even before we have turned on the camera. Even if we happen to have just stumbled upon this good-looking cop with a black eye standing against a brick wall and bleeding from the mouth, it's our decision not only to film him but to use that footage in our film. If we decide to use the footage, we have made an expressive statement with it. And we have done so with only one shot that's maybe six seconds long. This is the power of mise-en-scene.

What's our next shot? A body lying nearby? An empty street? Another cop? A giant slimy alien? All of these things are possible, and all of them are going to give our audience even more information about the first shot. Subsequent shots stand in relation to the first shot, and by the time you get to the tenth or twentieth or hundredth shot, the sheer amount of expressive information—the content of individual shots, and the relationships from shot to shot—is staggering. But we're getting ahead of ourselves; this is the subject of chapter 4.

THE SHOT

By the way: what is a SHOT? *A shot is the basic element of filmmaking—a piece of film run through the camera, exposed, and developed; an uninter-*

rupted run of the camera; or an uninterrupted image on film. That's it: you turn the camera on, you let it run, you turn it off, and the result—provided that you have remembered to put film in the camera—is a shot. It's an unedited shot, but it's a shot nonetheless. It's the basic building block of the movies.

Despite the use of the word *scene* in the term *mise-en-scene*, mise-en-scene describes the content not only of a sequence of shots but of an individual shot. A shot is a unit of length or duration—a minimal unit of dramatic material; a scene is a longer unit *usually* consisting of several shots or more.

Even at the basic level of a single shot, mise-en-scene yields meaning. The first shot of an important character is itself important in this regard. Here's an example: Imagine that you are going to film a murder movie, and you need to introduce your audience to a woman who is going to be killed later on in the film. What does the first shot of this woman look like? What does *she* look like? Because of the expressive importance of mise-en-scene, every detail matters. Every detail is a statement of meaning, whether you want it to be or not. (These are precisely the questions Alfred Hitchcock faced when he made his groundbreaking 1960 film, *Psycho*.) Is she pretty? *What does that mean?* What is she wearing? *What does that mean?* If she's really attractive and wearing something skimpy—well, are you saying she deserves to be killed? What if she's actually quite ugly—what are you saying there? Do you want your audience to like her or dislike her? It's your choice—you're the director. So what signals are you going to send to your audience to get that emotion across? Let's say you're going to put something on the wall behind her. And it's . . . a big stuffed bird. No, it's . . . a pair of Texas longhorns. No, it's . . . a broken mirror. No, it's a crucifix. Or maybe it's just a big empty wall. Each of these props adds meaning to the shot, as does the absence of props and decorative elements.

This is why mise-en-scene is important: it tells us something above and beyond the event itself. Again: *mise-en-scene is the totality of expressive content within the image.* And every detail has a meaningful consequence.

Let's say you're filming a shot outdoors and a bird flies into the camera's field of vision and out the other side. Suddenly, a completely accidental event is in your movie. Do you keep it? Do you use that shot, or do you film another one? Your film is going to be slightly different whichever TAKE you choose. (A *take* is a single recording of a shot. If the director doesn't like something that occurs in Take 1, she may run the shot again by calling out "Take 2"—and again and again—"Take 22"—"Take 35"—"Take 59"—until she is ready to call "print!") If you're making the kind of film in which everything is formally strict and controlled, then you probably don't want the bird. If however you're trying to capture a kind of random and unpredictable quality, then your little bird accident is perfect. When film students discuss your work, they'll be talking about the bird—the significance of random events of nature, perhaps even the symbolism of flight. That bird is now part of your film's mise-en-scene, and it's expressing something—whether you want it to or not. Whether critics or audiences at the multiplex specifically notice it or not, *it's there*. It's a part of the art work. It's in the film, and therefore it has expressive meaning.

Here's an example from a real film called *Gentlemen Prefer Blondes*, a 1953 musical comedy starring Marilyn Monroe and Jane Russell. There's a scene in which Jane Russell performs a musical number with a crew of athletes on the American Olympic team. The number was supposed to end with a couple of the muscle boys diving over Jane Russell's shoulders as she sits by the side of a swimming pool. As it turned out, however, one of the actors accidentally kicked her in the head as he attempted to dive over her into the pool. With the camera still running, the film's glamorous star got knocked violently into the water and came up looking like the proverbial drowned rat. It was obviously an accident. But the director, Howard Hawks, decided to use that take instead of any of the accident-free retakes he and his choreographer subsequently filmed. Something about the accident appealed to Hawks's sensibility: it expressed something visually about sex and sex roles and gender and animosity and the failure of romance. There's a sudden and shocking shift in mise-en-scene, as Jane Russell goes from being the classically made-up Hollywood movie star in a carefully composed shot to being dunked in a pool and coming up sputtering for air, her hair all matted down, and improvising the end of the song. Hawks liked that version better; it said what he wanted to say, even though it happened entirely by chance. The shot, initially a mistake, took on expressive meaning through its inclusion in the film.

SUBJECT-CAMERA DISTANCE—WHY IT MATTERS

At the end of Billy Wilder's *Sunset Boulevard* (1950), an aging star turns to her director and utters the famous line, "I'm ready for my close-up." But what exactly is a close-up? Or a long shot? And why do these terms matter?

One way directors have of providing expressive shading to each shot they film is to vary the distance between the camera and the subject being filmed. Every rule has its exceptions, of course, but in general, the closer the camera is to the subject, the more emotional weight the subject gains. (To be more precise, it's really a matter of how close the camera's lens makes the subject seem to be; this is because a camera's lens may bring the subject closer optically even when the camera is physically far away from the subject. See the glossary's definition of TELEPHOTO LENS for clarification.) If we see an empty living room and hear the sound of a telephone ringing on the soundtrack but we can't immediately find the telephone onscreen, the call may seem relatively unimportant. But if the director quickly cuts to a CLOSE-UP of the telephone, suddenly the phone call assumes great significance. Because the director has moved the camera close to it, the phone—once lost in the living room set—becomes not only isolated within the room but enormous on the screen.

A close-up is a shot that isolates an object in the image, making it appear relatively large. A close-up of a human being is generally of that person's face. An **extreme close-up** might be of the person's eyes—or mouth—or nose—or any element isolated at very close range in the image.

Other subject-camera-distance terms are also simple and self-explanatory. A MEDIUM SHOT appears to be taken from a medium distance; in terms of the human body, it's from the waist up. A THREE-QUARTER SHOT takes in the human body from just below the knees; a FULL SHOT is of the entire human body. A LONG SHOT appears to be taken from a long distance. Remember: lenses are able to create the illusion of distance or closeness. A director could conceivably usea *telephoto lens* on a camera that is rather distant from the subject and still create a close-up. The actual physical position of the camera at the time of the filming isn't the issue—it's what the image looks like onscreen that matters. The critical task is not to try to determine where the camera was actually placed during filming, or whether a telephoto lens was used to create the shot, but rather to begin to notice the *expressive* results of subject-camera distance onscreen.

There are gradations. You can have **medium close-ups**, taken from the chest up; **extreme long shots**, which show the object or person at a vast distance surrounded by a great amount of the surrounding space. If, at the end of a western, the final shot of the film is an extreme long shot of an outlaw riding off alone into the desert, the director may be using the shot to convey the character's isolation from civilization, his solitude; we would see him in the far distance surrounded by miles of empty desert. Imagine how different we would feel about this character if, instead of seeing him in extreme long shot, we saw his weather-beaten face in close-up as the final image of the film. We would be emotionally

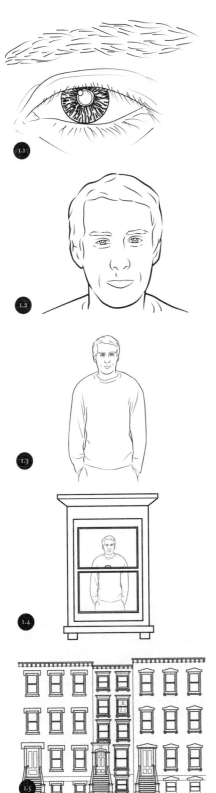

FIGURE 1.1 Extreme close-up: a single eye dominates the image.

FIGURE 1.2 Close-up: the character's face fills most of the screen.

FIGURE 1.3 Medium shot: the character appears from the waist up.

FIGURE 1.4 Long shot: because the camera has moved back even further, the character now appears in a complete spatial context.

FIGURE 1.5 Extreme long shot: the camera is now very far away from the character, thereby dwarfing him onscreen. What are the emotionally expressive qualities of each of these illustrations (figs. 1.1 through 1.5)?

as well as physically closer to him at that moment because we would be able to read into his face the emotions he was feeling. His subtlest expressions—a slightly raised eyebrow, a tensing of the mouth—would fill the screen.

Here's a final observation on subject-camera distance: Each film establishes its own shot scale, just as each filmmaker establishes his or her own style. Whereas Orson Welles in *Citizen Kane* (1941) employs an extreme close-up of Kane's lips as he says the key word, "Rosebud," Howard Hawks would never push his camera so close to a character's mouth and isolate it in that way. The Danish director Carl Theodor Dreyer shot his masterpiece *The Passion of Joan of Arc* (1928) almost entirely in close-ups; as a result, what would be a long shot for Dreyer might be a medium shot for John Ford or Billy Wilder. If we begin with the idea that the human body is generally the measure for subject-camera distance, then the concept's relativity becomes clear: a close-up is only a close-up *in relation to something else*—the whole body, for example. The same holds true for objects and landscape elements. In short, we must appreciate the fact that subject-camera distances are relative both within individual films—the sequence in *Citizen Kane* that includes the extreme close-up of Kane uttering "Rosebud" begins with an equally extreme long shot of his mansion—and from film to film: Dreyer's close-ups differ in scale from those used by Ford or Wilder.

CAMERA ANGLE

In addition to subject-camera distance, directors employ different camera angles to provide expressive content to the subjects they film. When directors simply want to film a person or room or landscape from an angle that seems unobtrusive and normal (whatever the word *normal* actually means), they place the camera at the level of an adult's eyes, which is to say five or six feet off the ground when the characters are standing, lower when they are seated. This, not surprisingly, is called an EYE-LEVEL SHOT.

When the director shoots his or her subjects from below, the result is a LOW-ANGLE SHOT; with a low-angle shot, the camera is in effect looking up at the subject. And when he or she shoots the subject from above, the result is a HIGH-ANGLE SHOT; the camera is looking down. An extreme overhead shot, taken seemingly from the sky or ceiling and looking straight down on the subject, is known as a BIRD'S-EYE VIEW.

The terms *close-up*, *low-angle shot*, *extreme long shot*, and others assume that the camera is facing the subject squarely, and for the most part

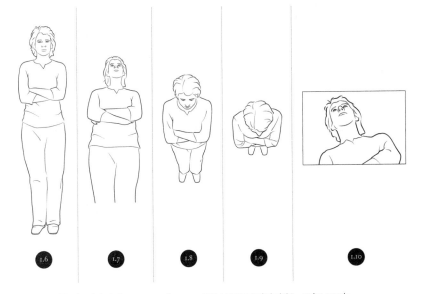

FIGURE 1.6 Eye-level shot: the camera places us at the character's height—we're equals.

FIGURE 1.7 Low-angle shot: we're looking up at her; low-angle shots sometimes aggrandize the shot's subject.

FIGURE 1.8 High-angle shot: we're looking down at her now; this type of shot may suggest a certain superiority over a character.

FIGURE 1.9 Bird's-eye shot: this shot is taken from the highest possible angle. What might be the expressive consequences of this shot?

FIGURE 1.10 Dutch tilt (or canted angle) shot: the camera is not on its normal horizontal or vertical axes, and the resulting image is off-kilter; Dutch tilts are sometimes used to suggest a character's unbalanced mental state.

shots in feature films are indeed taken straight-on. But a camera can tilt laterally on its axis, too. When the camera tilts horizontally and/or vertically it's called a DUTCH TILT or a **canted angle**.

Of everything you read in this book, the opposite also may be true at times, since every attempt to define a phenomenon necessarily reduces it by ignoring some of the quirks that make films continually interesting. There's a fine line to tread between providing a useful basic definition that you want and need and alerting you to complications or outright contradictions that qualify the definition. This is certainly true with any discussion of the expressive tendencies of low-angle and high-angle shots. Typically, directors use low-angle shots to aggrandize their subjects. After all, "to look up to someone" means that you admire that person. And high-angle shots, because they look down on the subject, are often used to subtly criticize the subject by making him or her seem slightly diminished, or to distance an audience emotionally from the character. At times, a camera angle can in fact distort the object onscreen. By foreshortening an object, for example, a very high angle shot does make an object or person appear smaller, while a very low angle can do the opposite.

But these are just broad tendencies, and as always, the effect of a particular camera angle depends on the context in which it appears. Film scholars can point to hundreds of examples in classical cinema in which a high- or low-angle shot produces an unexpected effect. In *Citizen Kane*, for instance, Welles chooses to film his central character in a low-angle shot at precisely the moment of his greatest humiliation, and a technical device that is often employed to signal admiration achieves exactly the opposite effect by making Kane look clumsy and too big for his surroundings, and therefore more pitiable and pathetic.

FIGURE 1.11 Two-shot: the definition is self-explanatory, but note the equalizing quality of this type of shot; these two characters have the same visual weight in a single shot.

FIGURE 1.12 Three-shot: the two-shot's socially balanced quality expands to include a third person, but note the greater subject-camera distance that goes along with it in this example.

FIGURE 1.13 Master shot: the whole set—in this case, a dining room—and all the characters are taken in by this type of shot.

1.12

1.13

Shots can also be defined by the number of people in the image. Were a director to call for a close-up of his protagonist, the assumption would be that a single face would dominate the screen. When a director sets up a TWO-SHOT, he or she creates a shot in which two people appear, generally in medium distance or closer, though of course there can be two-shots of a couple or other type of pair walking that would reveal more of their lower bodies. The point is that two-shots are dominated spatially by two people, making them ideal for conversations.

A THREE-SHOT, of course, contains three people—not three people surrounded by a crowd, but three people who are framed in such a way as to constitute a distinct group.

Finally, a MASTER SHOT is a shot taken from a long distance that includes as much of the set or location as possible as well all the characters in the scene. For example, a scene set in a dining room could be filmed in master shot if the camera was placed so that it captured the whole dining table, at least two of the four walls, all of the people sitting around the table, and maybe the bottom of a chandelier hanging over the table. The director could run the entire scene from beginning to end and, later, intercut close-ups, two-shots, and three-shots for visual variation and dramatic emphasis.

SPACE AND TIME ON FILM

Like dance and theater, film is an art of both space and time. Choreographers move their dancers around a stage for a given amount of time, and so do theater directors with their actors. But a dance can run slower or faster some nights, especially if it isn't connected to a piece of music. And if the actors in a play skip some of their lines or even talk faster than usual in a given performance, the play can run shorter some nights than others.

But a 110-minute film will be a 110-minute film every time it is screened, whether on the silver screen at a multiplex or on a standard-speed DVD player in your living room. This is because sound film runs at a standard **24 frames per second**, and it does so *not only through the camera when each shot is individually filmed but also through the projector when it is played in a theater.* In the early days of cinema, camera operators cranked the film through their cameras by hand at a speed hovering as close as possible between 16 and 18 frames per second. If camera operators wanted to speed actions up onscreen, they would UNDERCRANK, or crank slower: fewer frames would be filmed per second, so when that footage was run through a standard projector at a standard speed, the action would appear to speed up. If they wanted to create a slow-motion effect, they would do the opposite: they would OVERCRANK, or crank faster, causing the projector to slow the movement down when the shot was projected. In short, undercranking produces fast motion, while overcranking produces slow motion.

The introduction of SYNCHRONIZED SOUND FILM—characters being seen and heard speaking at the same time onscreen—in the late 1920s meant that the IMAGE TRACKS and the SOUNDTRACKS had to be both recorded and projected at the same speed so as to avoid distortion. 24 frames per second was the standard speed that the industry chose. You'll learn more about sound technology in chapter 5. And although videotape—unlike film's celluloid—is not divided into individual frames, the same principle applies: video's electromagnetic tape is recorded at the same speed at which it is transmitted and screened. A 60-minute video will always run 60 minutes—no more, no less.

There is a philosophical point to film's technical apprehension of time. Unlike any other art form, motion pictures capture a seemingly exact sense of real time passing. As the great Hollywood actor James Stewart once described it, motion pictures are like "pieces of time." Then again, a distinction must be made between **real time**, the kind measured by clocks, and **reel time**—the pieces of time that, for example, Spike Lee manipulated by editing to create *Malcolm X*, a film that covers the central events of a 39-year-old man's life in 202 minutes.

One familiar complication, of course, is that when films are shown on television they are often LEXICONNED to fit them into a time slot and squeeze in more commercials. *Lexiconning* involves speeding up the

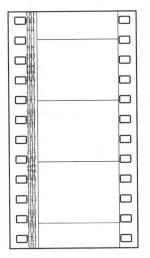

FIGURE 1.14 A strip of celluloid, divided by frames, with the soundtrack running vertically down the left alongside the image frames.

standard 24 frames per second by a matter of mere hundredths of a frame per second to as much as one frame per second, which may shorten the film by as much as 6 or 7 percent of its total running time. Also note the familiar warning that accompanies movies on TV: "Viewer discretion is advised. The following film has been modified from its original version. It has been formatted to fit this screen and edited to run in the time slot allotted and for content." People who love films hate this Procrustean process. (Procrustes was a mythical king who had a bed to which he strapped and tortured his victims. Those who were too short for the bed were stretched to fit it, and those too tall had their heads and legs chopped off.) Would an art gallery trim the top, bottom, and sides of a painting just so it would fit into a preexisting frame?

COMPOSITION

One confusing aspect of film studies terminology is that the word FRAME has two distinct meanings. The first, described above, refers to each individual rectangle on which a single image is photographed as the strip of celluloid runs through a projector. That's what we're talking about when we say that film is recorded and projected at 24 *frames* per second: 24 of those little rectangles are first filled with photographic images when they are exposed to light through a lens, and then these frames are projected at the same speed onto a screen.

But the word *frame* also describes the borders of the image onscreen—the rectangular frame of darkness on the screen that defines the edge of the image the way a picture frame defines a framed painting or photograph. Sometimes, in theaters, the screen's frame will be further defined by curtains or other masking. Your television set's frame is the metal or plastic edge that surrounds the glass screen. In fact, you can make three-quarters of a frame as you sit reading this book simply by holding your hands in front of you, palms out, and bringing your thumbs together. The top of this handmade frame is open, but you can get a good sense of why the frame is an important artistic concept in the cinema just by looking around your room and framing various objects or even yourself in a mirror.

Note that your literally handmade frame is more or less a square if you keep your thumbs together. Now create a wider rectangle by touching your right forefinger to your left thumb and vice versa. See how this framing changes the way the room looks. And be aware of the subject-camera distance and camera angle of the imaginary shots you create. Ask yourself why certain "shots" look better than others. Do you find that you have a taste for oblique angle close-ups, for example, or do you see the world more at eye level?

The precise arrangements of objects and characters within the frame—the picture-frame kind of frame—is called COMPOSITION. Each time you moved your handmade frame, you created a new composition, even if you didn't move any objects around on your desk or ask your roommate to move further away.

As in painting, composition is a crucial element of filmmaking. In fact, composition is a painterly term. (Few if any art critics ever refer to the mise-en-scene of a painting.) Composition means the relationship of lines, volumes, masses, and shapes *at a single instant* in a representation. Composition is relatively static, though few elements remain truly motionless in a motion picture; mise-en-scene is more dynamic. Mise-en-scene is the relation of everything in the shot to everything else in the shot *over the course of the shot*, though sometimes film critics can extend their discussion of compositional consistency to individual spaces represented in the film and even over the course of the entire film. One could write a great paper on any of these diverse mise-en-scenes, paying particular attention to their compositional elements: the courtyard in Hitchcock's *Rear Window* (1954), the bar's basement in David Fincher's *Fight Club* (1999), Rick's Café in Michael Curtiz's *Casablanca* (1942), or Sal's Pizzeria in Spike Lee's *Do the Right Thing* (1989).

Like a painter, a director's particular arrangement of shapes, masses, vectors, characters' bodies, textures, lighting, and so on within each film image is one of the cornerstones of his or her cinematic style. Think again of the bird that flew into the hypothetical shot described above. That example was not only an instance of meaning being produced unintentionally; it was an instance of compositional change as well. Here's a related example: If a director had taken several hours to set up a landscape shot with an eye toward a strict, static composition—a western butte on the left seen at sunset with a flock of sheep standing more or less still at closer distance on the right, and a ranch hand on a horse in near distance at more or less precisely the center of the image—and suddenly one of the sheep bolted away from the herd and went running across the camera's field of vision, that director may insist on a RETAKE with the errant sheep safely put away in a faraway pen. Why? Because he considered his composition ruined. Then again, another director might use the take with the running sheep because she might see its sudden, rapid, *lateral* movement across the screen as a beneficial if accidental addition to her composition.

Adding to the problems of cinematic composition is the fact that motion pictures are (clearly) all about *motion*, so to a certain extent almost every composition is fluid: people move, the wind blows things around, cars speed by, and the camera itself may move. Moreover, as you will learn in chapter 4, shots are connected to other shots in a process called EDITING, and the composition of one shot ought to have something to do not only with the shot that follows it but with the shot that precedes it.

One final concept in this introductory chapter: the shape of the image. Conceivably, movies could be round, couldn't they? Indeed, Thomas Edison's first films *were* round. Obviously films aren't round anymore.[1] They take the form of rectangles of various widths. The term ASPECT RATIO describes the precise relation of the width of the rectangular image to its height. Historically, aspect ratios are problematic. The silent aspect ratio was actually 1.33:1, a slightly wide rectangle, the width of the image being one and one third the size of its height. Making matters more confusing, the film industry standard—the so-called ACADEMY RATIO (named after the Academy of Motion Picture Arts and Sciences, the group that gives the Oscars, and that instituted the standard ratio in 1932)—is often referred to as being 1.33:1, but in actual fact the Academy ratio is 1.37:1—a very slightly wider rectangle than that of silent films.

All Hollywood films after 1932 were made with the standard Academy aspect ratio of 1.37:1—that is, until the 1950s, when various widescreen technologies were developed as a way of competing with television. But again, that's the subject of a later chapter.

1. One exception is the IMAX Dome or OMNIMAX system, which projects a rounded (but not circular) image on a tilted dome.

STUDY GUIDE: ANALYZING THE SHOT

You will learn through the course of reading this book that film is a complicated art form with many technical and expressive aspects, and one of the key problems in analyzing motion pictures is that that their images are in fact in motion. So to simplify things here at the beginning of the course, try the following exercise:

Get a videotape or DVD of a feature film from any period in film history. In fact, if possible, get one you've already seen and enjoyed. Fast forward to any point you choose, and then freeze-frame the image.

You are now looking at a single frame of a single shot. What do you notice about its mise-en-scene? Properly speaking, since this is a static image, a single frame, you are being asked to notice elements of its composition rather than the totality of expressive content in an entire shot. Remember what mise-en-scene means: *all of the elements placed in front of the camera to be photographed: settings, props, lighting, costumes, makeup, and figure behavior (meaning actors, their gestures, and their facial expressions).* And composition: *the relationship of lines, volumes, masses, and shapes at a single instant.* Composition is relatively static; mise-en-scene is dynamic.

Your assignment is to notice the various compositional elements in the image. Write them down in the form of a list, and be as descriptive as possible. (Instead of saying simply "Julia Roberts," for instance, describe in detail what Julia Roberts looks like—the color of her hair, the color and style of her costume, and so on.) Describe the room or the landscape in terms of its colors. How well lit is the room or outdoors space? Is it day, night, dusk, or dawn? What kind of furniture is in the room, or what landscape elements are in the image?

Is the shot taken at eye level or low angle? Is it a close-up or a long shot? Is there anything you notice about the composition?

Put all of your observations into words, and be as clear as possible.

Here is an example, drawn from *Fight Club* (David Fincher, 1999—Chapter 9, minute 21:54):

Close-up, eye-level
Man, about 30 years old, blandly handsome
Dark hair
Top of gray suit jacket
White collar of dress shirt
Man is centered on the screen
Top part of head cut out of image
Airplane interior
Blue seat with white headrest
Man in focus; background out of focus
Blue curtains center-left of image in background
Bright curved windows on right in background

FIGURE 1.15 The unnamed narrator (Edward Norton) of *Fight Club* (1999) (frame enlargement).

Aspect ratio—wide rectangle

Man in row behind, out of focus—no other people

Light on forehead and nose of man in close-up

Eyes in shadow

Dark circles under eyes

He is staring straight ahead

WRITING ABOUT THE IMAGE

The first step in writing about film is to translate the content of film images into words using the new technical vocabulary you are learning. So your first writing assignment is a simple one: take the detailed description of the shot you created above and turn it into a coherent paragraph. Don't worry about forming a thesis statement or making any sort of argument. Forget about assigning meanings to what you see onscreen or discussing the symbolism of anything. Concentrate instead on creating a single paragraph of prose that succeeds in translating an image into words. Spell-check your work when you are finished. If your word-processing application's dictionary does not contain some of the technical terms you have used, add them (after consulting the glossary at the back of this book to make sure you have spelled them correctly to begin with).

Here's an example using the above list of compositional elements from the *Fight Club* image:

The image is a close-up of a blandly handsome man who appears to be about thirty years old. He has dark hair with a conservative, businessman-type haircut. We can see the shoulders of his gray, conservative suit jacket and the white collar of his dress shirt. The man is centered on the screen; the very top part of his head is cut out by the frame. The image shows the interior of an airplane. The man is seated on a blue seat with his face framed by a white strip of material that serves as a headrest. The man is in crisp focus, but the background is out of focus. Still, we can clearly see some blue curtains in the center-left of the image, with some bright curved airplane windows on the far right in the background. The curtains match the blue of the seat; the windows, appearing white, match the headrest. The aspect ratio is that of a fairly wide rectangle. There is another man in the image—he is seated in the row behind the man in close-up—but he is the only other person in the image. The man in close-up has a bright light shining on his forehead and nose, but his eyes are notably in shadow, although we can clearly see dark circles under his eyes, indicating tiredness and a lack of sleep. The man is staring straight ahead.

CHAPTER 2

MISE-EN-SCENE: CAMERA MOVEMENT

MOBILE FRAMING

Motion pictures share a number of formal elements with other arts. The shape of a particular painting is essentially its aspect ratio—the ratio of width to height of the image—and the composition and lighting effects created by the painter play a central role in that painting's meaning, as does the distance between the artist and his or her subject. (A portrait might be the equivalent of a close-up; a landscape is usually a long shot or an extreme long shot.) The term *mise-en-scene* is derived from the theater: the arrangement and appearance of a play's sets and props, its characters' gestures and dialogue and costumes, the STORY and PLOT—all come together toward an expressive goal, just as in motion pictures. Novels, too, have stories and plots that can (and should) be analyzed for meaning.

Film offers something unique: MOBILE FRAMING. In the first chapter of *Film Studies*, we made an assumption that turns out to be false: that the camera is static. All the definitions and examples implied that characters and objects move within the frame, but the framing stays the same within each shot. In fact, this is not the case at all. The camera can move from side to side, up and down, backward and forward, all of the above, and more. Editing from shot to shot or scene to scene changes the position of the spectator from shot to shot or scene to scene, but camera movement shifts the spectator's position *within the shot.*

No other art form is able to accomplish this feat. In painting, Cubism plays with the idea of expressing multiple perspectives of a single subject, but Cubist paintings inevitably and necessarily have an immobile frame owing to the nature of painting as an art form. Similarly, one can walk around a sculpture, but the sculpture remains on its pedestal. A particularly dynamic sculpture may *suggest* movement, and in fact some sculptures have motors that make parts of them move, but they still remain essentially in place. A rotating stage may shift from one scene to another in the theater, but the audience does not itself experience the sensation of movement.

Film and video are different. Films offer shifting positions and perspectives. Shots aren't limited in terms of subject-camera distance or angle of view. A single shot may begin from a position so high off the ground no human being could achieve it unaided by a machine or a structure and proceed to lower itself to the level of a person, travel on the ground for a while, look around, follow a certain character, change direction and follow another character for a while, or maybe follow *no* particular character at all and go out on its own, thereby revealing a sense of spatial coherence and expressive fluidity that no static shot could ever achieve. Camera movement is an especially significant aspect of mise-en-scene.

TYPES OF CAMERA MOVEMENT

How does film studies describe various kinds of camera movements? First, when the camera itself is stationary but pivots on its axis from side to side, it's called a PAN. If the camera is stationary but tilts up and down, it's called a TILT (or a VERTICAL PAN). Both of these camera movements are like moving your head but not your body: you can take in a whole panorama without taking a single step simply by turning your head from side to side (a pan) or nodding up and down (a tilt). By panning and tilting, the camera reveals more space without itself moving from its fixed position on the ground—which is to say on a tripod or other supporting device. You can create the effect of a pan and a tilt right now simply by moving your head.

As you can see, you can take in large expanses of the room you're in without getting up from your seat. But you're still grounded; you're stuck in the same place. But just as you can get up and walk around, the camera itself can move. Camera movement is one of the most beautiful and yet underappreciated effects in any art form. However much we take it for granted, movement through space on film can be extraordinarily graceful. And by its movement alone, a camera reveals much more than simply the space through which it moves. It can express emotions.

The simplest way of moving a camera is to place it on a moving object, such as a car or a train or a ship. That's called a MOVING SHOT. The camera can also be placed on its own mobile device. When the camera moves parallel to the ground, it's called a TRACKING SHOT or a DOLLY. If it moves up and down through space it's called a CRANE. For a *crane shot*, the camera is mounted on a kind of cherry-picker, which enables it to rise very high up in the air—to ascend from ground level into the sky or descend from the sky to ground level.

With both of these devices, tracking shots and cranes, the camera moves physically through space. In classical Hollywood filmmaking, crews used to mount actual tracks on the ceiling or the floor, thus ensuring that the camera would move in a very smooth and precise fashion (hence the term *tracking shot*). Actors being filmed in tracking shots would therefore sometimes have to play their scenes squarely on the tracks, and when they walked they had to make sure to lift their legs high enough to clear the railroad ties that held the tracks in place. More often, cameras were—and still are—mounted on wheels, or dollies, thus enabling them to move freely in a variety of directions: forward and backward, sideward, diagonally, or around in a circle.

In the 1960s, technology developed to the point at which the size and weight of a motion picture camera, which had formerly been large and cumbersome, was reduced so much that a camera operator could actually carry the camera while filming. These are called **hand-held cameras**, which create HAND-HELD SHOTS. In any number of '60s (and later) films, directors used hand-held shots as a convention of realism—the jerkiness of hand-held shots seemed to suggest an unmediated reality, a lack of intervention between camera and subject. Audiences still tend to read hand-held shots that way: witness *The Blair Witch Project* (1999), which depends on the shakiness of the camera work to convey the homemade quality of the filmmaker-characters' attempt to document the supernatural. In fact, of course, a hand-held shot isn't any more "realistic" than any other kind of shot. It is a stylistic convention—a visual sign that people still read as expressing heightened realism.

In a still later development, cameras are now able to be mounted on an apparatus called a STEADICAM, which fits onto a camera operator's body (via a vest) in such a way that when he or she walks, the effect is that of very smooth movement, as opposed to a hand-held camera that records every bump in every step.

Finally, there's a kind of fake movement, an impression of movement that isn't really the result of a moving camera but rather of a particular kind of lens. That's called a ZOOM. With a zoom, the camera operator creates *the impression* of movement by shifting the focal length of the lens from wide angle to telephoto or from telephoto to wide angle, *but the camera itself does not move.* Zoom lenses are also known as *varifocal lenses.* A zoom is therefore a kind of artificial movement. There is no *real* movement with a zoom, just an enlargement or magnification of the image as the lens shifts from wide-angle to telephoto or the opposite, a demagnification, as it shifts from telephoto to wide-angle.

In other words, a zoom has two extremes—telephoto and wide angle. The telephoto range tends to make space seem flatter, while the wide-angle range (like any WIDE-ANGLE LENS) enhances the sense of depth.

Please note: when you say or write "zoom," you should specifically mean "*zoom.*" Be careful not to describe a shot by saying or writing "the director zooms forward" unless you are convinced that the director actually used a zoom lens to achieve the impression of camera movement. Granted, it can be difficult for beginners to appreciate the difference in appearance between a tracking shot and a zoom. One way of differentiating between the two is that a forward tracking shot actually penetrates space whereas a zoom forward (or *zoom in*) has a certain flatness to it—an increasing lack of depth owing to the shift from the wide-angle range to the telephoto range.

One way of understanding the difference in visual effect between a tracking shot and a zoom is to realize that film creates the illusion of a three-dimensional world—height, width, *and depth*—on a two-dimensional screen. We're usually fooled into perceiving depth where there is none. A forward tracking shot enhances this illusion of depth; the camera passes through space as it moves forward, and the resulting image re-creates that spatial penetration. A forward zoom, in contrast, does nothing to alleviate the screen's actual flatness. The camera doesn't move with a forward zoom, so we perceive the resulting image as being seemingly flatter than usual. In fact, the image is *always* flat. Forward zooms just do nothing to make us think it isn't. (In a *zoom out*—a zoom that begins in the telephoto range and ends in wide-angle—the flatness of the telephoto gives way to the sense of depth created by the wide-angle.)

Finally, filmmakers and film scholars alike make a distinction between MOTIVATED AND UNMOTIVATED CAMERA MOVEMENTS. It's the film's characters who determine whether the movement is motivated or not. For example, if a character begins to walk to the left and the camera tracks with her, the camera movement is considered to be *motivated*. If the character stands perfectly still but the camera tracks forward toward her, it's *unmotivated*. This is a useful distinction to the extent that it defines the characters' world as being separate and distinct from the filmmaker's commentary on that world. *Motivated camera movements are those that are prompted by the characters and events in the film; unmotivated camera movements are those that pertain to the filmmaker's commentary on characters and events.* At the same time, the term *unmotivated* is a poor choice of words to describe a filmmaker's expressive, artistic choices. There's a motive there, after all. It's just that of the director, not that of a character.

EDITING WITHIN THE SHOT

No matter whether a given camera movement is called motivated or unmotivated, all camera movement, like all editing, is a matter of human decision-making. In fact, an extended camera movement may function in much the same way as editing. They are each a way of selecting, arranging, and presenting information in a sequential manner to the audience.

Imagine a film that begins with a crane shot of a movie marquee that contains the name of the film's location. Let's say it's the Reseda Theater in Reseda, California. Without cutting, the camera pans left and cranes down to street level just as a large car pulls up at a nightclub across the street; using a Steadicam, the camera operator continues the shot by following the driver of the car and his girlfriend as they get out of the car and are greeted by the nightclub manager, who follows them inside the nightclub, where—still in the same shot—the man and woman are led to a booth, where they sit and place an order for drinks. The shot continues even further as the camera operator follows the nightclub manager as he says hello to a club-goer wearing an out-of-style western shirt, then returns to the couple at the booth just as a woman on roller skates appears and engages them in a brief conversation. This lengthy camera movement is neither solely unmotivated nor solely motivated; it contains elements of both.

Film buffs will recognize this as the opening shot of Paul Thomas Anderson's *Boogie Nights* (1997). But even if you have not seen the film, you can appreciate the degree of planning and skill required in creating a shot of this extraordinary duration. A single actor flubbing a line or sneezing would have ruined the take, as would an EXTRA—an actor who has no lines in a crowd scene—bumping into the Steadicam operator. Notice also the amount of *selection* involved in executing the shot. First we see the marquee; then we see the car; then we see the couple in the car; then we see the nightclub manager . . . It's a kind of *editing within the shot*—an arrangement and sequential presentation of discrete pieces of information within a single shot.

The first shot of *Boogie Nights*—and any such shot—is called a LONG TAKE, meaning that the shot continues without a cut for an unusually long time. The director of *Boogie Nights* could easily have carved up his opening sequence into individual shots—of the marquee, the car, the driver, his girlfriend, the nightclub manager, and so on—but he chose to unify both space and time by filming it in one continuous take—a *long take*. (If you have seen the film, or when you see the film, ask yourself what Anderson's long take expresses in terms of the overall theme of his movie.) This particular long take lasts for almost three minutes. Another famous long take, the opening shot of Orson Welles's *Touch of Evil* (1958), lasts for about four minutes. But it's important to note that long takes are like subject-camera distances in that they are defined relatively, so in an otherwise highly cut movie a shot lasting thirty or forty seconds could be considered a long take in the context of that particular film.

A single shot may serve, somewhat paradoxically, as its own sequence or scene; the term for this is a SEQUENCE SHOT. The opening of Hawks's *Scarface* (1932) is a classic example of a sequence shot; the shot chronicles the last minutes in the life of a mobster. Hawks begins with a low-angle shot of a streetlamp atop a street sign; the names of the streets are set perpendicular to each other to form the first of the many X shapes that appear throughout the film whenever anybody is about to get rubbed out. The camera tracks back as the light dims and goes out, tilts down, and pans right past a milk delivery man to reveal a man with an apron coming out of a private club doorway and yawning and stretching. The camera then tracks laterally right—seemingly through the exterior wall of the club—through the lobby, and into the ballroom, where the aproned man begins to clean up after what has evidently been a wild party. He removes streamers from the many potted palms that define the foreground as the camera continues to track and pan right. The man stops sweeping for a moment, and as the camera tracks forward, he reaches down and pulls a white brassiere out of the pile of streamers that litters the floor. (It certainly *was* a wild party.) As the man examines the bra, Hawks continues to track right and forward to reveal three men seated at a table set amid streamers hanging from the rafters; the man in the middle, a portly fellow called Big Louie, is wearing a paper party crown. The camera remains stationary as the three men converse for a few moments, after which the men get up from the table; Hawks tracks left with them as they move in that direction. After the two other men depart offscreen left, the camera remains on Big Louie, who walks toward the right; the camera tracks with him as he moves through the ballroom and into a telephone booth. He begins to place his call, and the camera stays motionless for a few seconds before tracking forward and then to the right to reveal the ominous silhouette of a man, who strolls in the direction of Big Louie; the camera tracks left with him as he walks; he is calmly whistling an opera aria. The camera stops on a frosted glass partition; the shadow of the man is framed by the partition as the man reaches into his pocket and pulls out a gun. "Hello, Louie," the man remarks before firing three times. Still in shadow, he wipes the gun off with a handkerchief and throws it on the floor. The man turns and leaves as Hawks tracks and pans left to reveal the body of Big Louie on the floor. The shot is still not over: the aproned man from the beginning of the sequence shot enters the image from the left. He stares at Louie's dead body, removes his apron, throws it in a closet, dons his hat and jacket, and runs left toward the door as Hawks completes the shot by tracking and panning left and slightly forward before ending with a DISSOLVE to the next scene. The shot is three and a half minutes long.

What makes this a sequence shot is that the single shot comprises the entire scene. The next shot takes place in an entirely different setting—that of a newspaper office, where editors debate the content of the headline announcing the killing. The lengthy opening shot of *Boogie Nights*, in contrast, does not contain the entire scene, which continues with more shots of the nightclub interior.

SPACE AND MOVEMENT

We are accustomed to thinking only about the content of each film image we see—the material actually onscreen. But if mise-en-scene, editing, and camera movement are all matters of decision-making, of selection, then it stands to reason that the information a director *leaves out* of the image is worth considering as well.

The film theorist Noël Burch has defined six zones of **offscreen space:**

1. *offscreen right*
2. *offscreen left*
3. *offscreen top*
4. *offscreen bottom*
5. *behind the set*
6. *behind the camera*

Imagine a medium shot of a woman, an aging actress, seated at a banquet table. We see her face and upper body; we see part of the table in front of her; we see an empty glass on the table. She reaches for something offscreen right, and when she brings her hand back into the image she is grasping a liquor bottle. She pours a few slugs of booze into the empty glass. Then, a hand enters the image (also from offscreen right); in the hand is a bottle of water. The actress bats the hand away before the otherwise unseen tablemate gets the opportunity to pour any water into the actress's liquor glass. The actress is casually but clearly refusing to have her drink watered down, and this action—together with the subtle smirk on the actress's face—establishes her character with great expressive efficiency.

This shot—which introduces Bette Davis's character in Joseph Mankiewicz's *All About Eve* (1950)—emphasizes the first of Burch's offscreen spaces: *offscreen right*. Although the director has framed the film's star in such a way as to emphasize her presence (he might have chosen instead to begin with a long shot of Davis seated at the same table surrounded by many other people and therefore not featured onscreen as an individual), he nevertheless indicates that someone else is sitting next to her. We naturally understand that the hand isn't disembodied. We assume that the space of the action continues beyond the frame—that there is a whole person there.

Audiences make similar assumptions about the other three spaces that border the image—*offscreen left*, *offscreen top*, and *offscreen bottom*. The director does not need to show these spaces to us directly for us to assume that they exist. And these four offscreen spaces are inevitably *diegetic*; in other words, they pertain to the world of the film's story. (See chapter 6 for a more complete discussion of the concept of *diegesis*.)

The other two offscreen spaces are important to consider, if only briefly, for the theoretical questions they raise. It's rare in narrative cinema for a director to move his or her camera behind the set, but it's conceivable. Such a shot would reveal that the set, which we have taken to be real, is in fact artificial—we might see the wooden supports holding up the walls, the lighting stands and a lot of electrical cords, the outer walls of the soundstage, and so on—and as such the shot would call attention to the fictional nature of what we've been seeing until that point in the film. That recognition is, of course, something that classical Hollywood cinema avoids. And because it does not have to do with the world of the film's story, the space behind the set is *nondiegetic*.

The sixth zone of offscreen space exists only in the imagination. We *know* that there is real space behind the camera, but the camera can never record it. Just as we don't have eyes in the back of our heads, so the camera can never have a separate lens that records the space behind itself. Only a second camera recording the first camera could record that space, but the space behind the second camera—the offscreen space Burch defines as being *behind the camera*—would be equally impossible for the second camera to record. Clearly, this impossible-to-record space is *nondiegetic*. It doesn't have to do with the film's fictional story but instead exists only in the world of the real people who are making the movie.

Individual shots could record the first five of Burch's offscreen spaces. Using the *All About Eve* example, the director could conceivably have cut from Bette Davis's character, the actress Margo Channing, to a shot of her tablemate to the left, her tablemate to the right, her legs under the table, the space above her head, and a final shot of the space behind the banquet room set. But by *moving* the camera, a director can actually reveal all five of the possible-to-record spaces in a single shot. By panning left and right, he could have shown us the spaces on either side of the character. By tilting up and down, he would have shown us the floor and the ceiling (or lack thereof—most sets have no ceiling so as to accommodate overhead lighting equipment). And by tracking laterally, then forward and around the walls of the banquet hall, he could have revealed the space behind the set. (Admittedly, following the logic of the impossible space behind the camera, none of the offscreen spaces can ever be recorded *as long as they are truly offscreen spaces*, but that's a subject for an upper-level film theory course to pursue.)

In short, mobile framing enables a director to unify diverse spaces within an individual shot. Even the tiniest, most minute readjustment, or REFRAMING, reveals and maintains spatial continuity from image to image without cutting. At the end of *City Lights*, which is analyzed in more detail in chapter 4, the director, Charles Chaplin, begins one shot by centering on the two characters' intertwined hands, then reframes the image to center on the Tramp's face and the flower he holds. What is key in this case, and in most cases of reframing, is the onscreen gesture or look or facial expression that the director wishes to emphasize. If a character moves her head slightly to the right in a close-up, for instance, it's likely that the director will reframe the shot by moving the camera slightly to the right so that part of her face will not be cut off by the original framing.

Ultimately, camera movement—like any other film technique—is about expressivity. There is no right or wrong way to film anything. Some directors, like Sergei Eisenstein, tend to carve the world up into individual static shots and edit it back together again, though even the famous "Odessa Steps" sequence from *Battleship Potemkin* contains several camera movements. Other directors, like F. W. Murnau and Max Ophüls are known for their elegant moving-camera work. Their films certainly contain static shots that are edited together, but as directors their style highlights camera movements rather than editing effects. Still others—the majority of contemporary filmmakers, in fact—like Paul Thomas Anderson, Martin Scorsese, Spike Lee, and others—choose to film certain scenes in the form of *long takes* with elaborate camera movements while others take the form of more rapidly cut sequences.

STUDY GUIDE: ANALYZING CAMERA MOVEMENT

To learn how to analyze camera movement, one must first be *aware* of camera movement. So get a DVD copy of your favorite movie, find a scene you know already, and watch it closely, this time paying particular attention to the camera movements it contains.

1. Pause the DVD after every camera movement you notice. If you are feeling particularly ambitious, write down each movement as you notice it.
2. Ask yourself the following questions after every pause:
   (A) What type of camera movement just occurred? Was it a single kind of movement (for example: a pan right, or a tilt down), or was it a combination of different types (a simultaneous crane down and pan left)?
   (B) What was the apparent motivation behind the movement? Did the camera move along with a character? Did it move away from a character? Or did it move seemingly on its own, without regard to a particular character?
   (C) To what does the movement draw your attention?
   (D) What ideas or emotions might it express by maintaining spatial unity?
   (E) As an aside, consider the offscreen spaces of each image and the assumptions you make about them.
3. Notice how often you are pausing the film—how often the camera moves. Is there a pattern of camera movements within the scene? For example, is there a series of tracking shots, or a series of pans? Is there any rhythm created by the way the camera moves?
4. Based solely on this particular scene (and bear in mind that the scene you choose may not be representative of the whole film), would you say that the director favors camera movements over cutting? Can you begin to perceive the director's overall style in this individual scene, or is it too soon to make such a generalization?

WRITING ABOUT CAMERA MOVEMENT

Given all these different terms and theoretical notions, how do you describe on a practical level the camera movements you see onscreen? It's not difficult; it just takes practice. The more familiar you become with the terminology, the easier it will be to describe and analyze what you notice.

"The camera tracks forward," "the camera tracks back," "the camera tracks laterally," and so on: just describe what you see using the technical terms at your command. "The camera cranes up." "The camera cranes down." "The camera cranes up, pans to the left, tilts down, cranes down, and tracks forward . . . " and on and on. However the camera moves, that's how you describe it. It makes for more precise analytical writing to write, "The camera tracks forward" or "the camera pans left," rather than fumbling around with "we go ahead" or "we go backwards" or "we turn and see . . . "

Be aware that cameras track *with* or *away from* characters. Here's an example from a Warner Bros. animated cartoon: "The camera tracks to the right *with* Elmer Fudd as Elmer tracks his prey, the 'wascally wabbit.'" (Yes, there are tracking shots in animated cartoons. Even though the camera that records each animation cel does not literally move, animators create *the effect* of all the different kinds of camera movements described in this chapter.)

What follows is a reasonably detailed description of the opening shot of *Boogie Nights*. Bear in mind that this description concentrates on camera movements. A full analysis of the shot would include many more details about mise-en-scene elements such as lighting, set design, color, costumes, makeup, and figure behavior, not to mention dialogue, music, and other sound effects, not to mention what it all adds up to in terms of meaning:

The first shot of *Boogie Nights* begins as a long shot of a movie marquee announcing that the film playing in the theater is titled *Boogie Nights*; the marquee fills the horizontal image, its shape echoing the film's widescreen aspect ratio of 2.40:1. The camera cranes slightly forward, pans slightly left, and rotates clockwise to reveal in an oblique angle the name of the theater—the Reseda. Just as the name "Reseda" fills the image horizontally, the camera reverses the direction of its movement: it now rotates counterclockwise and cranes down to reveal some people exiting the theater and walking under the marquee. The camera continues its movement by craning down and panning rather rapidly to the left just as a car moves forward on the street next to the theater. The camera continues to pan left and crane down—at one moment, the car, now traveling from right to left across the image, fills the screen—until it is at ground level.

Owing to the camera having panned, the car is now facing away from the camera. As a subtitle appears—"San Fernando Valley 1977"—the car makes a left turn and pulls up in front of a nightclub with a gaudy neon sign that reads: "Hot Traxx." The camera tracks forward on the street toward the car; the camera operator is evidently using a Steadicam, because the movement is very smooth.

A crowd has gathered in front of the entrance to the club. The driver gets out of the car and raises his arm in a greeting gesture but is momentarily cut out of the image because the camera is moving rapidly forward toward the club's entrance. The camera continues to track forward until it singles out the nightclub manager, who rushes forward and to the left of the image with his arms outstretched.

In a very rapid movement, the camera circles around the nightclub manager and pans left to reveal the moment at which the manager reaches the driver and his girlfriend, who has also gotten out of the car (an action we only assume has occurred, because we have not actually seen it).

The camera then tracks backward, and the three characters follow the camera as it backs into the doorway of the nightclub, through the small entrance hall, and into the club, at which point the camera makes a left turn; this allows the characters to pass the camera, and as they continue to walk they make a left turn as they head away from it. The camera operator reframes the image with a slight pan left as the characters make a similar adjustment in their direction. For a few seconds, the image is a three-shot of the characters walking away from the camera in silhouette.

The characters then turn right and head toward an as-yet-unseen booth; their destination is revealed in dialogue. The driver and his girlfriend continue walking away, but the manager stops, and the camera stops with him; as he walks back in the direction from which he came, the camera reverses its direction and tracks backward. When he turns toward the left of the image, the camera pans left and tracks forward, following him. He gestures toward the left side of the image, and the camera quickly pans left to reveal a waiter dressed in a striped white shirt and turning away from the camera. The waiter begins to walk toward the back of the club, but the camera quickly pans right away from him and returns to the manager, who is now walking toward the camera while the camera tracks backward.

The manager turns toward his left as he walks, and the camera pauses to allow him to pass it; he then walks away from the camera, and the camera follows him through a crowd of people. He jumps up on the dance floor and greets a man who is dancing there.

The camera follows the manager onto the dance floor and then begins to circle the group of people to whom the manager is speaking: the dancing man, who is white; a woman; and a black man wearing a western shirt. The camera travels in two full 360-degree turns before panning and tracking left, following the waiter in the white shirt, who is walking left in the distance and carrying a tray of drinks.

The camera tracks rapidly left and then slightly forward around some tables full of people and slows down when it nears the driver and his girlfriend, now seated at their booth; the driver is on the left, his girlfriend is roughly in the center of the image, and the waiter is slightly to the right. The couple says something to the waiter, who turns and begins to walk away. The camera follows him for a moment or two, cutting the couple briefly out of the image, but then a young blonde woman on roller skates enters the image from the background. As she passes the waiter, the camera changes direction and begins to track backward until it is more or less at the same position it took during the exchange with the waiter. The woman on skates stops at the table and begins a conversation with the driver and his girlfriend. But the camera is restless and begins to track forward and around the woman on skates. At one moment, the driver's girlfriend is alone in the image in medium shot facing at a three-quarter angle to the left.

The camera then tracks backward and pans to the left to form what is essentially the reverse angle to the one that first captured the waiter and the couple and was repeated with the woman on skates and the couple: now the woman on skates stands just to the left of center, the driver sits in the center, and his girlfriend sits on the right.[1]

The woman on skates makes a hopping gesture and turns and skates away from the camera, but the camera quickly follows her. She turns left; the camera pans left with her. The camera tracks left as she skates in that direction, after which she turns

---

1. For a definition of the term *reverse angle,* see SHOT/REVERSE-SHOT PATTERN in the glossary.

and skates toward the background. The camera tracks forward, following her, until she disappears into the crowd in the center of the image. But the camera continues to track forward and pan to the left to reveal a young man wearing a white shirt. The camera finally stops moving as the young man, seen in medium close-up, gazes toward the left.

Cut! The first shot of *Boogie Nights* terminates here.

CHAPTER 3
MISE-EN-SCENE: CINEMATOGRAPHY

MOTION PICTURE PHOTOGRAPHY

CINEMATOGRAPHY—photography for motion pictures—is the general term that brings together all the strictly photographic elements that produce the images we see projected on the screen. *Lighting devices and their effects; film stocks and the colors or tones they produce; the lenses used to record images on celluloid; the shape of the image, how it is created, and what it means*—these all constitute the art of cinematography. This, too, is an aspect of mise-en-scene.

The word *cinematography* comes from two Greek roots: *kinesis* (the root of *cinema*), meaning movement, and *grapho*, which means to write or record. (*Photography* is derived from *phos*, meaning light, and *grapho*.) *Writing with movement and light*—it's a great way to begin to think about the cinematographic content of motion pictures.

ASPECT RATIO is the relation of the width of the rectangular image to its height. As you may remember from the first chapter, silent pictures had an aspect ratio of 1.33:1, a rectangle a third again as wide as it was tall. And while the so-called ACADEMY RATIO, standardized by the Academy of Motion Picture Arts and Sciences in 1932, is usually referred to as being 1.33:1, in point of fact the Academy ratio is 1.37:1—a very slightly wider rectangle than that of silent films.

After 1932, all Hollywood films were made in the Academy ratio of 1.37:1 until the advent of television in the 1950s. Although TV provided a new market for old movies, it also gave audiences the opportunity to enjoy audiovisual entertainment without leaving their homes. So as a way of offering people something they could not get for free in their living rooms, Hollywood emphasized the enormity of motion picture screens by developing technologies that widened the image far beyond the 1.37:1 Academy ratio.

CINEMASCOPE, introduced by 20th Century-Fox for the biblical drama *The Robe* (1953), used what is called an ANAMORPHIC LENS on the camera to squeeze a very wide image onto each frame of standard-sized film stock and another anamorphic lens on the projector to spread it back out again. CinemaScope's aspect ratio used to be 2.35:1; it was later adjusted to 2.40:1. PANAVISION, another system with a 2.40:1 ratio, is the most commonly used anamorphic process today.

There were still other WIDESCREEN processes in the 1950s, including CINERAMA and VISTAVISION. Cinerama used three interlocked cameras to record three separate images which, when projected across a specially curved screen, yielded a single continuous widescreen image with an aspect ratio of 2.77:1. The first film released in Cinerama was a display of the process called *This Is Cinerama* (1952). It was an enormous box office success, but the process proved too cumbersome, not only for filmmakers but also for exhibitors, who had to fit the huge curved screen into their theaters in order to show Cinerama films, which were mostly travelogues. Moreover, every theater had to be outfitted with three separate projection booths, each staffed by two people. Cinerama, in short, was an expensive proposition for exhibitors. Only two narrative films were made in three-strip Cinerama: *The Wonderful World of the Brothers Grimm* and *How the West Was Won* (both 1962).[1]

VistaVision, developed by Paramount Pictures, was first used for the 1954 film *White Christmas*. Instead of the film frames running vertically on the celluloid, with the sprocket holes on the sides, VistaVision's frames

1. Cinerama continued as a trade name used for single-strip widescreen films such as Stanley Kubrick's *2001: A Space Odyssey*.

FIGURE 3.1 An anamorphic frame as it looks to the naked eye—*Scary Movie 3* (2003). (Photofest)

FIGURE 3.2 The same anamorphic frame as it looks projected onto the screen—Agent Thompson (Ja Rule) and President Harris (Leslie Nielsen). (Photofest)

ran horizontally; the sprocket holes were on the top and bottom of each frame. This system yielded an aspect ratio of 1.5:1, though most VistaVision films used MATTES or MASKING to produce ratios from 1.66:1 and 1.85:1 to 2:1. Still another widescreen process was **Todd-AO** (named for the producer Mike Todd and the American Optical Company), with an aspect ratio of 2.20:1; Todd-AO was an early 70mm process, whereas the others used 35mm film.

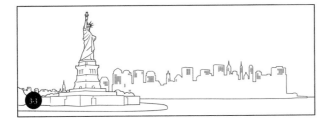

FIGURE 3.3 Cinerama with an aspect ratio of 2.77:1.

FIGURE 3.4 VistaVision with an aspect ratio of 1.85:1.

FIGURE 3.5 The full frame at the Academy ratio, 1.37:1. Knowing that the top and bottom portions of the image will be masked when the film is projected, the director doesn't care that the boom is visible at the top of the image and electrical cords can be seen at the bottom.

FIGURE 3.6 The same frame masked at 1.85:1; the hatch marks indicate the parts of the image that were photographed during shooting but are masked when projected onto the screen. Now that the image has been properly masked, the composition makes visual sense; the filmmaking equipment still exists on the celluloid, but it can't be seen on the screen.

Simply masking the image was—and continues to be—the easiest way to produce a widescreen effect. Masking means covering the top and bottom of the image with an *aperture plate* in the projector in order to produce any of a number of widescreen aspect ratios.

ASPECT RATIO: FORM AND MEANING

Unless you are an aspiring film director or CINEMATOGRAPHER, you may find yourself asking what the point of all these aspect ratios is. If learning about the variety of cinematic aspect ratios were just a matter of memorizing technical specifications, the lesson would be all but useless. But the shape of every film is basic to its expressive meaning. Each aspect ratio yields a different way of looking at the world. It is meaning, rather than just numbers, that's important.

If you watch films on DVD, you may have come across the terms LETTERBOX and LETTERBOXING. Letterboxing means preserving the original aspect ratio of a widescreen film when transferring the film to DVD or broadcasting it on television. Letterboxed films have blank areas above and below the image, making the image's shape resemble a business envelope, or letter. Despite the rise in sales of widescreen, flatscreen televisions, many TVs still maintain an aspect ratio of 1.33:1, and broadcasters as well as video distributors often simply chop off the sides of widescreen films in order to fit the image to the almost-square screen. Rather like slashing off the edges of a painting so it fits a preexisting frame, this crude practice ruins movies. When you watch films made after 1954 on DVD, you should always make sure that they are letterboxed.

To see why, consider the differences between figures 3.7 and 3.8:

In figure 3.7, a woman is seen in close-up. We can read her facial expression clearly: she is frightened at what she is seeing. But because the aspect ratio is 1.37:1, there is no room in the image to maintain both a close proximity to her face and, at the same time, to see what she is looking at. To reveal that information, the director would have either to move the camera or cut to another shot. Figure 3.8, with an aspect ratio of 2.40:1, not only provides the emotional intensity of the woman's close-up but also reveals what she is seeing *in the same image*. Please note: neither image is superior. There is no single, *correct* way of framing and filming this shot, or *any* shot. One director may prefer to shoot in the narrower aspect ratio of 1.37:1, while another may choose the wider, more expansive 2.40:1. It's a matter of personal style. There is, however, a single and correct way of *showing* a given film: if it was filmed with an aspect ratio of 2.40:1, it should be shown and seen only in 2.40:1.

FIGURE 3.7 A non-letterboxed video image, chopped off so it conforms to the shape of a television screen.

FIGURE 3.8 Properly letterboxed on video and restored to its original cinematic aspect ratio, the same shot makes narrative as well as visual sense once more.

The point is this: each aspect ratio brings with it a set of aesthetic, expressive consequences. As a key facet of mise-en-scene, each film's aspect ratio presents a kind of creative limitation to the filmmakers—rather like the way in which the 14-line, iambic pentameter form of a sonnet offers a poet a strict framework in which to write. If, for example, a director chooses to film in Panavision's 2.40:1 aspect ratio but wants to create the impression of cramped spaces, she must follow through by somehow counterbalancing the expansive nature of the extra-widescreen process—crowding her sets with objects, say, and blocking her actors to move closer to one another. (*Blocking* is a term derived from theater and simply means planning where and when actors move around the stage or film set.) It's all a question of *composition*—the arrangement of people and things within the rectangular frame. Conversely, a director may choose to film in 1.37:1, the Academy ratio, and yet create the impression of spatial emptiness by consistently framing his characters at a distance from one another, keeping the set design relatively spare, and refraining from image-filling devices such as close-ups. Once again, it's a matter of creating expressive compositions that are coherent and meaningful throughout the film.

As you begin to notice the aspect ratio of the films you see, ask yourself what relation the shape of the image has to what you're feeling and what the film is subtly expressing simply by way of its shape.

LIGHTING

Consider how futile it would be to film a scene set in a pitch black room. There can be no cinematography—or still photography, for that matter—without light. The light source may be only a flaming match, some sparks, the tip of a cigarette, or a bit of light shining in through the gap between a door and the floor, but without some form of lighting nothing can be registered on film.

Film studies, at least on the introductory level, is less concerned with the technical means by which lighting effects are created than with their expressive results. Your goal at this point is not to try to determine how a given effect was created by a cinematographer but rather to begin to appreciate the way in which that effect bears *meaning*. Imagine filming a scene set in a courtroom, where a woman stands accused of murdering her husband. You could light the scene any number of ways, depending on the particular story you were telling and the mood you wanted to create. You might suggest that justice was being served, for instance, by lighting the room brightly and warmly, with sun streaming in through unblinded windows. On the other hand, you might want to generate some visual tension to suggest that the defendant has been unjustly charged with the crime, in which case you could light the room very unevenly; a sort of gray light could shine through half-closed Venetian blinds in the windows, and a few bluish fluorescent lights overhead could shine down on the courtroom to create a room full of shadows. One thing you would probably *not* want to do is simply use the lights that are available in a real courtroom and nothing more. Why not? Because the expressive results would be left entirely to chance. You might find, when you get the film back from the processing lab, that what looked great in a real courtroom doesn't look nearly as good on film: shadows that weren't noticeable in the real room may appear in the filmed scene, and there might be areas of overexposure as well. Even more important, the available lighting in a real courtroom might not express artistically what you want to say.

THREE-POINT LIGHTING

The first motion pictures were lit by the most powerful light source in the solar system—the sun. Not only were many of these movies set outdoors, but even interior sets, too, were constructed in the open air simply so that there would be strong enough lighting to register images clearly on film. The development of more light-sensitive film stocks, together with more powerful electric lights, enabled filmmakers to be much less dependent on direct sunlight as their chief source of illumination.

The most basic lighting setup is known as THREE-POINT LIGHTING, which consists of a **key light**, a **fill light**, and a **backlight**. The *key light* (A in fig. 3.9) aims directly at the subject—most likely the main character or object in the shot—and is the brightest light source for the shot. The *fill light* (B) is a softer light, and is usually placed opposite the key light; the fill light cuts down on shadows created by the bright key light. And the *backlight* (C) shines behind the subject or object, separating him, her, or it from the background—in other words, enhancing the sense of depth in the shot. Backlighting sometimes creates a halo effect around a character's head, particularly at the edges of the hair.

The term *key light* is the source of two commonly used adjectives: *low key* and *high key*. To call something *high key* is to say that it's intense, whereas *low key* means subdued. The overly cheerful atmosphere of a television game show would be described as *high key*, whereas the smoky mood of a jazz club would be called low key. These expressions come from cinematography. When cinematographers, also known as DIRECTORS OF PHOTOGRAPHY (DPs) use a high proportion of fill light to key light, it's called high-key lighting; the effect is both brighter and more even than when they use a low proportion of fill light to key light, which is called low-key lighting. The lower key the light, the more shadowy the effect. The distorting, spooky nature of extremely low-key lighting is perfectly illustrated by a trick almost every child has played: in the dark, you shine a flashlight up at your face from below your chin. That flashlight was your key light, and since there was no fill light at all, the proportion of fill to key was as low as you could get.

To hammer the point home: the object is not to determine where the key light was on the set, or what the real proportion of fill light to

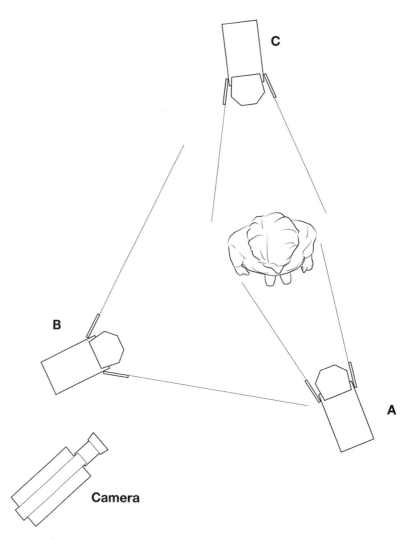

C

B

A

Camera

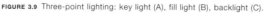

FIGURE 3.9 Three-point lighting: key light (A), fill light (B), backlight (C).

key light was, or whether there was some **top lighting** (lighting from overhead). Instead, your goals are to notice the *effects* of the lighting in a given scene, to describe these effects accurately, and to venture analytically some ideas about what the effects mean. See the Study Guide, below, for tips on how to reach these goals.

Bright, even high-key lighting is often used in comedies and musicals to enhance a sense of liveliness and high energy (fig. 3.10).[2] Conversely, the shadows created by low-key lighting (fig. 3.11) work so well in mysteries and horror films that they have long been an important convention of those GENRES. And of course many films use a combination of high-key and low-key setups, depending on the nature of the

FIGURES 3.10 AND 3.11 High-key lighting and low-key lighting: In the publicity still from Ernst Lubitsch's musical-comedy *The Merry Widow* (1934) (fig. 3.10), the image is ablaze in brilliant, even light shining not only on the character (Jeanette McDonald) but also on her surroundings—the carpet, the walls, and the ridiculous bed. The fact that the set is almost completely white only adds to the image's luminous quality; had the fill lighting been less intense, the effect of all that whiteness would have been greatly diminished by shadows. The still from John Ford's downbeat drama *The Fugitive* (1947) (fig. 3.11, p. 48) demonstrates the opposite effect of low-key lighting. Here, the key light shines onto only half the face of the central character (Henry Fonda), leaving the other half in darkness. The shadow of the prison bar could have been reduced or even eliminated had Ford wanted the character's face to be brightly and evenly lit, but that was clearly not his expressive intent. And there is little if any backlighting, so the top of the character's head all but blends in with the completely unlit back wall.

individual scene. Imagine a western outlaw, for instance, walking from a brilliantly lit, high-key exterior into a darker, more low-key saloon. The director might be contrasting the external world of bright nature with the confining, darker, interior world of civilization.

It's important to understand that the high-key exterior—in this case, the outside of the saloon—was probably filmed using artificial lighting as well as actual sunlight; audiences never see the many **reflectors** and **lamps** that the filmmakers have aimed at the outlaw character as he walks toward the saloon's swinging wooden doors so as to even out the shadows that would have resulted if the bright midday sun overhead had been the only light source.

FILM STOCKS: SUPER 8 TO 70MM TO VIDEO

DPs are in charge of selecting the type of FILM STOCK—raw, unexposed footage—that is used to make a given film. Film stock is categorized in several ways: (1) by **gauge**; (2) by **type**; (and 3) by **exposure index**. The film's *gauge* is simply its width, which ranges in standardized increments from 70mm, the widest, through 65mm, 35mm, and 16mm, to the narrowest—Super 8mm and 8mm. (In point of fact, 70mm films are actually shot in 65mm; the added five millimeters comes from the soundtrack.) The gauge for most theatrical film releases is 35mm. In general, the wider the gauge, the better the picture quality. Motion picture film contains a flexible **base**—it has to be flexible so it can run through cameras and projectors—the surface of which is covered with an **emulsion**. So when the film is shot, a wider gauge has more surface area, and therefore more emulsion on which to record the light patterns that form the image. Second, when the film is projected, a wider gauge has more surface area through which to shine the projector's light beam, thereby yielding a clearer, less grainy image than a narrow gauge film projected on the same large screen. As with snapshots, the more you attempt to blow up a small image to greater and greater proportions, the grainier the result will be.

There are five *types* of film stock: **black-and-white negative, color negative, intermediate stock, black-and-white print,** and **color print.** *Negative* film is film that is run through a camera and exposed to light frame by frame. The images contained on it are inverted in two ways: they are upside down, and their tones are reversed. Black-and-white negative has dark areas in place of light areas, and vice versa, and color negative has magenta in place of green, yellow in place of blue, and cyan (blue-green) in place of red. Processing this film creates a *positive print*, which reverses the tones back to normal. Intermediate stocks—*internegative* and *interpositive*—are used during postproduction.

Exposure index refers to the film's sensitivity to light. It's also called *film speed*. So-called *slow film* requires longer exposure to light, whereas *fast film* needs a much briefer exposure. A key consequence of the decision to use a faster or slower stock is the degree of *contrast* one desires. Faster stock yields higher contrast—bright areas are very bright and dark areas are very dark—whereas slower stock yields lower contrast.

BLACK, WHITE, GRAY, AND COLOR

Almost all narrative films produced today are shot in color. Today's audiences are so used to seeing color cinematography that they sometimes fail to appreciate the beauty and range of black-and-white filmmaking.

It may surprise you to learn that many silent films were released in color, though not the kind of color you are used to seeing. Through the related processes of **tinting** and **toning**, cinematographers turned the grays into equally monochromatic blues or sepias (light browns) or reds. *Tinting* means dyeing the film's base; *toning* means dyeing one component in the emulsion. Interiors and landscapes would sometimes be tinted sepia. Night scenes were often tinted or toned blue, and in fact this convention became so standard that such scenes were often filmed in broad daylight with the expectation that they would be tinted later.

Color cinematography began, in a way, in 1903, when a French film company, Pathé, began hand-stenciling colors onto each frame of film. Color film stock, however, was not commonly used in commercial filmmaking until the 1930s and 1940s, when a famous company called Technicolor began to put its three-color processing system to wide use. Technicolor, which was actually founded in 1915, used first a two-color and later, much more extensively, a three-strip system to render super-saturated colors on motion picture film. Light entered the camera's lens, but instead of registering an image more or less directly onto film stock, it passed instead through a prism that separated it into red, green, and blue values, each of which was registered on its own stock; later, these strips were dyed and processed onto a single strip of color stock. (In point of fact, calling Technicolor film "color stock" is inaccurate; the process originally used black-and-white stock with filters for each of three colors, and release prints were made on blank, black-and-white stock on which color dyes were stamped. Color negative was not used until the late 1940s and 1950s.)

Black-and-white cinematography is inaccurately named. In fact, it's **monochromatic**, meaning that it is comprised of a single color—usually gray—in a variety of shades. From the late 1930s to the 1960s, filmmakers saw the difference between black and white or color cinematography as a matter of choice, the decision being based on economic as well as aesthetic factors. Technicolor was an expensive process, adding about 25 percent more to the cost of an average film production. At the same time, cost was not the only issue, since certain genres—most notably the gritty, urban genre known as film noir—worked particularly well in black and white, whereas others—lavish musicals and costume dramas, for instance—were better suited to color. The development of Eastman Color, a simpler and less expensive color system, in 1952 led to more and more films being made in color, and eventually artistic choice gave way to audience expectation. At this point in the twenty-first century, black-and-white cinematography is rarely employed in commercial filmmaking.

A WORD OR TWO ABOUT LENSES

Because most if not all of the movies you have seen in your life have not been full of distorted visuals—they don't reflect the world the way a funhouse mirror would—you may assume that there is such a thing as a *normal* lens, and that most films are shot with it. But this is not the case. In fact, most filmmakers use a wide variety of lenses during the course of shooting an individual film. While most of these lenses yield images that resemble "normal" human vision, the word *normal* means something extremely varied in this context; the human eye is remarkably flexible and creates an enormous variety of effects without our being aware of the minute physical changes the eye performs. Lenses are not nearly as adaptable. They are hard pieces of unbendable glass, and they need to be changed frequently to create the impression of apparently simple, so-called "normal" vision.

Look at the book you are reading. Focus on the print of this **word** in this sentence. Notice that even the other words surrounding it are somewhat out of focus, let alone the edges of the book, the desk at which you are sitting, and the surrounding room. There is nothing *abnormal* about this particular view of the world, is there? It's specific, but it's not at all unusual.

Now focus on a whole paragraph. The print is in focus (more or less), but individual words are somehow not. This view is also particular but not strange looking. Look at the page as a whole with this concept in mind. Look up from the book, focus on an object nearby, and notice that while you can see the rest of the room, the object you have selected seems clearer than things in the background. Look out a window (if you can) at something or someone in the distance, and literally *see* the way your eyes automatically bring that object or person into clear focus while the objects in the room become fuzzier, less distinct. All of these visuals are your eyes' successful attempts to select objects for your attention. None of them is distorted in any way, but each of them is different.

In order to guide your eyes to particular people and things onscreen, filmmakers must use individual lenses that are suited to certain applications. There is no need for you to learn the technical terms for most of the lenses used in motion picture production, but a few of the basic concepts are worth knowing.

Just as your eyes keep objects at a certain distance in focus while the rest of the room seems to blur, so every lens has what is known as a specific **depth of field**—the area of the image between foreground and background that remains in focus. If, for example, a filmmaker wants to direct your attention to a particular row of spectators in a crowded football stadium, she and her DP might choose a lens with that particular depth of field; everyone behind that row and in front of that row would be slightly out of focus.

In some instances, filmmakers choose to shoot in what is called **deep focus**, which means that objects near the camera, midway, and far from the camera are all in sharp focus. In a deep focus shot, we can see objects and/or characters in all three planes in equally clear focus. A number of shots in *Citizen Kane* are in deep focus; *Citizen Kane*'s cinematographer, Gregg Toland, pioneered the technique.

Lenses run in a spectrum from WIDE-ANGLE to TELEPHOTO. A *wide-angle lens* has a wide depth of field, which means that objects in the foreground, middleground, and background are all in focus. A *telephoto lens*, on the other hand, has a narrow depth of field, as it appears to bring distant objects closer. A lens that is capable of shifting from wide-angle to telephoto and back is called a ZOOM LENS. Unlike forward and reverse tracking shots, zoom shots do not involve moving the camera through space. And finally, a **rack focus shot** (sometimes called a *focus pull*) changes the plane of focus within the shot by way of a change

FIGURE 3.12 Deep focus in *Citizen Kane* (1941): all planes of depth are in focus—the woman in the foreground, the man standing in the near-middle ground, the window frame and wall in the background, and even the boy playing outside in the snow in the far background (frame enlargement).

in focus, rather than by way of a zoom. For instance, a character in the foreground is in sharp focus; he hears a noise and turns to look at the far background; the focus then shifts—the man becomes blurry while a car exploding in the distance becomes clear. Notice the difference between a zoom and a rack focus: in a zoom, all the depth planes remain in focus, whereas in a rack focus only one plane at a time is clear and sharp.

STUDY GUIDE: ANALYZING CINEMATOGRAPHY

To begin to analyze the various components of cinematography, get a film on DVD, randomly select a scene, and freeze frame any image that strikes you as worth pursuing in detail.

First, notice the aspect ratio. Can you tell what aspect ratio it is by sight? Probably not, though you can certainly distinguish a widescreen film from one shot in the Academy ratio.

Although the use of freeze framing has its drawbacks—what, after all, is a motion picture without motion?—you can tell a lot about a shot from an individual frame. In terms of composition, how do the people and objects in the image relate to the film's aspect ratio? Are they centered, or clustered on one side, or spread out across the expanse of the screen? (If it's a widescreen film, imagine what it would look like if it hadn't been letterboxed. What would have been cut out?)

What about the lighting? Would you describe it as high key or low key? If there are shadows, where do they fall? Is the lighting naturalistic or not? In other words, does it look like the world you live in, or have the filmmakers juiced it up with lighting effects? Write your responses to these and other issues in a notebook, because you may need them for reference in the writing exercise that follows.

Now examine the image with an eye toward the effects created by the camera's lens. Is the entire image in the same sharp focus, or is one depth plane clearer than the others? Can you even distinguish the foreground from the background, or is the shot one that contains only one plane? (If the shot is a close-up, for instance, there can be only one plane because the image contains only one object or face.)

WRITING ABOUT CINEMATOGRAPHY

Given the fact that this chapter is the most technically oriented one so far, what with its array of cinematographic facts and figures, you may be overwhelmed by the idea of writing about this aspect of filmmaking. In fact, the challenge of writing about cinematography is the same as writing critically about movies as a whole: you must find a way not only to describe what you see clearly but also to figure out what the filmmakers are expressing in terms of meaning.

One of the problems beginning film students face is how to move beyond simple description to meaningful analysis. Just as it's not enough to provide a summary of the film's story and pass it off as criticism, a simple description of a scene's cinematography won't cut it either. You must learn how to find meaning onscreen—in this case, through cinematography.

Don't be afraid to state the obvious. Or, better, begin with the obvious—what does the film look like?—and use reason to explore the implications of those visuals. Take the example of the western outlaw entering the saloon, above, and break down the observations made about it into basic logical steps that lead to a conclusion about what the scene is actually about:

1. The character moves from one type of lighting (bright, high key) to another (dim, low key).
2. The character is an outlaw—a person who operates *outside* the laws of society.
3. The character moves from *outside* to *inside*.
4. *Outside* is full of light and space; *inside* is shadowy and confining.
5. Conclusion: by way of this shift in cinematography, the filmmaker is actually contrasting the openness and freedom of nature with the constraints of society.

In this case, the conclusion is not particularly profound, nor is it unexpected. As they say, it isn't rocket science. But it gets the job done, which is to say that it moves from simple, surface visual description to deeper analytical thinking. It identifies and ascribes thematic meaning to formal artistic decisions. In short, it's a start.

Go over your notes from the study guides and writing exercises in the previous two chapters. Note whether you included any descriptions of cinematographic elements along with your observations about mise-en-scene and camera movement. What visual information about lighting did you fail, however inadvertently, to notice and specify in your notes? If you have the time and inclination, compare your previous notes with the notes you took for this chapter. See what you have learned to see.

Most important of all: ask yourself how you can use the raw material of your descriptions to draw inferences and implications about what the films are about. Based on what you know so far, and using reason to guide you, what can you logically conclude about what each unique combination of mise-en-scene, camera movement, and cinematography *means*?

CHAPTER 4

EDITING: FROM SHOT TO SHOT

TRANSITIONS

With all but a very few exceptions, films—especially narrative feature films—are made up of a series of individual shots that filmmakers connect in a formal, systematic, and expressive way. There are practical as well as artistic reasons for directors to assemble movies from many hundreds if not thousands of shots. For one thing, film cameras are able to hold only a limited amount of celluloid film—not enough for a feature-length motion picture. (Digital cameras, however, can capture multiple hours.) More important, narrative films generally compress time considerably by leaving out the boring parts of the stories they tell. Imagine how dull it would be to watch even the most intriguing characters go through the humdrum motions of everyday life—doing the laundry, brushing their teeth, spending an hour stuck in traffic—simply because the filmmaker had no way of eliminating these necessary but irrelevant

FIGURE 4.1 Editors work manually at an editing table in this undated photograph. Now, most editing takes place on computers. (Photofest)

activities. Even those rare films that try to duplicate real time—the story of two hours in a woman's life could conceivably take exactly two hours to tell on film—generally require the filmmaker to carve up the action into discrete shots and reassemble them coherently, if only to hold the audience's visual interest, let alone to make expressive points by way of close-ups, long shots, high- and low-angle shots, and so on.

Alfred Hitchcock's 1948 film, *Rope*, is an attempt to film an entire feature-length narrative in a single shot. The fact that film *magazines* (lightproof containers that hold, feed, and take up film in the camera) of that era could only hold about ten minutes of film was a big constraint, but Hitchcock uses two devices to mask the technically necessary edits:

he makes straight cuts at certain reel changeovers and tracks forward into the backs of men wearing dark suits in order to black out the image before cutting at certain others. Still, by moving the camera and reframing the image within these 5- to 10-minute shots, Hitchcock effectively carves each shot into discrete units for expressive purposes.

This chapter describes the methods by which filmmakers link individual shots to one another in a process called EDITING, or CUTTING. These links are broadly called TRANSITIONS.

The simplest transition is the CUT. A director films a shot, the basic unit of filmmaking, and has it developed. She films another shot and has it developed as well. She trims each shot down to the length she wants, and she attaches the two strips of film together with a piece of tape. That's it: she has *cut* from one shot to another. In this example, the filmmaker is using celluloid. She can create the same effect electronically with two shots taken in video, though in that case, of course, she has no need for tape.

Bear in mind that editing is a human activity. Unlike the camera's mechanical recording of images, editing is quite specifically a matter of active decision-making—the product of human choice. So when describing editing, it makes no sense to say or write "the camera cuts." Cameras can only record; directors and editors cut.

Other important transitions include the FADE-IN and FADE-OUT; the IRIS-IN and IRIS-OUT; the DISSOLVE, and the WIPE, but because these effects are used mostly as transitions from scene to scene—in other words, from the final shot of one scene to the first shot of the next scene—and this chapter concerns transitions from shot to shot *within* a scene, let's postpone describing them until chapter 6.

MONTAGE

One of the key terms in film studies is MONTAGE. Taken from the French verb *monter*, meaning *to assemble*, montage describes the various ways in which filmmakers string individual shots together to form a series.

The term *montage* has three different but related definitions. The first definition is the easiest. In France, the word *montage* simply means editing—*any kind of editing*. As described in the example of a simple cut, above, the filmmaker takes two pieces of exposed and processed celluloid, trims them down to the length she wants—decisions made on the basis of the expressive and/or graphic content of the image, or the dialogue, or a combination of both—and literally tapes them together. In France, what she has done is known as montage.

In the United States, the term *montage* refers more specifically to *a film sequence that relies on editing to condense or expand action, space, or time.* The effect is often that of a rapid-fire series of interrelated images. Imagine that a director is telling the story of a rock band that forms in Omaha, and he needs to move them quickly to Hollywood, where they will perform live on a television show. Since there is neither the need nor the time to watch the group drive the entire way from eastern Nebraska to southern California, our director begins by filming a shot of the band members packing up their van in Omaha; he cuts quickly from this shot to a shot of the van on the interstate making its way across the Great Plains. From this he cuts to a shot of oil derricks next to the highway, then to a shot of cattle in a field, and then to a shot of the van heading toward the snowcapped Rockies. Cut to a shot of the band members in the van; cut to a shot of the van driving down the Las Vegas Strip at night. An image of Death Valley follows. From the desert the director cuts to a shot of a sign reading "Los Angeles—30 miles" and then to a shot of the van pulling up at an office building on Sunset Boulevard.

In this American-style montage sequence, the band has moved all the way from the Midwest to L.A. in less than a minute. This montage condenses time and space—a 1,700-mile trip that would take several days in real time shrinks down in screen time to about 45 seconds.

Here's an example of the way in which an American-style montage can *expand* time and space: Imagine a pitcher on the mound of a baseball field preparing to fire a fastball to the catcher. But instead of presenting the pitch in one single shot taken from high in the stands, the director assembles an American-style montage sequence in order to enhance the game's suspense: a full shot of the pitcher winding up; a long shot of the crowd in the bleachers; a medium shot of the manager looking tense in the dugout; another shot of the pitcher, this one a close-up, a moment later in his windup; a shot of a middle-aged guy watching the game on television in his den; a long shot of a group of fans beginning to stand up; a medium shot of the batter looking defiant; a close-up of the ball leaving the pitcher's fist; a full shot of the batter beginning to swing; a shot of the ball hurtling across the screen . . . None of these shots needs to be in slow motion for real time to be stretched out in reel time by virtue of montage. By assembling an American-style montage in this manner, the filmmaker has expanded an action that would take only a few seconds in real time into a 60-second montage.

There's a third definition of montage, and it is the most complicated to describe and comprehend. In the Soviet cinema of the immediate post-Revolutionary period—which is to say the twentieth century's late 'teens and '20s—filmmakers conducted a fierce debate about the nature and effects of montage. Soviet filmmakers were excited by the 1917 Marxist revolution that sought to transform their country from a feudal state to a modern industrial empire overnight, and they wanted to find ways of expressing this political energy on film. The key filmmakers involved in this blend of polemical debate and cinematic practice were **Sergei Eisenstein, Vsevolod Pudovkin,** and **Dziga Vertov.** Pudovkin believed that shots were like bricks that were carefully placed, one by one, to form a kind of cinematic wall, and that montage was effectively the cement that held them together; the resulting film, like a wall, was more meaningful than the simple sum of its bricklike parts *because montage added meaning to the individual shots' content.* Vertov, being essentially a documentarian, was not interested in the narrative cohesion montage could produce; his most famous film, *Man with a Movie Camera* (1929), is a kaleidoscopic assemblage of shots put together with the attitude of a symphonic musician rather than a storyteller.

For Eisenstein, montage meant a kind of *dynamic editing used both to expose and explore the dialectics, or oppositional conflicts, of a given situation, and to create in the mind of the viewer a revolutionary synthesis.* The most famous example of Soviet-style montage in film history, in fact, is the "Odessa Steps" sequence from Eisenstein's *Battleship Potemkin* (1925). The situation Eisenstein depicts is a fictional re-creation of the 1905 uprising of sailors on the eponymous battleship; they mutinied against the harsh czarist government and received a strong measure of popular support from the people of Odessa, who in the sequence in question have gathered on the city steps to voice their solidarity with the sailors. The czar's soldiers march down the flight of steps and begin firing their guns at the citizens. Not only does Eisenstein edit this sequence of shots very rapidly in order to intensify the sense of conflict between the monarchy and the people, but the compositions within each shot are themselves full of conflict—strong contrasts of lights and darks, lots of diagonal vectors, and so on. There is nothing static about this sequence—not in its editing, not in its individual shots. It is the classic Soviet-style montage.

For Eisenstein, shots were meant to *collide*; his style of montage was the opposite of smooth, apparently seamless continuity editing (which is defined below). And his goal was to create in the minds of his audience a revolutionary synthesis of all these conflicts—to encourage the viewer, through montage, to *think* and *see* in a new and, he hoped, radical way. By editing these conflict-filled shots together in a way that intensifies conflict rather than smoothing it over, Eisenstein hoped to inspire in his audiences a kind of revolutionary thinking. For him, the creative act was not only that of the filmmaker who shoots and assembles the film. An equally creative act is performed by those of us who see the film; we take

FIGURE 4.2 Four images from the "Odessa Steps" sequence, *Battleship Potemkin* (1925) (frame enlargements).

in all of these images by way of montage and consequently put the pieces together in our own minds in our own ways.

What links all of these definitions of *montage* is not only the splicing together of individual shots. What makes *montage* worthy of study in any of its three forms and definitions is that it is a fundamentally creative act—the product of artistic decision-making. As the French film theorist André Bazin once wrote, montage yields "the creation of a sense or meaning not proper to the images themselves but derived exclusively from their juxtaposition." As the rest of the chapter will make clear, editing compounds information and creates evocative associations that form a cornerstone of any film's expressive meaning.

THE KULESHOV EXPERIMENT

Film studies illustrates editing's ability to create new associations and ideas in the viewer's mind with another example from Soviet cinema—an apolitical example, but one that still neatly describes the way Soviet filmmakers viewed montage as imaginative and dynamic. By splicing together snippets of photographed reality, these filmmakers understood that something new was being created—something that didn't exist on a brute material plane but *did* exist in the minds of a movie audience—and *only* in those minds. The film director and theorist **Lev Kuleshov** is said to have conducted an experiment involving the effects of montage on an audience's perception of emotion. He filmed the great Russian actor **Ivan Mozhukin** in medium close-up, with a sincere-looking but neutral expression on his face. Kuleshov then filmed a shot of a bowl of soup, a shot of a coffin, and a shot of a little girl playing. Figure 4.3 shows how Kuleshov edited the sequence.

Audiences are said to have marveled at the great actor's extraordinary range and subtle technique. Mozhukin could express great hunger! Mozhukin could express extraordinary grief! Mozhukin could express exactly the kind of pride and joy a parent feels when watching his child at play! *What a great actor!*

In fact, of course, it was the same shot of Mozhukin, and he wasn't expressing anything other than neutrality. It was the audience members who provided the emotional content of the sequence simply by making associations in their own minds from one shot to the next.

One of the underappreciated aspects of Kuleshov's experiment is that Kuleshov didn't just create emotional content by way of editing. He also defined and constructed three continuous but distinct *spaces*: Mozhukin and the bowl of soup in one, Mozhukin and the coffin in the second, Mozhukin and the child in the third. The actor was seen as being in the same place as the soup bowl; the same place as the coffin; and the same place as the little girl—spaces created solely by way of editing.

The dirty little secret of the Kuleshov experiment is the fact that nobody is on record as ever having seen the film itself. In point of fact, Kuleshov may never have screened or even filmed the sequence. But then he didn't have to. He knew it would work.

CONTINUITY EDITING

Classical Hollywood style, which film studies defines as the set of predominant formal techniques used by most American narrative filmmakers through the twentieth century and to the present day, relies on several editing principles to achieve its central goal: to keep audience members so wrapped up in the fictional world created onscreen that they cease to be conscious of watching a movie and, instead, believe that they are witnessing something real. Whether it's a romance between two

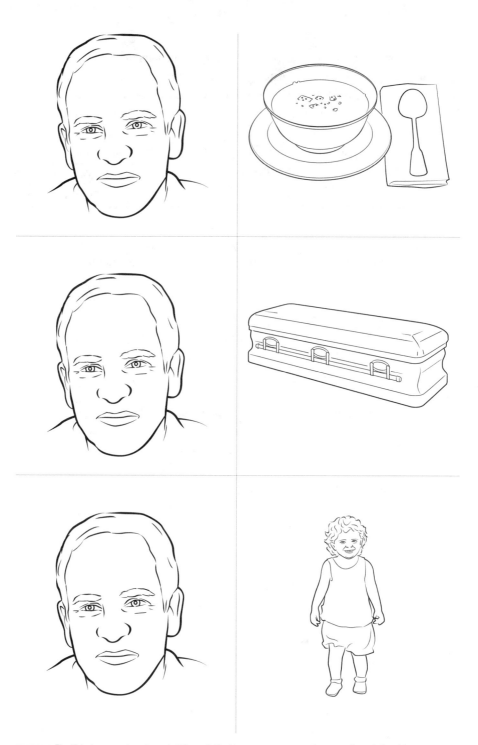

FIGURE 4.3 The Kuleshov experiment created three distinct screen *spaces* as well as narrative relationships.

believable characters or an action film with a larger-than-life hero or a horror film featuring a preposterous monster, classical Hollywood films want us to believe that we are watching reality, if only for the duration of the picture.

For example, have you ever noticed that film characters rarely turn and look precisely at the camera and speak directly to you in the audience? Although direct addresses from characters to audiences have happened from time to time—*Annie Hall* (1977) and *Wayne's World* (1992) contain notable examples of this violation of formal convention—it's startling when it occurs precisely because it occurs so rarely. The effect of such direct addresses is to jolt us out of our dreamlike immersion in the film's story into a sudden awareness of the film's artificiality: we know we weren't there when the movie was being filmed, and we know that the character isn't really talking to *us* at all. This jolt makes us aware that we're watching a movie.

Classical Hollywood style strives to avoid calling attention to the means and forms of its own construction. Through strictly formal techniques, Hollywood films attempt to smooth over the many cuts that occur. They try to maintain a sense of spatial unity within each individual sequence. They attempt, to use loftier critical discourse, *to efface themselves*—to render themselves unnoticeable. The overall term that describes this formal system is CONTINUITY EDITING, also known as INVISIBLE EDITING. Continuity editing is *a set of editing practices that establish spatial and/or temporal continuity between shots*—in other words, any of the various techniques that filmmakers employ to keep their narratives moving forward logically and smoothly, without jarring disruptions in space or time, and without making the audience aware that they are in fact watching a work of art. Continuity editing strives not only to keep disruptions to a minimum but to *actively promote a sense of narrative and spatial coherence and stability in the face of hundreds or even thousands of the discrete bits of celluloid called shots*. What are these techniques?

The first set of continuity editing techniques involve ways to downplay the jarring effect of cutting. They are called **editing matches**. There are three essential ways of matching one shot to another, and they are defined according to how the match is made.

1. Matching on action
2. Eye-line matching
3. Graphic matching

MATCHING ON ACTION occurs when a piece of physical action in the first shot continues in the second shot. Here's a simple example: In the first shot, a character opens a door; in the second shot, she goes through the doorway. Her movement provides the continuity that matches the two shots. If the shots are set up well and the editor knows his stuff, the audience will slide visually from the first shot to the second, thanks to the seemingly continuous, apparently uninterrupted movement of the character through the doorway.

Let's use another baseball game as a more complicated example. The pitcher throws a pitch in Shot 1: we see him hurl the ball from the right side of the screen to the left. In Shot 2, the ball flies into the image from … which side? Yes, from the right side of the screen to the left. This makes it appear that it's the same ball pitched by the same pitcher at the same time. How odd and disruptive it would be if the ball flew from the pitcher's mound to home plate in one direction in the first shot and entered the succeeding shot from the opposite direction. It would make no sense visually. An experimental filmmaker may choose to create such a disruptive effect, but most narrative filmmakers seek to avoid that kind of visual illogic.

Now the batter takes a swing and connects: it's a line drive, and the ball goes flying out of the image on the … right. When the ball reenters the image in the next shot—the second baseman is waiting for it—where does it enter the image and in which direction is it traveling?[1]

EYE-LINE MATCHING works on a similar principle, but instead of using the direction of a physical action to determine the way that shots are set up, filmed, and edited together, it's the direction of characters' gazes that determines where the camera is placed, in which direction the actors are looking when they're filmed, and how the two (or more) resulting shots are edited together. Before our pitcher throws the ball to the batter, he takes a long look at the catcher, who uses some hand signals to communicate with him. He then turns to the first baseman to check on whether the runner there was preparing to steal second. The director films the sequence in four shots, and when he edits them all together, these four shots make sense *spatially* because of eye-line matching:

SHOT 1:   Full, eye-level shot of PITCHER on mound looking off-screen *left*.

SHOT 2:   Full, eye-level shot of CATCHER crouching and forming hand signals behind batter; the catcher is looking offscreen *right*. The impression created is that the pitcher and the catcher are looking at each other, even though they are not in the same shot.

SHOT 3:   Full, eye-level shot of PITCHER turning on his heels and looking offscreen *right*.

1. If the ball flies out of the right side of the image after the batter hits it, it must enter the image again on the left for the rules of continuity editing to be observed.

SHOT 4:   Full, eye-level shot of FIRST BASEMAN guarding OP-
POSING PLAYER and looking offscreen . . .[2]

2. If the pitcher is looking offscreen right, the first base-man must look off-screen *left* if we are to believe that the two men are looking at each other.

When audiences see this sequence projected as part of an action sequence in a baseball movie, they will understand that the players are looking at one another. Why? Because the rules of eye-line matching have
been respected. Imagine the spatial disorientation the audience would
experience if the pitcher was filmed looking in the "wrong" direction; the
sequence would make little spatial sense and would be much more chal-
lenging to follow. Many people in the audience would be bewildered.
Confusion may be a legitimate artistic goal, and a truly radical filmmaker may choose to baffle people to make a point. But that filmmaker
would find it difficult to succeed with most commercial moviegoers—a
legitimate artistic goal in itself, perhaps, but whoever financed the picture would probably not see it that way.

The term *eye-line match* can also be used to describe an edit that occurs between a shot of a person and a following shot of an object though
there is also a particular term that describes it, too— GLANCE-OBJECT
MATCH. Say in the first shot we see a hungry-looking little girl in profile
staring toward the left of the image; we would not be jarred or jolted in
the slightest to find that the second shot in the sequence contained the
image of a large dish of ice cream, and we would assume—given the
fact that the director has set up the shots and matched them well—that
the little girl is looking at the ice cream. The fact that the little girl was
filmed on a Friday afternoon and the ice cream was filmed separately the
following Monday would not matter in the slightest: the glance-object
match would bring the little girl and the ice cream together spatially and
temporally in a meaningful and coherent way.

The term *eye-line match* may seem odd to describe this two-shot sequence because although the girl's eyes are directed offscreen left, the
dish of ice cream can't look back at her. But eye-line matching is not
limited to two or more sets of eyes. Even with two characters, only one
set of eyes needs to look in a certain direction for an eye-line match to
be made.

Of the three types of matches, GRAPHIC MATCHING may be the
most difficult to describe. It refers to matching made on the basis of a
compositional element—a door or window frame, for example, or any
prominent shape. Graphic matches are made by cutting (or dissolving,
fading, or wiping) from one shape in the first shot to a similar shape—in
the same relative position in the frame—in the second shot. If instead
of the easily catchable line drive straight into the second baseman's mitt
in the example above, the batter had hit a high but long fly ball that

FIGURE 4.4 A graphic match in *2001: A Space Odyssey* (1968): from the prehistoric to the futuristic (frame enlargements).

appeared to be heading out of the park, the director could have made a point about the batter's quick demise by matching a shot of the catcher's empty rounded glove with the similarly sized and shaped fielder's glove that receives the batter's ball with a thwack.

If the batter had been successful, on the other hand, a graphic match could have expressed the point by comparing the shape of the flying ball to a round comet hurtling through the sky leaving a fiery trail in its wake. There is a famous graphic match in Stanley Kubrick's *2001: A Space Odyssey* (1968) in which a prehistoric ape tosses a bone in the air in one shot. After it begins to fall to earth in a subsequent shot, Kubrick matches it with a rectangular spaceship, thereby signaling not only the passage of millions of years but also equating a primitive weapon with a futuristic means of space travel. Usually, graphic matches are not so clearly designed to add additional meaning to the sequence; graphic matches, like eye-line matches and matches on action, are generally employed to smooth over cuts rather than call attention to them.

THE 180° SYSTEM

In addition to these three types of matches, classical Hollywood cinema developed a so-called rule in order to maintain a sense of coherent space within a given film sequence: the 180° rule. Because it is a rule that is often broken, film studies tends more and more to call it THE 180° SYSTEM. Terminology aside, the 180° system provides a simple but crucial way for filmmakers to preserve spatial coherence within a given scene.

Imagine a scene taking place in a living room; there are two chairs set at three-quarter angles to one another, and in these chairs sit two women.

The 180° system suggests that the best way for a director to establish and maintain spatial coherence in this scene (or any scene) is to draw an imaginary line across the axis of the action (the middle of the set), dividing it in two. In figure 4.5, the 180° axis is represented by a dotted line.

If the director keeps the camera on one side of the dotted line for the duration of the sequence—and she would probably choose the side that includes the characters' faces—when the film is edited and projected onto a screen, the woman on the left in the illustration will always be on the right. This seems simple.

FIGURE 4.5 The 180° system: the cameras generally stay on one side of the dotted line. See figure 4.6 for the corresponding images shot by each camera.

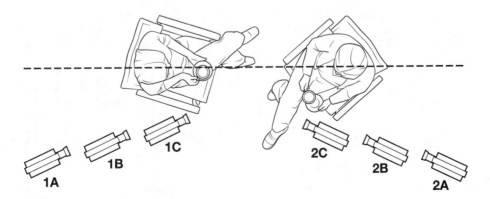

But what happens if she shoots a shot or two from the other side of the imaginary line?[3]

Please note: the director can *move* the camera across the line while filming without disrupting spatial coherence because the camera movement would make it clear that the space is whole and unified. It is only when *cutting* across the imaginary line that spatial confusion may occur.

SHOT/REVERSE-SHOT PATTERN

One of the most common, efficient, and effective editing patterns developed by classical Hollywood cinema is the SHOT/REVERSE-SHOT PATTERN. To define this technique, let's use the above example of the living room scene illustrated immediately above. The two women are seated in living room chairs set at a three-quarter angle toward each other, and they are having a conversation. Establishing and maintaining the 180° system, the director chooses her first shot to be taken from position 1 (see fig. 4.6). The resulting image onscreen is that of the woman in medium shot facing at a three-quarter angle to the left of the image. Since our director has chosen to film and edit this sequence using a shot/reverse-shot pattern, she then positions the camera to film the so-called "reverse angle," namely from position 2: now the camera faces the other woman, who is seen onscreen in medium shot, also at three-quarter angle, looking toward the right of the screen.

The word "reverse" in this instance does not really mean an absolute reversal of the camera's place; the camera does not cross over to its truly opposite position because that would mean violating the 180°

3. By cutting across the axis and shooting from the other side of the line, the characters when projected would appear to flip from their regular side of the screen to the opposite side. For most audiences, this would be jarring and disruptive.

FIGURE 4.6 The shot/reverse-shot pattern: If the first shot of a shot/reverse-shot pattern is 2A, the second shot—the reverse shot—would be 1A. If the director then cuts to a close-up of the woman on the left (1C), the reverse shot would be 2C. Now imagine editing a scene between these two characters, using the framings indicated.

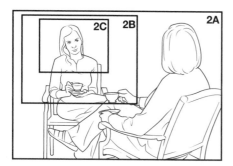
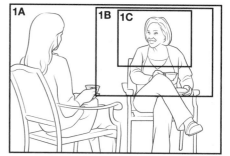

axis system. Instead, *shot/reverse-shot* means that the shots alternate not between the two characters but between the two *camera positions*, one pointing right, the other pointing left. The shot/reverse-shot pattern can be used to reveal both characters in both shots—the camera pointing over the shoulder of one to the face and upper body of the other—or we can see them as individuals appearing to look at each other by virtue of eye-line matching. Or the shots can be imbalanced: in shot 1 we might see over the shoulder of one character to the face and shoulders of another character, while the so-called reverse shot might only be an angled close-up of the first character. The point is that the director shoots an *apparent* reverse angle while maintaining the 180° axis system, thereby showing both characters from more or less equal but appropriately reverse angles.

STUDY GUIDE: ANALYZING SHOT-TO-SHOT EDITING

To learn to analyze editing, you are going to begin with an exercise of your imagination. You are a beginning filmmaker, and your assignment is to film—in exactly three shots—a character whom you will reveal, mostly by way of editing, to be mentally disturbed.

Other filmmakers might take the easy way out and use mise-en-scene elements like makeup (darkened, hollow-looking eyes, for instance, or a lot of stage blood smeared across the face) or a piece of outrageous physical action or dialogue (the character falling down on the ground and rolling around swearing incoherently, and so on). Still another lazy director could telegraph the character's insanity at the beginning of the sequence by starting off with a close-up of a sign that reads "Pittsburgh Home for the Criminally Insane."

Not you. You will convey this character's insanity by way of editing. You have precisely three shots to do it with, too; not one, not two, not four, but *three*. Yes, the content of each of these three shots will convey information. But your primary task is to consider the shots' contents *in relation to one another*.

Give yourself some time to consider the possibilities.

Once you have thought about the problem for a few minutes, begin to construct the three-shot sequence in your mind at the very least and, if you have even the most rudimentary drawing skills, on paper.

What is your first shot? If you must convey a character's craziness chiefly by way of editing, how do you begin the sequence?

Here are some potential opening shots:

1. An extreme close-up of a single eye staring blankly out from the screen.
2. A very high angle shot of a young man standing in an empty room and looking out the window.
3. A close-up of a young woman's hand nervously twisting a pencil around, seemingly unable to stop.

Bear in mind that the second shot of the sequence will need to relate in some way to the first shot, and that some form of transition must be employed.

Let's concentrate on example 2, above, and decide on a second shot with which to follow it. Here are some potential second shots:

2A. An even higher-angle extreme long shot of the young man taken from outside the building. There is no one else in the shot: nobody on the sidewalk outside the building, and nobody in any of the other windows.
2B. A close-up of his foot tapping anxiously and continually on the floor.
2C. Linked by an eye-line match, an extreme close-up of a pigeon on the sidewalk far below.

Notice that not much is happening in our sequence. Except for the foot-tapping and pencil-twisting, there is very little physical action. But as the sequence begins to take shape, the relation of shot to shot begins (or should begin, anyway) to convey a certain uneasiness—a sense of anxiety that is enhanced if not entirely created by the relationship of one shot to another. It's true that the character's extreme solitude is expressed by the content of the shots of him looking out the window, but that effect is strongly enhanced by the relationship between the two shots. And the pigeon is disturbing not because it is a pigeon—we might be filming a benign sequence in a city park instead of a three-shot indication of a character's madness—but because it is seen in relation to the first shot of the young man, and the bird's relationship to him is unexplained and therefore troubling.

Let's finish up by following through with 2A, above—the extreme long shot taken from outside the building. What kind of shot would drive home the point of the sequence? It's your decision.

WRITING ABOUT EDITING

As you learned in chapter 1, there are seemingly innumerable mise-en-scene elements within a single shot if you look at it closely and carefully enough. Rapidly cut sequences only compound the extraordinary amount of visual information available for analysis. So to begin to learn how to write about shot-to-shot editing, take a DVD of the film of your choice and choose a simple and fairly short sequence to work on—say five to ten shots in a sequence lasting between 30 seconds and 1 minute. Be sure to choose an individual sequence or part of an individual sequence rather than the end of one sequence and the beginning of another; that's the subject of chapter 6. A **sequence** is simply a series of interrelated shots that form a coherent unit of dramatic action.)

Describe the content of each image thoroughly, but concentrate on the methods by which the director effects transitions from shot to shot. What type of matching does he or she employ, if any? Does the sequence use a shot/reverse-shot pattern?

Here's an example drawn from the end of Charles Chaplin's *City Lights* (1931). It's longer than ten shots, but it is one of the most famous sequences in world film history; not only is it exceptionally emotionally satisfying, but it contains a fascinating lapse in continuity:

SHOT 1:   A two-shot of the Tramp and the Girl; the Girl is standing in the doorway of the flower shop on the right side of the screen, and the Tramp is standing on the sidewalk on the left side of the screen. The Girl reaches out with her right hand and offers the Tramp a flower she is holding. The Tramp turns and reaches out to take the flower with his left hand. The flower is in the center of the screen as he takes it. As the Tramp pulls his left hand back with the flower, the Girl steps toward him as he puts the flower in his right hand and quickly pulls him by the left hand toward her. Chaplin cuts on this action to:

SHOT 2:	A closer two-shot taken from the reverse angle. This shot is taken over the Tramp's right shoulder. The Girl is seen at a three-quarter angle; both characters are in medium shot. The Girl, now holding the Tramp's left hand in hers, looks the Tramp in the eye and smiles, but as she begins to pat the Tramp's left hand with her right hand (the Tramp is still holding the flower in his other hand), her expression changes to one of newfound understanding: she recognizes the touch of her previously unseen benefactor's hand and realizes that this ridiculous homeless man has enabled her vision to be restored. She now appears to be looking not only at him but into him; her gaze is penetrating. Chaplin cuts on the action of the Girl patting the Tramp's hand to:
SHOT 3:	A reverse-angle shot, taken at a closer distance (but not a close-up) of the two people's hands clasped in the center of the image. The Tramp's right hand is raised to his face. The camera tilts up and pans slightly left to reveal a closer medium shot of the Tramp, who is holding the flower in front of the right side of his face, his hand covering his mouth. The side of the Girl's head is visible on the right side of the image; her left hand is now touching the lapel of the Tramp's worn jacket. She begins to withdraw her left hand as Chaplin cuts on the action to:
SHOT 4:	A reverse angle two-shot (the same as Shot 2). She now pulls her right hand back and touches her own face in a gesture that indicates comprehension; the weight of her recognition grows. Oddly, the flower the Tramp holds is no longer at the level of his face but is now in front of his chest. The Girl mouths the words, "It's you?" before Chaplin cuts to:
SHOT 5:	A TITLE CARD that reads, "You?" Cut to:
SHOT 6:	More or less the same shot as Shot 3, only a bit closer; now only the barest sliver of the Girl's head is visible at the very edge of the right-hand side of the image. The Tramp nods in response to the Girl's question. The flower is back up at the Tramp's face, and his index finger appears to be touching his lips. Chaplin cuts on his slight nodding action to:
SHOT 7:	The same as Shot 4. The flower is again at chest level. Chaplin cuts rather quickly to:
SHOT 8:	The same as Shot 6; the flower is again at the Tramp's face. He points to his own right eye and mouths the words, "You can see now?" Cut to:
SHOT 9:	A title card that reads, "You can see now?" Cut to:
SHOT 10:	The same as Shot 8. The Tramp smiles. Cut to:
SHOT 11:	The same as Shot 7. The flower is once again at chest level as the Girl nods and mouths the word, "Yes." She swallows, indicating the depth of her emotion, and mouths the words, "I can see now." Cut to:
SHOT 12:	A title card that reads, "Yes, I can see now." Cut to:
SHOT 13:	The same as Shot 11. The Girl appears to mouth the word "yes" twice as she gazes at the Tramp. Chaplin cuts to:

SHOT 14:   More or less the same as Shot 10: Not quite close enough to be a close-up of the Tramp, because not only is his face visible but also his shoulders, but close enough to register the depth of emotion in his face as he begins to giggle with pleasure at the Girl's recognition of him. The flower is once again at the level of his face, and his hand partially covers his mouth. Fade out.

What do you notice about the sequence? Film scholars have puzzled over the ending of *City Lights* since the film's release in 1931; the sequence is one of the most emotionally satisfying endings ever filmed, and yet the director, Chaplin, violates one of the cardinal rules of continuity editing by not matching the position of the flower from shot to shot. Is this simply an error—an editing glitch? Or is there an expressive purpose behind it? Could it be a glitch *and still have expressive meaning?* These questions could form the basis of a great final paper for your course.

CHAPTER 5
SOUND

A VERY SHORT HISTORY OF FILM SOUND

We call them *silent movies*, those early films that did not have a soundtrack. But they weren't actually silent. Most motion pictures of that era were screened with some form of live music. In large, urban theaters, exhibitors would often hire a full orchestra to accompany the movies they showed, while in small venues there would simply be a pianist. Organs, too, were commonly used to accompany films in those years. Not only could a single pipe organ or electric organ simulate a variety of instruments from clarinets to violins, but it could also provide a variety of sound effects such as bells and knocks.

It cannot even be said that silent films lacked spoken dialogue. Characters spoke to each other all the time. But instead of hearing their words, audiences read them onscreen in the form of TITLE CARDS—some of those words, anyway, since not every line of dialogue was printed in full.

Title cards also conveyed information about characters, when and where scenes were set, and so on.

Experiments with synchronizing the image with audible, recorded dialogue, music, and sound effects began in Hollywood in the 1910s. By the early 1920s, there were two competing systems—SOUND ON FILM and SOUND ON DISC. The latter system recorded sounds on phonograph discs (otherwise known as records), which then had to be cued to begin playing at precisely the correct instant in order to match the images that were projected onscreen. The sound-on-film system, which proved less cumbersome and which ultimately was adopted around the world, records sound onto photographic film in the form of light waves, which are then read optically by the projector and converted back into sound.

In October 1927, Warner Bros. released *The Jazz Singer*, the first feature film with synchronized dialogue and songs. Starring the popular song-and-dance man Al Jolson, it's the story of a young Orthodox Jew who defies his father by becoming a jazz singer instead of a cantor (a vocalist who sings prayers during Jewish services). Jakie Rabinowitz leaves home, Americanizes his name to Jack Robin, and turns up ten years later at a cabaret, where he sings a synchronized song and then addresses not only the audience onscreen but the movie audience as well: "Wait a minute! Wait a minute! You ain't heard nothin' yet!" *The Jazz Singer* was a successful moneymaker for Warner Bros., and although it took several more years for synchronized sound to become standard in world cinema, the film effectively signaled the end of the so-called silent era and the beginning of feature-length TALKIES, an era that continues today.

Perhaps needless to say, there have been many technological developments since *The Jazz Singer*—advances in microphones, sound recorders, and speakers—but the details of these improvements are best left to upper-level filmmaking and film history courses. One common term that you might be curious to know a bit about, though, is DOLBY, since many if not most commercial films carry that particular credit and logo. Dolby Laboratories specializes in the noise reduction system invented by Ray Dolby in 1965 for use first in the recording industry and, a few years later, in the cinema. (The first film that used Dolby technology was Stanley Kubrick's *A Clockwork Orange*, 1971.) The Dolby system greatly reduces background noises, enhances the clarity of voices, sound effects, and music, and currently offers a total of six separate channels that play sound from speakers placed behind the screen on the left, center, and right, a subwoofer, and surround-sound speakers on the left and right in the auditorium. The digital information for each of these channels is placed, ingeniously, between the sprocket holes of the film.

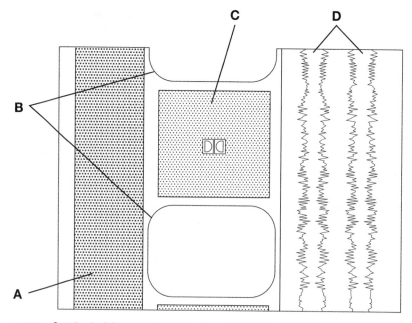

FIGURE 5.1 Soundtracks (*left to right*): (A) the Sony Dynamic Digital Sound (SDDS) track; (B) sprocket holes; (C) the Dolby Digital track; (D) the analog soundtrack.

RECORDING, RERECORDING, EDITING, AND MIXING

The process of creating, manipulating, and playing back cinematic sound is typically long, expensive, and increasingly complex from a technical and personnel standpoint, and since the specific technologies involved in filmmaking are, here as elsewhere, less important to film studies than the *meanings* generated by the finished films, there is no point in an introductory class to overwhelm you with technical details. Still, you should be aware of the enormous amount of time, effort, and skill that go into every feature film soundtrack you hear.

Just as the creation of the image track begins with light entering the camera's lens, the soundtrack's genesis is the sound that enters a microphone. A scene can be miked by way of a BOOM, a glorified broom handle onto which a microphone is attached before being held out over the actors' heads just out of camera range, or by way of mikes attached to the actors' bodies, heads, or clothing. RADIO MICROPHONES have the virtue of being small and wireless—and therefore easy to hide. In addition, there are SHOTGUN MICROPHONES that pick up sounds at some distance but must point exactly in the direction of the sound being miked—usually an actor's speech.

It's not only dialogue that requires one or more mikes. Sound effects, too, must be picked up by a mike before they can be recorded, as does music. This is not only for amplification. Microphone filters reduce if not entirely eliminate unwanted or unnecessary frequencies, thereby rendering the recorded sound even clearer than the original.

Sound is recorded and edited in either **analog** or **digital** form. In an analog system, sounds are recorded onto magnetic tape that is edited in much the same way as the image track; the magnetic tape, like the film, is literally cut into strips of varying lengths and spliced together sequentially. Editors rely on the clacking of the clapboard described in chapter 8 to synchronize the image track with its corresponding magnetic tape. Contemporary digital editing systems rely on a DIGITAL AUDIO WORKSTATION (DAW), a computer and specialized application that match the digital recording with the image.

Much of the work of creating the soundtrack is done during POST-PRODUCTION, the period after the images have been shot. In a way, the term *postproduction* is something of a misnomer, precisely because the production process goes on long after the photography has been completed. This is certainly the case with the soundtrack.

FOLEY ARTISTS are sound effects creators who duplicate certain sounds in a special recording studio called a Foley stage or Foley studio. Various kinds of footsteps, for instance, don't sound quite right when they are recorded at the time they are photographed. It takes a Foley artist, specifically a **Foley walker**, to re-create a more accurate effect by walking on, say, sand or gravel and recording the sounds that result.

Foley artists and other sound technicians may strive to create or enhance the audience's sense of realism, but others can be said to work toward a different aesthetic goal. We take film SCORES for granted as a part of our experience of motion pictures, but unless we walk around listening to our iPods all day, our real lives do not have musical accompaniments to set and develop the mood of the moment the way movies do. The effect of a score, then, cannot be considered to be simply "realistic." Appropriate to the particular film, yes—"realistic," no. Whether it's chords from a single guitar or the rich, symphonic sound of a full orchestra, the elements of a film's musical score augment the audience's emotional response to the characters, story, and images irrespective of whether the moment is meant to be real-seeming or not.

An original score may be written by a **composer**, though many films also (or even exclusively) utilize preexisting recorded songs.

Finally, the **sound mixer** takes all the different components—the dialogue tracks, the sound effects, the score, and so on—and brings them together in an aesthetically balanced way. Adjusting volume and tone by bringing parts of the dialogue up while bringing certain sound effects down, and manipulating the tracks so that sounds seem to move around the theater—these are some of the critical tasks in MIXING. And just as there is no single, correct way to film any given scene, there is no single and correct way to mix sound. It's all a matter of honoring the director's vision (or in this case *hearing*). A horror director, for example, may want her sound mixer to produce an unnerving, echo-like quality on the soundtrack—a quality that might not be what the director of a romantic comedy would want. (Then again, it might be, depending on what the director is trying to achieve.) A composer may create an especially beautiful piece of orchestration, but if the director doesn't think its use is of value to the scene for which it was written, the sound mixer will remove it from the soundtrack.

ANALYTICAL CATEGORIES OF FILM SOUND

Because the goal here and throughout *Film Studies* is not to try to figure out how a given cinematic element—in this case *sound*—was created, but rather to locate, define, and analyze elements of expressive meaning, you may be wondering how to deal with film sound productively. Let's begin by categorizing some of the various sounds you actually experience when watching and listening to films.

The three main categories of film sound are **dialogue, music,** and **sound effects.** *Dialogue* includes all the spoken words in a film. Dictionaries define the word *dialogue* as *a conversation between two people* (as opposed to *monologue—a speech, usually long, by one person*). But in film terminology, *dialogue* refers to *any* spoken words, including conversations, monologues, random words audible in crowd scenes, and voice-over narration. The term *music* is self-explanatory, but it is important to remember that in film, music may be *diegetic* or *nondiegetic*; it may be sourced within the world of the story (we see someone with an iPod and earphones onscreen and we hear the music she is hearing) or not (we hear music playing as a bear walks alone through the woods). *Sound effects* are all other noises, including both diegetic and nondiegetic sounds. The crash of ocean waves, birds chirping, a cannon's boom, comical honking sounds—every noise that isn't spoken words or music is considered a sound effect, whether it's diegetic or not.

One key distinction to make among types of film sound is whether it is SYNCHRONOUS or NONSYNCHRONOUS. *Synchronous* means *occurring at the same time*, which in cinematic sound terms means that a sound is heard at the same instant as its source appears on the screen. We see a woman's lips move, and we hear the matching words. A visitor presses a doorbell, and we hear the bell. A high school kid turns on a car radio, and music begins to play. These sounds and images are temporally and spatially matched: *synchronous sound*.

Not all sounds are synchronous. *Nonsynchronous sounds*, in contrast, are sounds that occur at a different time and/or in a different space than what appears onscreen. Directors and editors often use nonsynchronous sounds to make cuts from scene to scene smoother, less jarring. These are called SOUND BRIDGES. For instance, at the tail end of one scene, a man is being handcuffed and led away in long shot. Anticipating the next scene, the sound of a cell door clanking shut is heard on the soundtrack for a second or two before the director cuts to a full shot of the man, now a prisoner, in his cell. For the last few seconds of the earlier scene, the clanking sound is nonsynchronous with the image; once the next scene begins, the sounds of the cell become synchronous.

Some nonsynchronous sounds are mismatched with the image, either by intention or by technological failure. When a film print becomes worn, for instance, or has been poorly printed to begin with, characters' speech may slip out of synch. Film dialogue that has been dubbed into another language is also nonsynchronous—characters' lips move to form words that are obviously different than those heard on the soundtrack.

A related term is ASYNCHRONOUS SOUND. Whereas the prefix *non-* means *not*, the prefix *a-* means *without*. *Asynchronous sound*, therefore, refers to those sounds that are heard without their sources being seen onscreen; the term *asynchronous sound* means the same thing as the term OFFSCREEN SOUND. For example, a shot of an office located in a large city may be accompanied by faint traffic noises. The cars and buses that are presumably producing the sounds aren't visible onscreen—the shot is of an interior, and there may not even be a visible window—but the offscreen sounds are understood to be occurring simultaneously with the visible action.

The term *offscreen sound* leads to yet another: AMBIENT SOUND—the background noises of the scene's environment. Very few places on Earth are perfectly silent. Car motors run and leaves rustle; pipes rumble and air conditioners hum. When film conversations are shot and recorded, edited, and screened without accompanying ambient sounds, they sound like they are taking place in a weirdly muffled or even totally sound-proofed room. Listen to the room in which you are sitting, and hear the particular ambient sounds of that particular space. Noises like the ones you are now hearing are generally recorded separately from the dialogue and added later during mixing. Even in the absence of car horns and alarms, barking dogs in the distance, and the like, every room has what is called ROOM TONE, which is also recorded apart from the dialogue and inserted into conversations to fill any gaps that may otherwise occur.

As you already know, another way of distinguishing cinematic sounds is to categorize them on the basis of whether they are DIEGETIC or NONDIEGETIC—in other words, whether the sounds are sourced in the world of the story or not. Almost all film dialogue is diegetic: characters speaking, whether synchronously, nonsynchronously, or asynchronously, usually do so within the world of the story. For a funny exception to this general rule, see the beginning of the comedy *The Girl Can't Help It* (1956), directed by Frank Tashlin. The star of the film, Tom Ewell, appears onscreen, looks toward the camera, and directly addresses the audience: "Ladies and gentlemen, the motion picture you are about to see is a story of music. I play the role of Tom Miller, an agent . . ." Ewell's dialogue *refers* to the story but remains outside of it; it is, therefore nondiegetic dialogue.

With the notable exception of so-called **backstage musicals**, a film's score is almost always nondiegetic; it is rarely sourced in the world of the story. (*Backstage musicals* are musicals that take place in the world of theater and film; their characters are themselves performers who are putting on a show, so their songs are often set in a real-world context). In a melodrama, the heartbroken mother of a dying baby begins to cry while, on the soundtrack, we hear the sound of violins. Or in a horror film, someone slowly approaches a closed door behind which lurk a group of flesh-eating zombies, and we hear a couple of beats of tense percussion. The violation of this general rule can be used to great comic effect. In Blake Edwards' Pink Panther comedy *A Shot in the Dark* (1964), Peter Sellers, as Inspector Jacques Clouseau, turns up at a nudist colony and walks ludicrously past an equally nude orchestra playing the familiar "Theme from *A Shot in the Dark*" by Henry Mancini. The film's score, which had previously been nondiegetic, suddenly and ridiculously becomes diegetically sourced in the world of the story.

In their book *The Film Experience*, Timothy Corrigan and Patricia White write: "One question offers a simple way to distinguish between diegetic and nondiegetic sound: can the characters in the film hear the sound?" If they can hear it, or if they could conceivably hear it, it's almost certainly diegetic. For example, a woman who is alone in her bedroom might not hear the faint footsteps of the intruder who is about to kill her, but the intruder can hear them—and we hear them, too: these footsteps are therefore diegetic sounds. The creepy music that accompanies the scene, however, cannot be heard by either the woman or the intruder and is therefore nondiegetic—unless, of course, that particular piece of music is coming from a radio or other sound source in the woman's bedroom;

in that case, both she and the intruder can hear it, which would make it diegetic.

Sometimes in a narrative film, a character seemingly speaks directly to the audience without appearing onscreen. This is called **voice-over** narration, or **VO**. Otto Preminger's classic film noir, *Laura* (1944), for instance, begins (after the opening credits, which are accompanied by the nondiegetic "Theme from *Laura*") with a voice-over: a dead man speaks to us from an entirely black screen for several seconds before an image appears. VO is also often used to convey a character's (otherwise) unspoken thoughts. For example, a shot of a college student looking attentively at his professor, who is discussing nondiegetic sound, may be accompanied by his voice in VO commenting on how boring the class actually is and how he would much rather be on a beach with his girlfriend.

SOUND AND SPACE

Ever since sound became standard in world cinema in the 1930s, film-makers have had to construct spaces aurally as well as visually. Because of technological limitations, the earliest synch sound films were especially cumbersome to create, and accordingly, the resulting sound space had an artificial quality. Microphones picked up not just the intended sound but *any* sound, including that of the camera; as a result, cameras had to be placed in soundproofed boxes. Moreover, all the sounds had to be re-corded simultaneously—there were no separate tracks and no mixing—so, if the film was to have an orchestral score, an orchestra had to be pres-ent on the set, playing alongside the actors as their dialogue scenes were shot. These technological requirements lent a certain canned quality to the sound of these films. The aural space created made every scene sound like—well, like it had been recorded in a cavernous studio soundstage. Interiors, exteriors—it didn't matter. It all sounded the same.

Improvements in microphones, cameras, recording devices, playback processes, and speakers have done much more than freed cameras from their soundproofing boxes (not to mention musicians from the set). Be-cause of the clarity of contemporary soundtracks, we are able to perceive and appreciate a more complete environment for every image we see—*because we can hear it in minute detail*. Whether the sound is synchronous, nonsynchronous, asynchronous, diegetic, or nondiegetic, various proper-ties of the sounds we hear contribute to the creation of aural space.

AMPLITUDE, otherwise known as *volume*, refers to the loudness or softness of the sound we hear. As always in film studies, it's the *effect* of amplitude that counts toward plausibility, not its strict realism. For instance, a scene set at a rock concert may begin with a master shot of the entire arena accompanied by deafening music on the soundtrack, but when the director cuts to a concertgoer saying something to her date in medium two-shot, the volume of the music drops—slightly perhaps, but no less significantly—to allow the audience to hear the character's dialogue. In reality, of course, musicians and their acoustical engineers don't accommodate even their most devoted fans' conversations in this way, but in the movies, audiences not only accept but even expect this particular sound convention. If the amplitude didn't drop, and the audience couldn't understand what the characters said to each other, they would likely become angry and frustrated.

The aural space is maintained in this example by virtue of the fact that the change in volume *is a subtle change*. If the amplitude fell to too low a level during the conversation, the aural space would no longer be plausible, and the scene would begin to seem unrealistic. Bear in mind: this could be a legitimate artistic strategy. Dropping the music's volume drastically might serve to make the two concertgoers seem to be living in their own world—a romantic world comprised of just the two of them despite the fact that they are in the company of 18,000 concertgoers. There's a scene in John Woo's *Mission: Impossible II* that tests the limits of plausibility in this regard: two characters (Tom Cruise and Thandie Newton) engage in a completely audible conversation while speeding alongside each other in competing convertibles on a winding oceanside highway. Plausible: barely. Realistic: not at all. Appropriate for the film: absolutely.

Amplitude is often used to establish and fortify the audience's sense of *distance*. An extreme long shot of a cowboy on horseback, for instance, may be accompanied by the sound of wind and dust blowing on the soundtrack, but if the director were to cut to an extreme close-up of the horse's hoofs, the likely accompanying sound on the soundtrack would be the sound of hoofs hitting dirt. (These sounds would probably have been created not by the horse but by a Foley artist.) This would not be the case, however, if the next shot in the sequence was of a man looking through a powerful telescope (the object of his gaze presumably being the horse's hoofs), in which case the implication would be that the watcher was at a far enough distance from the cowboy that he would not hear the hoofbeats—and neither would we.

Variations in amplitude may also indicate a character's subjective awareness of the world around her. In the Korean horror movie *The Host* (2006), for instance, a young girl is preoccupied with something that has just happened to a family member when she leaves her father's snack bar and goes outside to walk in a riverside park. There is relative silence on the soundtrack—that is, until she gradually becomes aware that she is in the midst of hundreds of screaming people who are fleeing a giant mutant river monster. The director, Bong Joon-ho, brings up the sound level of the screaming, thus indicating a shift in the girl's awareness. (Tragically, she is soon lassoed by the hideous serpent's tail and spirited away to its foul lair deep in the Seoul sewer system.)

Amplitude is an important signifier of closeness or distance, but it is not the only factor. The term **sound perspective** describes the aural equivalent of three-dimensional vision. Just as we perceive depth, the third dimension (the other two being height and width), largely on the basis of the relative size of objects in the foreground, middleground, and background, we hear in perspective, too. *Sound perspective* describes the relative proportion of **direct sound** and **reflected sound**. *Direct sound* is created (directly!) from its source: an actor's mouth is miked, and the sound it produces is recorded. This is direct sound. *Reflected sound* is sound that bounces off the floor, ceiling, and walls and reaches the microphone a phase later than direct sound. (P*hase* refers to the distance between sound waves.) The actor's voice creates such sounds as well. Sound perspective is created by mixing direct and reflected sound together. A high ratio of direct sound to reflected sound suggests closeness; a low ratio of direct sound to reflected sound suggests distance.

Two other sound properties are PITCH and TIMBRE. *Pitch* is a sound's fundamental frequency, *timbre* its tonal quality. Women's voices are generally pitched higher than men's, meaning that their vocal cords tend to be smaller and the resulting frequencies higher. A violin playing a particularly high note produces a particularly high pitch; a bass violin's pitch is much lower. *Timbre*, meanwhile, covers virtually every other aspect to a given sound—it's also called *tone quality*. Does a piece of music sound *rich* or does it sound *tinny*? Is a man's voice *nasal*? Is a child's voice *shrill*? Does a sound effect have a particular *depth*, or does it sound *thin*? All of these characteristics, and more, fall under the general category of timbre. Timbre, in short, is difficult if not impossible to define precisely, but we know it when we hear it.

You do not need to become an acoustical engineer to appreciate the variations in pitch and timbre that affect your perception of film sound. Just try to increase your awareness of the differences in recorded human voices that affect your understanding of different characters and the particular characteristics of any film sound you hear. Practice describing what you hear using the concepts of pitch, timbre, and amplitude as a jumping-off point.

STUDY GUIDE: HEARING SOUND, ANALYZING SOUND

The first step in analyzing film sound is, of course, to notice it in the first place. It's easy to become so distracted by what you're seeing that you fail to notice what you're hearing—the particular qualities of a given sound, its relationship to the image that accompanies it, and so on. Consider the information you receive solely by way of sound, as opposed to what you learn solely from the image.

As an exercise in distinguishing sound information from image information, read the following shot breakdown of the opening, pre-credits sequence of John Turturro's 2005 film, *Romance & Cigarettes*:

SHOT 1:   An extreme close-up of a pattern of flesh-colored waves. The camera tracks back to reveal that they are the friction ridges of the big toe on a man's right foot. The foot twitches. The camera continues to track, now in a circular right lateral movement, around the left side of a gray couch; the foot and leg are surrounded by gray pillows. The darkness of the room as a whole and the couch area in particular lead to the image being almost entirely indecipherable at one moment of this tracking shot before the man's bare arms, folded over his beefy chest, become visible. The camera is now positioned over the man's head; the man (James Gandolfini), whose eyes remain closed throughout the sequence, appears upside down in the image.

SHOT 2:   A long shot of a woman entering the shadowy room; the shot is taken from the vicinity of the man's head. She is in silhouette. As she approaches the bed, the director cuts to:

SHOT 3:   A close-up of the man's face; his mouth twitches.

SHOT 4:   A medium shot of the woman, now in dim light. She flicks a lighter and lights a cigarette.

SHOT 5:   A **POV** medium shot, from her POINT OF VIEW, of the man lying on the couch.

SHOT 6:   Same as Shot 4: a medium shot of the woman. The camera tilts down slightly as her hand, now holding the lit cigarette, moves down toward the bottom of the image.

SHOT 7:   A slightly closer shot of the man. He is smiling. The camera tracks forward.

SHOT 8:   A slightly closer shot of the woman. The camera tracks forward as she blinks and looks away.

SHOT 9:   A close-up of the man's bare foot. A hand reaches into the image from the top of the frame. The hand carefully places the lit cigarette between the man's big toe and the toe next to it; the lit end is on the side of the foot's sole.

SHOT 10:   A brief shot of the woman.

An extreme close-up of James Gandolfini's big toe in *Romance & Cigarettes* (2007) (frame enlargement).

SHOT 11: A shot of the man's head and shoulders; he jerks his head and quickly opens and closes his mouth.

SHOT 12: A close-up of the toes holding the cigarette.

SHOT 13: Same as Shot 10. The woman begins to turn, and Turturro cuts on the action to:

SHOT 14: A full shot of the woman completing the turn and walking away from the couch in the general direction of the camera. In this light, her outfit is revealed in more detail: she is wearing a tight, deep-cut black vest with no blouse underneath. Fade out.

Based only on the information contained in this description of the visuals, what do you understand about the relationship between the man and the woman? Who is he? Who is she? And what happened with the lit cigarette?

SHOT 1: An extreme close-up of a pattern of flesh-colored waves. ***The sound of snoring is heard***. The camera tracks back to reveal that they are the friction ridges of the big toe on a man's right foot. The foot twitches. ***A loud snort accompanies the twitch***. The camera continues to track, now in a circular right lateral movement, around the left side of a gray couch; the foot and leg are surrounded by gray pillows. The darkness of the room as a whole and the couch area in particular lead to the image being almost entirely indecipherable at one moment of this tracking shot before the man's bare arms, folded over his beefy chest, become visible. The camera is now positioned over the man's head; the man (James Gandolfini), whose eyes remain closed throughout the sequence, appears upside down in the image. ***The snoring continues***.

SHOT 2:	A long shot of a woman entering the shadowy room; the shot is taken from the vicinity of the man's head. She is in silhouette. ***She makes no sound at first, then says,* "Dad?"** As she approaches the bed, ***she says,* "Daddy?"** and the director cuts to:
SHOT 3:	A close-up of the man's face; his mouth twitches ***and he snorts again***.
SHOT 4:	A medium shot of the woman, now in dim light. She flicks a lighter—***the flicking sound is heard***—and lights a cigarette. ***The snoring sound continues***.
SHOT 5:	A POV medium shot, from her point of view, of the man lying on the couch.
SHOT 6:	Same as Shot 4: a medium shot of the woman. The camera tilts down slightly as her hand, now holding the lit cigarette, moves down toward the bottom of the image.
SHOT 7:	A slightly closer shot of the man. He is smiling. ***A short snort is heard as the snoring continues***. The camera tracks forward.
SHOT 8:	A slightly closer shot of the woman. The camera tracks forward as she blinks and looks away.
SHOT 9:	A close-up of the man's bare foot. A hand reaches into the image from the top of the frame. The hand carefully places the lit cigarette between the man's big toe and the toe next to it; the lit end is on the side of the foot's sole.
SHOT 10:	A brief shot of the woman.
SHOT 11:	A shot of the man's head and shoulders; he jerks his head and quickly opens and closes his mouth. ***A snort is heard***.
SHOT 12:	A close-up of the toes holding the cigarette. ***The snoring continues***.
SHOT 13:	Same as Shot 10. The woman begins to turn, and Turturro cuts on the action to:
SHOT 14:	A full shot of the woman completing the turn and walking away from the couch in the general direction of the camera. ***Unlike her entrance, her footsteps are now heard***. In this light, her outfit is revealed in more detail: she is wearing a tight, deep-cut black vest with no blouse underneath. Fade out. ***After a few moments, the snoring sounds stop, and we hear a roar of agony***.

Aside from the fact that the scene's payoff depends on our *not* seeing the man's reaction to having his toes burned by the cigarette, but instead solely *hearing* it, Turturro's soundtrack also reveals a crucial piece of narrative information: the woman is actually the man's daughter. They're merely two words of simple dialogue—"Dad? Daddy?"—but without hearing them we would probably come to a very different conclusion about who these two characters are and what their relationship is.

To get your own sense of the differences between visual information and information conveyed by sound, try watching a scene from any film with the volume turned off. Note what you learned only by way of the images. Note also what the images failed to tell you on their own. Then, after watching the same scene again with the volume back up, determine what you got only from the soundtrack. Finally, just listen to the scene, either by turning away from the screen or by turning your laptop in the other direction. Try to distinguish one character from another solely by virtue of their individual vocal qualities.

WRITING ABOUT SOUND AND SOUNDTRACKS

The beginning of any film analysis is awareness. The second step is pinning down in words what you see and hear. In the analysis of the *Romance & Cigarettes* sequence, consider in particular the writer's description of the sound the man makes after the fade-out—*roar of agony*. There are lots of words that describe the noises human beings make when we're in distress: *scream, shriek, yelp, shout, squeal* . . . In this case, the particular timbre and pitch of the sound is better described by the word *roar* than the word *squeal*. Given the man's bearlike size, *roar* conveys a sense of depth that other words do not. Finding the right words to describe what you see and hear is a key element of any analysis.

As a matter of fact, a precise description is itself analytical. *Rhetoric* is the art of persuasion. When you write a paper, you are trying to persuade your professor that you have seen (and heard) the film, that you have thought about what it means, and that you have a point to make about it—an argument. As rhetorical strategies go, there are few more effective than a clear and accurate verbal account of a film's exceedingly complex blend of images and sounds. It proves that you have noticed things other people might have taken for granted or missed altogether. It leads the reader to see and hear and understand the film the way *you* see, hear, and understand it. And that's your primary goal in writing the paper.

Academic prose is often dull and labored, but it doesn't need to be. All too often, academic writers confuse analysis with obfuscation. They phrase their points in a showy, unnecessarily complicated way in the mistaken belief that they will seem more intelligent than they are. From a rhetorical standpoint, it doesn't work; it doesn't persuade anyone that there's anything worth arguing about. Finding and explaining meaning in a film is not nearly as difficult or boring as most academic writing makes it seem.

Here are two sentences about John Turturro's use of sound in the opening sequence of *Romance & Cigarettes*. Both attempt to convince the reader not only that the student who wrote it knows what she is talking about but also that she has something worthwhile to argue in terms of what the film means. One works, the other doesn't:

"By privileging sound over image at the conclusion of the sequence—by maintaining the aural space of the room while purging the screen of visual content—Turturro further problematizes the already contested relationship between the paternal and the filial."—Phyllis Dietrichson, senior, Harvard University

"The sequence ends visually with a blackout, but Turturro maintains the room's sound space long enough to include the father's roar; the sound of his agony is the first punchline to the feature-length joke Turturro is making of the American nuclear family."—Laura Hunt, junior, Wagner College

The first sentence appears to say more than it actually does. Its use of academic jargon (*privileging*, *problematizes*, *contested*) is self-defeating. The student's point is actually clearer than she makes it out to be; by overloading the sentence with big but empty words, she reduces its rhetorical effectiveness. It sounds terribly important and meaningful, but it isn't really.

The second student makes more or less the same point—that the sound of a father in pain is Turturro's funny comment on the family—but she does so with more persuasive power. Her concise but colorful description of what happens on the soundtrack is just as analytical as the first student's, but because it's clearer, it's more convincing, not to mention much more fun to read.

CHAPTER 6

NARRATIVE: FROM SCENE TO SCENE

NARRATIVE STRUCTURE

Even the simplest stories can be broken down into component parts:

1. Boy meets girl
2. Boy loses girl
3. Boy tries to get girl back
4. Boy and girl get together in the end

If this conventional story takes the form of a feature-length film, each of its four parts is composed of hundreds of individual shots. Each shot contains mise-en-scene elements that convey expressive information, and each transition from shot to shot compounds that information by creating relationships. But what about *the story*? How does the boy meet the girl? Why does he lose the girl? What does he do to get her back, and what stands in his way? What changes does the boy go through. What does he learn? This chapter is about how film studies addresses questions like these by analyzing film narratives.

First of all, what does the term NARRATIVE mean? Narrative simply means *storytelling*. Not all films are narrative films. There are DOCUMENTARIES—nonfiction accounts of real people and events that may or may not tell a story in the process. And there are AVANT-GARDE or experimental films that may be composed of nothing but shapes or colors or shots of people and things that are not assembled in the form of a tale.

But most of the films you will see in your life—and most of the television shows as well—are narratives. They tell stories, and their stories follow broad patterns or conventions. How do we begin to analyze these patterns?

STORY AND PLOT

The first step is to distinguish between STORY and PLOT. What's the difference? In everyday conversation, we use the two terms interchangeably. But in film studies, *story* refers to the events the tale tells, while *plot* refers to its structuring. Using the boy-meets-girl example, this particular story concerns Josh and Jennifer and how they meet, get to know each other, and end up married and having children and grandchildren. The *plot*, on the other hand, is as follows:

1. A little girl named ELSIE asks a 60-year-old JOSH and JENNI-FER how they met; the little girl is their granddaughter. Jennifer begins to tell their story.
2. YOUNG JOSH, a 25-year-old rookie cop, arrests YOUNG JEN-NIFER for speeding.
3. The 60-year-old Josh laughs and says, no, that's not what happened at all.
4. Young Josh arrests Young Jennifer for driving without a license . . .

The story, in other words, tells what happened to Josh and Jennifer from the beginning (they meet) to the end (they have a granddaughter). The plot, on the other hand, is the order in which the filmmaker reveals these story elements to the audience: first we see that they have a granddaughter, then we see how they met.

A more formal definition of *story* is this: *all the events of the narrative as they occur in chronological order from beginning to end, including not only those that we see and hear, but those we infer.* In this example, we infer that Josh and Jennifer had at least one child because we see that they have a grandchild; the child him- or herself may not appear in the film.

Here is a more formal definition of *plot: the ordering and structuring of narrative events as they are presented in the film.*

In sum, the story of Josh and Jennifer begins with him arresting her for one reason or another and ends with them as late-middle-aged people telling their granddaughter how they met, whereas the plot begins with the two characters as elderly people telling conflicting stories.

To further complicate matters, film studies uses a term to describe *the world of the story*: DIEGESIS. The diegesis of a film is *all the story elements presented by the narrative, no matter whether they are actually seen or heard onscreen or not.* Perhaps the best way to describe the diegesis is by giving an example of its opposite: the musical score of a film is generally NON-DIEGETIC. If a character turns on the car radio and music comes on, that music is DIEGETIC. However, the music played over the opening credits or closing credits, or any music that does not originate within the story, is nondiegetic. The theme from *Star Wars* is nondiegetic; Luke Skywalker doesn't hear it in the background, but the audience does. But if, on the other hand, Josh and Jennifer are seen onscreen watching *Star Wars* on DVD on their first date, the theme music from *Star Wars* would be diegetic because the music originates in their story world; *the characters can hear it.*

And finally, there are two more terms, drawn from the school of literary criticism known as Russian Formalism, that distinguish between the events of the story and their presentation to the audience: FABULA and SYUZHET. As defined by the film historian and theorist David Bordwell, the *syuzhet* is essentially the film's plot—it's the specific ordering of narrative elements within the film. The *fabula*, however, is more than simply the story being told; it's the story that each of us constructs as we watch and hear the syuzhet unfold. It's all the story material presented by the filmmaker, but it's also the story material and associations we bring to the film as individuals—the stories we tell ourselves based on the stories we are being told. Just as every story has an unlimited number of plots that could tell it, so every syuzhet sparks an infinite number of fabulas. Why? Because every audience member brings his or her own personal experience to the movies we watch, the stories we're told.

SCENES AND SEQUENCES

If the story of Josh and Jennifer were written in screenplay form, it might begin this way:

SAMPLE SCREENPLAY

FADE IN:

INT [abbreviation for *Interior*]. JOSH AND JENNIFER'S LIVING ROOM,
2050—DAY

JOSH, a 60-year-old man with gray hair, is sitting on a couch with his wife,
JENNIFER, also 60, though her hair is dyed bright red. In Jennifer's lap is
ELSIE, age 7. She is wearing a futuristic plastic T-shirt and sweatpants and
shoes in the shape of rockets.

                  ELSIE
Grandma, how did you meet Grandpa?

                JENNIFER
   (grinning)
Well, dear, your grandfather and I met between exits 5 and 6 on the New
Jersey Turnpike.

EXT [abbreviation for *Exterior*]. NEW JERSEY TURNPIKE, 2015—DAY

Cars are whizzing by as YOUNG JOSH sits in his patrol car, which is hidden
behind some trees by the side of the road. One car goes by particularly fast,
and Young Josh reacts immediately by gunning his engine, causing his back
tires to shoot gravel behind them as he takes off after the speeding car . . .

The "Sample Screenplay" box shows how a typed screenplay actually looks. The following shows the same elements of the preceding screenplay, but this time these elements are identified and also indicate the proper indentations for your screenplay.

SAMPLE SCREENPLAY ELEMENTS

[ALWAYS THE FIRST ITEM ON THE FIRST PAGE]
FADE IN:

[SCENE HEADING]
INT [abbreviation for *Interior*]. JOSH AND JENNIFER'S LIVING ROOM,
2050—DAY

[CHARACTER'S FIRST APPEARANCE (USE ALL CAPS)
and CHARACTER DESCRIPTION]
JOSH, a 60-year-old man with gray hair, is sitting on a couch with his wife,
JENNIFER, also 60, though her hair is dyed bright red. In Jennifer's lap is
ELSIE, age 7. She is wearing a futuristic plastic T-shirt and sweatpants and
shoes in the shape of rockets.

[CHARACTER CUE
and DIALOG]
                    ELSIE
Grandma, how did you meet Grandpa?

[CHARACTER CUE
and PERSONAL DIRECTION
and DIALOG]
                    JENNIFER
    (grinning)
Well, dear, your grandfather and I met between exits 5 and 6 on the New
Jersey Turnpike.

[SCENE HEADING]
EXT [abbreviation for *Exterior*]. NEW JERSEY TURNPIKE, 2015—DAY

Cars are whizzing by as YOUNG JOSH sits in his patrol car, which is hidden
behind some trees by the side of the road. One car goes by particularly fast,
and Young Josh reacts immediately by gunning his engine, causing his back
tires to shoot gravel behind them as he takes off after the speeding car . . .

Note: Formats and software for screenplays can readily be found on the
Internet (for example, see scriptbuddy.com or screenplayguide.com).

This screenplay already makes several notable distinctions: between
scenes; between *interior* and *exterior*; between *time periods* (2055 and 2015);
and between *characters* (JOSH, JENNIFER, ELSIE, and YOUNG
JOSH). But because this is a film and not simply a written narrative, a
full analysis of what we see onscreen would have to include a shot-by-
shot breakdown:

SHOT 1:   Long shot of JOSH, a 60-year-old man with gray hair, sit-
            ting on a couch with his wife, JENNIFER, also 60, though
            her hair is dyed bright red. In Jennifer's lap is ELSIE, age

7. She is wearing a futuristic plastic T-shirt and sweatpants and shoes in the shape of rockets. Jennifer begins bouncing Elsie on her knee. Cut on the action to:

SHOT 2:   Close-up of Elsie's feet, which do not reach the floor, bouncing up and down. Cut on this action to:

SHOT 3:   Close-up of Elsie's bouncing face as Elsie laughs. Elsie says, "Grandma, how did you meet Grandpa?"

SHOT 4:   Same as shot 1: Long shot of Josh, Jennifer, and Elsie on the couch. Jennifer, grinning, says, "Well, dear, your grandfather and I met between exits 5 and 6 on the New Jersey Turnpike." Cut to:

SHOT 5:   Long shot of SIGN ON TURNPIKE that reads "Speed limit 75 mph." Cut to:

SHOT 6:   Long shot of cars whizzing by. Cut to:

SHOT 7:   Medium shot of YOUNG JOSH through the window of his patrol car, looking bored.

SHOT 8:   Long shot of patrol car, which is hidden behind some trees by the side of the road.

SHOT 9:   Same as Shot 6, but now one car goes by particularly fast.

SHOT 10:   Same as Shot 7, but now Young Josh reacts immediately by gunning his engine (sound of engine roaring).

SHOT 11:   Close-up of back left tire shooting gravel behind it as the car begins to move. Cut on action to:

SHOT 12:   Same as Shot 8, but now the patrol car is moving forward out of its hiding place and onto the highway . . .

This shot-by-shot breakdown is itself not a complete descriptive analysis because it leaves out such important elements as lighting, most of the costume details, and all of the camera angles. (For example: Are these all eye-level shots, or are they varied?) And because this movie has not yet been cast, let alone filmed, we do not know what any of the characters looks like beyond the barest descriptions of their ages and hair color. Still, this analysis suggests another important distinction: between the terms SCENE and SEQUENCE. *A scene is defined by the unity of time, space, and action.* In other words, a scene is a unified action that takes place in one location during a single time period. (A single scene set in a hospital emergency room might include a waiting room, a hallway, and an examining room *if the camera moves continually from one room to the next*). Scenes are defined by their location and time period; sequences are defined by the patterns of shots within each scene. Both are units of dramatic action. In this example, there are two scenes: one inside, the other outside; the first in 2055, the second in 2015.

A *sequence*, on the other hand, *maintains one or more of these unities while introducing a discontinuity*. In a classical Hollywood montage sequence, for example, this discontinuity occurs temporally—time is usually speeded up in a montage sequence. In a crosscutting sequence, the discontinuity occurs spatially. In the example here, the first scene—Shots 1 through 4—contains one sequence. The second scene contains another sequence: Shots 5 through 12 are at least the beginning of an action sequence that might go on to include shots of Young Jennifer at the wheel of the speeding car, close-ups of Young Josh as he chases her, a long shot of Young Jennifer's car with Young Josh's car entering the image from the right, and so on.

Note also the reversal of chronological time in the plotting of this story. Filmed stories are not always told in the order in which the events happened. The terms FLASHBACK and FLASHFORWARD describe two of the ways time can be manipulated in motion pictures. We would describe Scene 2 as a *flashback—a shot, sequence, or scene that takes place in the past, before the present-day time frame established by the film*. In this example, the year 2055 is established as the film's present day despite its being in *our* future, so anything that happens before that year must occur in the form of a flashback. A *flashforward* achieves the opposite effect: it's *a shot, sequence, or scene that takes place in the future, after the present-day time frame established by the film*. Our film might end, for instance, with a flashforward of Elsie, herself aged 60, telling her own grandchild a story.

TRANSITIONS FROM SCENE TO SCENE

Nowadays, most transitions from scene to scene occur with a simple cut, as in the example above, in which the director cut from Scene 1 to Scene 2 without using any special transitional technique. But throughout film history, directors have employed more elaborate means to shift from one scene to another. These devices are the FADE-IN and FADE-OUT; the IRIS-IN and IRIS-OUT; the DISSOLVE, and the WIPE.

With a *fade-in*, the screen often begins as an entirely black field (though sometimes it's entirely white), with the image gradually appearing until it is at full strength and clarity; with a *fade-out*, the opposite occurs: the image gradually disappears until the screen is either all white or all black.

An *iris-in* is created when the image begins as a small circle in the middle of an all-white or all-black screen and widens until it covers the screen. An *iris-out* is the reverse: the full rectangular image shrinks in a circular form until it disappears in the middle of the screen. *Irises* are not restricted to transitions. The effect of looking through a telescope could be achieved by a fixed, nonmoving iris that masks the rectangular edges of the image into a circular form. A character looking through a pair of binoculars might be expressed by masking the rectangular image into two circular forms connected at the center.

With a *dissolve*, one image fades out while the subsequent image fades in, thereby creating the impression of a multiple exposure. With a *superimposition*, two separate and distinct images overlap. At the midway point of a dissolve, when the two images are of equal intensity, the effect is a superimposition.

And a *wipe* is created when one image appears to push another image off the screen. Wipes may occur in any direction—horizontally, vertically, or diagonally. Or they may take the form of a shape: a *star wipe*, for instance, is a wipe in which the second image appears in the center of the screen in the shape of a star and expands outward, appearing to "wipe" the first image off the screen. Wipes, which are optical effects created in the processing lab, were popular transitional devices in the 1930s and 1940s, but they fell out of favor until video technology made them easy to achieve, and they became popular again in music videos beginning in the 1980s.

Finally, there is a technique known as CROSSCUTTING. *Crosscutting is defined as editing that alternates two or more lines of action occurring in different places or times, thereby connecting them.*

Here's a classic example of crosscutting used countless times in so-called *B westerns*—and by the way, when film studies refers to a **B movie**, B is not short for *bad*; a *B movie* is a film that was made to fill the B side of a double feature and was probably less expensive to produce than the **A picture** that preceded it. In any event: a crosscutting example from a B western is a shot of a woman tied to the railroad tracks; a shot of a man riding on a horse; a shot of the woman on the railroad tracks; a shot of the man on the horse; a shot of a speeding train; a shot of the woman on the tracks; a shot of the man on the horse; a shot of the speeding train . . . and so on.

What do you assume from these separate shots? You are likely to connect them all in your mind, rather like the Kuleshov experiment, and understand that the woman is about to be run over by the train unless the man on the horse arrives in time to save her. It wouldn't make a bit of difference if the woman was tied to the tracks in Kentucky, the train was in fact in California, and the man on the horse was in Saskatchewan, and the shots were filmed three months apart. When the director edits them all together into a crosscutting sequence, he or she is *telling an interconnected story by drawing two or more lines of action together by way of editing.*

Bear in mind that crosscutting is different than simple cutting. If a director cuts back and forth between two characters in the same space, it's CUTTING. If a director cuts from one character to another character *not* in the same space, then back to the first character, then back to the second character, then perhaps to a third character in still a different space, that's *crosscutting*. Different spaces or times being linked temporally by editing: that's crosscutting.

CHARACTER, DESIRE, AND CONFLICT

That narrative films are often about an individual character in search or pursuit of a goal is a convention so basic to Americans' experience of motion pictures that we often take it completely for granted. In the conventional "boy meets girl" story, we simply assume that what the boy really wants (however little he may be aware of the fact at the beginning of the film) is to get together with the girl in the end. If he didn't, there would be little substance to the tale. "Boy meets girl and doesn't care" might make an out-of-the-ordinary comedy, but unless the boy wants something else—money and fame, for instance, or maybe another boy—his lack of a goal would likely result in a very short movie.

We also assume that something will get in the way of the central character's pursuit of his or her goal. Boy meets girl, boy gets girl—the end? Once again, this scenario would make for a very brief film.

Film studies tends to describe the central character's pursuit of a goal with the word *desire*. In the conventional boy-meets-girl story, the desire is essentially sexual in nature, but films deal with other forms of desire as well: knowledge, for example. The narrative of *Citizen Kane* unfolds around the basic question of what "rosebud," Kane's dying word, means. On a more abstract level is the question of who the title character actually is beyond his public image; a journalist attempts to unlock the secret of Charles Foster Kane's identity by interviewing his friends and business associates, and we, the audience, share the reporter's desire for information. (Kane himself turns out to be a man whose desire knows no bounds, though precisely what he wants remains elusive at the end.) Characters may also express desire by seeking a better life for themselves. What is *The Wizard of Oz* (1939) if not a quest for a more colorful and exciting world over the rainbow?

Fortunately for audiences, characters almost always find their desire thwarted by something. If film characters got what they wanted right away, they would be satisfied—and audiences would be bored. (Murder mysteries go out of their way to delay the delivery of information.

"*Who did it?*" "*She did!*"—a two-minute film.) Narratives require *conflict*. In *Citizen Kane*, for instance, the reporter discovers that Kane's friends each saw a slightly different side of Kane—they offer subtly conflicting accounts of the man, and the journalist's attempt to learn the meaning of Kane's final utterance, "rosebud," ends in failure. Kane himself, meanwhile, cannot achieve what he sets out to achieve because other people and circumstances get in the way. His desire, too, is left unfulfilled.

Imagine *The Wizard of Oz* without the Wicked Witch of the West. If she didn't appear from time to time to block Dorothy's progress to Oz, the film would be not only shorter but duller. Dorothy would simply skip happily down the Yellow Brick Road with her friends, and that would be that. Who wants to watch somebody happily skipping for two hours?

Desire and conflict come into play even in those relatively rare instances in which a narrative film does not center on a single protagonist or group of protagonists. In Eisenstein's *Battleship Potemkin*, for instance, the conflict is not between an individual sailor and something that stands between him and his goals but between two opposing collective forces: the czarist government and its officers and soldiers on the one hand and the people of Odessa and the sailors on the battleship on the other. *Battleship Potemkin*'s narrative unfolds as a conflict of these two groups: the desire to preserve the czarist government and the class structure it represents and the desire to change it.

ANALYZING CONFLICT

In the next chapter, you will learn how to break down cinematic stories in a process called SEGMENTATION. Segmentations can be rather detailed, so for the time being, let's simply break down a familiar movie into its broadest component parts.

> *The Wizard of Oz*: locations
> Beginning: Kansas
> Middle: Oz
> End: Kansas

> *The Wizard of Oz*: main characters
> Dorothy
> Miss Gulch / the Wicked Witch of the West

The Wizard of Oz: secondary characters

    Auntie Em and the farmhands / Scarecrow, Tin Man, Cowardly Lion

    Professor Marvel / the Wizard

The Wizard of Oz: desires

Beginning:	Dorothy wants to leave home
Middle:	Dorothy wants to return home
End:	Both desires are fulfilled by the end

The Wizard of Oz: conflicts

Beginning:	Dorothy vs. Miss Gulch over the possession of Toto
Middle:	Dorothy vs. the Wicked Witch over the possession of the ruby slippers
End:	Both conflicts are resolved by the end

What do you notice about *The Wizard of Oz*'s structure? If you have seen the film, you have experienced the effects of its structure, but what occurs to you now that you have seen it broken down into its basic elements?

FIGURE 6.1 A publicity still from *The Wizard of Oz* (1939)—Dorothy (Judy Garland) and Toto in Kansas. (Photofest)

First, you should be able to see that that there is a symmetry to its locations: the film ends where it began, in Kansas—specifically, on Auntie Em's farm.

There is also a doubling of characters—primarily Miss Gulch and the Wicked Witch, and secondarily Professor Marvel and the Wizard and the farmhands/Oz trio.

This doubling repeats itself in terms of the film's major conflicts: Dorothy and Miss Gulch are in conflict over Toto in Kansas, and Dorothy and Miss Gulch's double, the Wicked Witch, fight over control of the ruby slippers in Oz.

The symmetrical narrative structure and doubling of characters in *The Wizard of Oz* are formal devices and are aesthetically pleasing as such, but they also convey meaning—or meanings. One may draw individual conclusions about what *The Wizard of Oz* is ultimately saying from an ideological perspective (or a psychological or sociological one), but the film's narrative structure provides a firm foundation for a basic claim: *The Wizard of Oz* is about the contradictory feelings a teenage girl harbors about her home. By comparing and contrasting an ordinary Kansas farm with the fantastic world of Oz, the film suggests both the virtues and limitations of conventional American life in the 1930s.

Does the film really embrace the idea that "there's no place like home"? Is Kansas ultimately more satisfying than Oz? Does the film espouse conservative values by showing Dorothy that she had everything she really wanted all along, and that her dreams of escaping conventionality were misguided? We may come up with our own answers to these questions depending on who we are and how we view the world, but the film's narrative structure provides a solid foundation for the individual arguments we make about its meaning.

STUDY GUIDE: ANALYZING SCENE-TO-SCENE EDITING

If you have not seen *The Wizard of Oz*, or if you don't remember it very well, watch the film and pay particular attention to its narrative structure and the formal, visual devices the director, Victor Fleming, uses to get from one scene to another. (In fact, you can watch *any* film and do the same thing. *The Wizard of Oz* is suggested here because of its familiarity and relatively simple narrative structure, not to mention its prominent place in this chapter, but any narrative film will work.)

Analyzing narrative structure, like any facet of formal film analysis, requires us to concentrate on one aspect of a particular film and, in effect, isolate it from the rest of the movie. With *The Wizard of Oz*, it's necessary to put aside our enjoyment of Judy Garland's beautiful voice and the Wicked Witch's spectacular nose and green makeup and keep our minds on transitions. It's tough not to let yourself get so caught up in the film that you fail to notice shifts from scene to scene. If you're watching the film (or any film) on DVD and you realize that your mind has wandered—you're in the middle of a new scene, and you don't know how you got there—just hit the reverse button and rewind to the previous scene. Come to think of it, the fact that you failed to notice a particular transition is itself noteworthy: what device or set of devices did the director use to make this transition so smooth that you didn't notice it?

If a structural pattern seems to be emerging, write it down.

If anything at all occurs to you, write it down.

At the end of the film, try to put into words at least one aspect of its narrative structure. Think about the film's representation of time. Did the events depicted occur completely chronologically, or were there flashbacks or flashforwards? Consider the film's locations. Did it take place in a wide variety of locales, or were the events set in only a few places?

What was the film about? To what extent did its narrative structure inform its meaning?

Finally, to return to *The Wizard of Oz* as an example, ask yourself the questions posed at the end of the previous section; if you have been thinking about another film, ask similar questions about it. What ideas did the film convey about culture, society, race, class, sex and gender, and even the meaning of life? *What did the film say?* Can you base your opinion on the evidence provided by the film's structure?

WRITING ABOUT NARRATIVE STRUCTURE

Citing evidence is an essential aspect of making an argument about a given film's meaning. One can simply assert that *The Wizard of Oz* is a conservative film because it says that women are better off staying at home on the farm, but the assertion remains a matter of opinion until it is proven by way of facts. In film studies, these facts are found in the film's formal details and structure.

Just as you have learned to describe a shot specifically and accurately by the camera's apparent distance from the subject (close-up, medium shot, long shot) or by its static or mobile framing (tracking shot, pan, crane), and in the same way that you have begun to analyze the relationship between one shot and another (cut, dissolve, eye-line match), so you can use the patterns created by a film's narrative structure to serve as a basis for any claims you make about what a film has to say about the world—what it means.

Let's say you do hold the opinion that *The Wizard of Oz* takes a very conservative view of the world—that the film does indeed say that women should learn to stay at home. (One could argue precisely the opposite, by the way; *The Wizard of Oz*, and narrative films in general, often support a variety of readings.) Your task as a critic is to support your argument with factual evidence from the film. In this case, you could use the movie's symmetrical narrative structure to help prove your point: even though the plot transports Dorothy to the colorful land of Oz and provides her with exciting adventures of the sort she craves when she sings "Over the Rainbow," the narrative structure returns her precisely to where she started out. That this is a way of saying that women are better off staying at home remains your opinion, but you have supported it with an undeniable fact.

CHAPTER 7

FROM SCREENPLAY TO FILM

DEEPER INTO NARRATIVE STRUCTURE

The screenwriter plays one of the key roles in the creation of a motion picture. He or she constructs a detailed story, maps out a scene-by-scene blueprint of the film's plot, and writes dialogue that may or may not sound like everyday life but that nonetheless fits the tone and style of the particular film. That's an important distinction. You may have the idea that movie dialogue must be realistic, but this is not the case. The script for Baz Luhrman's *Romeo + Juliet* (1996) features dialogue written by Shakespeare (and adapted by Luhrman and the screenwriter Craig Pearce), much of which is rhymed poetry. It's hardly "realistic," and yet it's perfectly appropriate for the film. Similarly, the tough-talking dialogue of a film noir ("We're both rotten, baby, only you're a little *more* rotten"—*Double Indemnity*, 1944) or the laconic speech of a western ("I wish I knew how to quit you"—*Brokeback Mountain*, 2005) may function beautifully in a particular work of film art despite the fact that you and your friends don't talk that way in everyday life.

It should be clear by this point that film studies does not ask you to be a movie reviewer. Your job is to examine rather than judge the films you see. You may like the characters or not or find the story uplifting or upsetting, but these personal responses—as important to you as they may be—are not crucial as far as the field of film studies is concerned. How, then, do you confront a film's story, if not to give it a thumbs-up or thumbs-down review?

The answer is: *analysis*. To analyze something means to break it down into its component parts. This holds true in chemistry as well as in film studies. In chapter 6, you read a fairly simple analytical breakdown of the locations, characters, desires, and conflicts in *The Wizard of Oz*. You may or may not like *The Wizard of Oz*, and you can certainly argue its merits with your family and friends, but film studies asks you to analyze and understand the film rather than enjoy it. Hopefully your deeper understanding of the films you study will lead to greater enjoyment of them, but such pleasure is secondary. All of this is to say that analyzing narrative structure is not especially fun. In order to analyze a film's story and plot, you must stand far enough apart from it that you can see it clearly. Given the fact that most narrative films try to draw you in rather than keep you at an analytical distance, it's not easy to enjoy them and analyze them at the same time.

SCREENWRITING: THE THREE-ACT STRUCTURE

Despite what you may have heard about narrative screenwriting, particularly Hollywood screenwriting, there are no *rules* governing a feature-length screenplay's structure—only *conventions*. A CONVENTION is *an artistic practice or process or device that is commonly accepted and understood within a given culture*. Examples of film conventions range from the outlaw in a western and the hostile alien in a science fiction film to the 180° axis system described in chapter 4 and the use of close-ups to express emotional intensity described in chapter 1. Audiences understand and accept these conventions not despite their familiarity but because of it; if we were confronted by an absolutely original, truly unique device in any art form, we would likely not know what to make of it. We often like to think that great art is always totally original, but in point of fact it's usually a matter of varying established conventions, sometimes radically, rather than dispensing with them altogether. In the case of screenplays, some screenwriting professors may insist that their precepts—in other words, what they teach—must be strictly followed, particularly in terms of structure, but this is only true if the screenwriter's goal is selling the screenplay to a large filmmaking corporation that expects to make not wildly original movies but movies that adhere to familiar conventions and thereby appeal to the largest possible audience.

One of the key conventions of narrative screenplays is known as the **three-act structure**. The origins of the idea that good dramas, which now include films, should have a beginning, middle, and end, can be traced to the ancient Greek philosopher Aristotle, who wrote his treatise *Poetics* around 335 BCE. In modern terms, Act One sets up the main character or characters and the situation in which he, she, or they find themselves. In Act Two, the middle, the main character or characters attempt to work out a problem caused at the end of Act One. The drama concludes in Act Three, in which the character or characters resolve his or her or their problems, usually by working through and resolving a crisis, which generally occurs at the end of the second act.

The three-act structure is a helpful tool for narrative screenwriters, who begin with a blank page and must fill about 120 such pages before they finish their first drafts. Having a three-part model to hold up as an ideal helps writers to build a series of incidents that will hold an audience's interest for two hours. It offers a basic blueprint for pacing the events of the story.

But because film studies is less about creating film art than analyzing it, we generally do not spend time trying to determine where the end of the first act is in a given film, or what constitutes the beginning of Act Three. Perhaps a better way of putting it is that such determinations are only the beginning. After all, many films do not follow precisely the three-act structure. Instead of trying to make the films we study conform to a preexisting model, we look closely, even minutely, at an individual film's plot to see the subtle narrative patterns that emerge. Every film's narrative has its own unique structure, and the process of discovering it is known as segmentation.

SEGMENTATION: FORM

In film studies, a formal analysis of a film's story and plot is called a SEGMENTATION. Segmentation provides a way to see and understand narrative patterns without being distracted by the tremendous sensory input of the rest of the film—without the loud sounds, exciting physical actions, and bright colors that contribute so much to the pleasure of moviegoing. Segmentations are straightforward, even dry outlines of what takes place in the film's narrative in the order in which the film-makers present the events.

You will recall that a film's STORY is *all the events of the narrative as they occur in chronological order from beginning to end, including not only those that we see and hear, but those we infer.* The PLOT, on the other hand, is *the ordering and structuring of narrative events as they are presented in the film.* Segmentations are about plot—the order in which narrative elements occur. If, for example, a killer confesses to his crime in the beginning of the film, after which a series of flashbacks present the events leading up to the murder, a segmentation of the film would begin, just as the plot begins, with the confession. The story, on the other hand, takes a chronological form: it begins with a man embarking on the path that will result in his murdering the victim and ultimately confessing to the crime. The story ends with the confession; the plot—and the segmentation—begin with it.

Film narratives can be long and complicated, so a segmentation of a whole film begins by breaking the narrative down into its largest component parts. Once again, these parts tend to follow the model proposed by Aristotle in the fourth century BCE. These *dramatic unities,* also known as the *classical unities,* are (1) the unity of action, meaning that the main character or characters pursue only one goal; (2) the unity of place, which is to say that the action occurs in a single general location; and (3) the unity of time, meaning that the action takes place during a single time period. But while Aristotle's theory of the dramatic unities sets forth the idea that plays (and, by extension into modern terms, films) should observe all three unities from beginning to end, most films (and many plays) observe only the first unity—that of action. Given cinema's ability to bring multiple locations and time frames together during the course of their 90-minute or two-hour running time, most films ignore the second and third unities when it comes to the entire film. *Within scenes,* however, these unities are still observed, and it is on this basis that the largest, most basic individual units of segmentation are concerned.

A segmentation of a well-known movie may make this point clearer. *The Wizard of Oz,* as we have seen, can be segmented into three broad units based on the unity of space:

1. Kansas
2. Oz
3. Kansas

If the screenwriters and director of *The Wizard of Oz* had been forced to observe Aristotle's three unities for the duration of the film, they would not have been able to move Dorothy from Kansas to Oz and back. The filmmakers do adhere to the unity of action—Dorothy desires a better, more exciting life "over the rainbow" but learns, through her experiences in Oz, that "there's no place like home." And they observe the unity of time as well, since the action of the film begins on the day of the tornado and ends with Dorothy waking up from what we assume to be a fairly brief period of unconsciousness afterward.

Within each of these three main segments, however, there are smaller units. The initial segment, taking place in Kansas, breaks down this way:

1. Kansas

(a) Auntie Em's farm, where Dorothy speaks of her fears for Toto's safety because of the evil Miss Gulch; to protect Toto, Dorothy decides to run away from home.

(b) On the road, Dorothy encounters the flamboyant Professor Marvel, who convinces her to go back to Auntie Em's.

(c) Auntie Em's farm, which is now deserted because of the impending tornado; the tornado strikes, Dorothy gets hit in the head, the house lifts off its foundation, and Dorothy and Toto are spirited into the air.

At this point, *each of the three segments (a, b, and c) observes all three classical unities*—action, place, and time. And there is a symmetry to the segments, one that matches the overall symmetrical pattern of the entire film; just as *The Wizard of Oz* moves from Kansas to Oz and back, the first segment moves from Auntie Em's farm to the road and back. When the house lands in the next segment, it lands in an entirely new location—"the merry old land of Oz," specifically Munchkin Land. And while time appears to be more or less continuous between the old location (the house sitting on its foundation in Kansas) and the new location (the house sitting on a dead witch in Munchkin Land), the unity of action shifts from Dorothy's desire to keep Toto away from Miss Gulch to Dorothy's desire to keep the ruby slippers away from Miss Gulch's double, the Wicked Witch of the West, the enraged sister of the (very) recently deceased witch.

SEGMENTATION: MEANING

Our partial segmentation of *The Wizard of Oz* is devoted to narrative form and its symmetrical, mirror-like structure. But as we explored its structure in chapter 6, we began to see how structure leads to meaning.

FIGURE 7.1 Dalton (Clive Owen) in the preface of Spike Lee's *Inside Man* (2006) (frame enlargement).

It is precisely by way of tools such as segmentation (and mise-en-scene, montage, and so on) that film scholars base whatever claims we make about a given film's politics and ideology. In film studies, it's not so much a question of *what happens* in a movie as *the way it happens*, and this is certainly true as far as plot patterns are concerned. Filmmakers use narrative structure not only to tell stories but to raise issues and make arguments, sometimes explicitly, sometimes implicitly.

Spike Lee's *Inside Man* (2006) is a good case in point. Based on a screenplay by Russell Gewirtz, *Inside Man* is—on the surface—a bank heist drama starring Denzel Washington, Clive Owens, and Jodie Foster. A segmentation of the film, however, reveals not only its formal structural patterns but also an implicit political argument about race and perception, or misperception as the case may be.

A SEGMENTATION OF *INSIDE MAN*

Preface: Unknown space: Dalton (Clive Owen), a white man, introduces himself and says he attempted a perfect bank robbery.

1. Alternation: outside and inside the bank: The robbery begins; detective Frazier (Denzel Washington), an African American is assigned; Arthur

Case (Christopher Plummer), the head of the bank, a white man, learns of the robbery; the robbers force the hostages to put on dark overalls and white masks that render them all but indistinguishable from one another; Captain Darius (Willem Dafoe) is introduced.

Interrogation: An African American man describes having been a hostage.

2. Inside the bank: Dalton in the bank's basement; Outside the bank: the penthouse of Madeleine White (Jodie Foster), who takes a phone call from Case.

Interrogation: Several hostages tell their stories.

3. Outside the bank: Frazier and Darius discuss the crisis; Case tells White about a secret safety deposit box; Alternation: outside and inside: Frazier attempts to call Dalton but Dalton doesn't pick up.

Interrogation: A female hostage.

4. Outside the bank: A Sikh hostage is released, and the cops remove his religiously mandated turban; the mayor's office: White convinces the mayor to let her intervene.

Interrogation: the Sikh complains about his racial treatment.

5. Outside the bank: Frazier, Mitchell, and Darius discuss Dalton's demands; Case attempts to join them but is rebuffed; the cops decide to send in pizza boxes outfitted with audio transmitters; Inside the bank: a hostage is beaten for taking off his mask.

Interrogation: a Jewish hostage.

6. Alternation between outside and inside the bank: the pizza is delivered; cops listen via the transmitters as the robbers seem to speak Russian; the female robber is disguised as a hostage.

Interrogations: two hostages are shown snapshots of other hostages.

7. Alternation between inside and outside: a hole has been chopped into the storage room floor; the language is identified as Albanian; Dalton and a young African American boy play a violent video game; Dalton opens (safety deposit) Box 392; White, the mayor, and Frazier discuss the situation.

Interrogation: an Armenian American hostage is asked if he is Albanian.

8. Alternation between inside and outside the bank: the robbers have bugged the command center; White enters the bank; Case's background as a Nazi collaborator is revealed; White insults Frazier.

Interrogations: the African American boy is asked if he recognizes anyone in the snapshots and says that "with the mask they all look the same"; a Latino hostage refers to a detective as "Wassa Wassa," which he defines as slang for "a person that don't come to your neighborhood"; a Jewish hostage; a female hostage.

9. Alternation between inside and outside the bank: Frazier is shown the hostages and tussles with Dalton; the robbers appear to shoot a hostage to death; Frazier discusses race and violence with a white cop; the cops storm the bank; the hostages are released, treated roughly by the cops, and taken away. Fade out.

10. Fade in: Frazier is told to "bury" a piece of information; Case confesses his past to White.

Unknown space: Dalton faces the camera and states his name—a repeat of the preface; this continues as voice-over into a flashback of Dalton in the bank's storage room fingering diamonds as the other robbers build a fake wall; Dalton is seen hiding behind it, then emerging.

11. Alternation between inside and outside the bank: three of the four robbers sit in a car outside the bank along with one of the supposed hostages; Dalton prepares to leave the bank; on his way out, Dalton bumps into Frazier, who is on his way in; Frazier opens Box 392.

12. Outside the bank: Frazier confronts Case; Frazier confronts White and the mayor; Frazier finds a diamond in his pocket.

13. Flashback: Inside: Dalton bumps into Frazier, shot from a different angle.

Coda: Frazier's girlfriend invites him into bed.

This segmentation of *Inside Man* divides the narrative into thirteen parts, with a preface and a coda framing them. These thirteen segments, in turn, are interrupted by seven interrogation scenes that take place in chronological terms after the hostages have been released but before Frazier has concluded his investigation. Notice in this context the difference between *Inside Man*'s plot and its story. In the story, which runs chronologically from beginning to end, the robbery is committed first; the story ends with Dalton confessing his crime. The plot, however, begins with Dalton's confession—the preface—and concludes with Frazier returning home to his girlfriend in the coda. In the story, the interrogations occur between segments 9 and 10 of the narrative; in the plot, they are interspersed at intervals between segments 1 and 9.

Inside Man appears to treat racial issues only incidentally. Compared to some of Spike Lee's other films, like *Do the Right Thing* (1989) and *Malcolm X* (1992), *Inside Man* may seem to be only mildly interested in perceptions of race and ethnicity. But in his book *American Film/American Culture*, the film scholar John Belton makes the case that the film's temporal shifts between the sequential events of the robbery and its aftermath on the one hand and the hostage interrogations on the other hand serve to reveal Lee's linking of race relations with perception and misperception, as two of the supposed hostages—who are in fact robbers or accomplices—slip past the detectives, while several of the real hostages are treated unfairly because of their race or ethnicity. Belton writes:

> Lee's playful manipulation of time and space foregrounds the problem of perception and misperception. Though the nominal subject of the film is the face-off between cops and criminals during a bank robbery, Dalton Russell and his gang harbor a hidden agenda that involves securing evidence that will expose Case's crimes against Jewish victims of the Holocaust. In other words, the film is also about race. New York City's multiculturalism is highlighted through a proliferation of characters representing different races and ethnicities, including African Americans, Albanians, Armenians, Asians, Hispanics, Jews, Poles, Saudi Arabians, and Sikhs. The title music—"Chaiyya, Chaiyya"—is an Islamic Indian love song from a popular Hindi film, further announcing the film's concern with other cultures.
>
> Lee's inclusion of seemingly random instances of racism provides a subtext on race that links racism to biased perception or misperception. The (white) cop on the beat who discovers the robbery tells Frazier, who is black, a story about his first violent encounter with a 12-year-old who stuck a gun in his face. He talks about breaking up a fight in which "one little spic is getting his clocked cleaned by another" when "a ni . . . , an African American" pulled a gun on him. With the n-word on his lips, he suddenly realizes who he's talking

to and says "African American" instead. Even Capt. Darius (Willem Dafoe) indulges in racist epithets, referring to "those ragheads at the Munich Olympics." A Sikh hostage is released; because he wears a turban, the police perceive him as an Arab terrorist and throw him to the ground.

Frazier's misreading of the bank robbery, though in no way racist, becomes the thematic center with which these other instances of biased perception resonate. Lee's choreography of the ending of the film involves the pooling of efforts on the part of the film's three major characters—a black man (Frazier), a white man (Russell), and a white woman (White)—to expose Case's criminal past. Three of the film's most visible non-racists take down the film's invisible racist. The moral imperative of the film is articulated by Russell in his final voice-over. Acknowledging that he robbed the bank for the money, he also admits to another motive, noting that the money's "not worth much if you can't face yourself in the mirror. Respect is the ultimate currency." Respect—both self-respect and respect for others—becomes the foundation on which a new, non-racist moral order can be built. (John Belton, *American Cinema/American Culture*, 3d ed., New York: McGraw-Hill, 2008)

STUDY GUIDE: STORY ANALYSIS AND SEGMENTATION

Segmentations can be time-consuming. You must stop and start the film many times in order to take notes, and if the film is at all entertaining to you, you will likely resent having to disengage yourself from what is happening in order to concentrate on the task at hand. The segmentation of *Inside Man* above took many hours to complete and was originally eight single-spaced pages long. Only after several more hours of whittling it down to its basic segments did the film's core narrative pattern emerge.

Unless your professor assigns you to write a segmentation of an entire film, here are two ideas for cutting down the sheer amount of work involved in doing a segmentation: (1) Segment a film with which you are already very familiar, and (2) Only segment part of a film.

Segmenting a film you know well will enable you to avoid getting so caught up in the action that you forget to analyze the narrative. Whether it is *Alien* (1979) or *The Sound of Music* (1965), your prior knowledge of the film's story will enable you to concentrate on its plot.

Segmenting only part of a film is also possible, although it may provide misleading results. You will save some time if you analyze, say, the first twenty minutes of a film instead of the whole thing, but while you will gain the experience of tracing a specific narrative's development, your analysis will be partial and possibly distorted. For example, were you to analyze only the first part of *Inside Man*, you would not see the larger pattern formed by the interrogations, only the first of which would appear in your segmentation. To avoid misrepresenting the narrative's structure, be sure to watch the rest of the film carefully, remaining aware of any broad patterns that emerge and noting them accordingly.

WRITING ABOUT WRITING

The search for meaning, and the articulation of ideas about meaning, continues as the central theme of this last section. Let's take a second look at John Belton's analysis of *Inside Man* to see specifically how Belton used segmentation and close observation to put together an argument about what the film means:

> 1. Lee's playful manipulation of time and space foregrounds the problem of perception and misperception. Though the nominal subject of the film is the face-off between cops and criminals during a bank robbery, Dalton Russell and his gang harbor a hidden agenda that involves securing evidence that will expose Case's crimes against Jewish victims of the holocaust. In other words, the film is also about race.

In this paragraph, Belton makes a logical connection between the film's nonchronological time structure and the theme of misperception, concluding that the combination of these elements— *unclear temporal structure* plus *theme of misperception* equals the film's otherwise hidden subject matter: *race*. It's an ingenious assertion. Here's how Belton supports it with evidence:

2. New York City's multiculturalism is highlighted through a proliferation of characters representing different races and ethnicities, including African Americans, Albanians, Armenians, Asians, Hispanics, Jews, Poles, Saudi Arabians, and Sikhs. The title music—"Chaiyya, Chaiyya"—is an Islamic Indian love song from a popular Hindi film, further announcing the film's concern with other cultures.

So far so good; Belton provides details of all the racial, ethnic, religious, and national communities represented by characters in *Inside Man*. By listing these groups, Belton is laying on details that support his argument that the film contains a social and political theme underlying its surface bank-robbery subject.

3. Lee's inclusion of seemingly random instances of racism provides a subtext on race that links racism to biased perception or misperception. The (white) cop on the beat who discovers the robbery tells Frazier, who is black, a story about his first violent encounter with a 12-year-old who stuck a gun in his face. He talks about breaking up a fight in which "one little spic is getting his clocked cleaned by another" when "a ni . . . , an African American" pulled a gun on him. With the n-word on his lips, he suddenly realizes who he's talking to and says "African American" instead. Even Capt. Darius (Willem Dafoe) indulges in racist epithets, referring to "those ragheads at the Munich Olympics." A Sikh hostage is released; because he wears a turban, the police perceive him as an Arab terrorist and throw him to the ground.

In this paragraph, Belton links incidents of racism to thematic questions about the nature of perception. He provides clear, accurate descriptions of three incidents in the film that relate to these issues, blends visual, aural and story descriptions, and methodically lays out his case.

4. Frazier's misreading of the bank robbery, though in no way racist, becomes the thematic center with which these other instances of biased perception resonate. Lee's choreography of the ending of the film involves the pooling of efforts on the part of the film's three major characters—a black man (Frazier), a white man (Russell), and a white woman (White)—to expose Case's criminal past. Three of the film's most visible non-racists take down the film's invisible racist. The moral imperative of the film is articulated by Russell in his final voice-over. Acknowledging that he robbed the bank for the money, he also admits to another motive, noting that the money's "not worth much if you can't face yourself in the mirror. Respect is the ultimate currency." Respect—both self-respect and respect for others—becomes the foundation on which a new, non-racist moral order can be built.

In this final paragraph, Belton ties up his assertion about misperceptions with clear, concise evidence from the film and offers a conclusion that spins out from the individual movie to the greater realm of politics and culture. Had Belton begun with his final sentence (" Respect—both self-respect and respect for others—becomes the foundation on which a new, non-racist moral order can be built") without logically leading the reader through his evidence-based argument step by step, his point would not stand; there would be no foundation for it to rest on. But by using logic, ingenuity, creative thinking, and accurate quotations from the film, Belton makes a solid case and a convincing argument. Keep this strategy in mind for any writing assignments you are asked to do, not only in this course but in your other courses as well.

CHAPTER 8
FILMMAKERS

FILM—A DIRECTOR'S ART?

You are probably used to hearing and reading reviewers refer to films as having been made by their directors: "Steven Spielberg's *Saving Private Ryan*," "Wong Kar-Wai's *2046*," "Michel Gondry's *Eternal Sunshine of the Spotless Mind* . . ." But consider this: of those three films, only *2046* was written by the person who directed it. Robert Rodat wrote *Saving Private Ryan*'s screenplay, not Steven Spielberg, and *Eternal Sunshine of the Spotless Mind* was written by Charlie Kaufman. Why is the director necessarily the film's creator? What about the screenwriter? Or the producer? Or the cinematographer? How about the actors? Shouldn't they be given some credit, too? Why not call it "Tom Hanks's *Saving Private Ryan*" or "Jim Carrey's *Eternal Sunshine of the Spotless Mind*"?

This chapter explores the nature of authorship in the cinema, the various roles played by the key creative personnel in a film's creation, and the collaborative nature of commercial filmmaking. After all, over eighty actors received credit in the CRAWL at the end of *Saving Private Ryan*; countless EXTRAS also appeared onscreen. (A *crawl* is a set of words that appear at the bottom of the screen and move upward; the END CREDITS of a film often take the form of a crawl. An *extra* is a performer who has no dialogue in a crowd scene and receives no credit.) A total of eight producers, coproducers, and associate producers helped make *Saving Private Ryan*, along with a cinematographer (Janusz Kaminski), an editor (Michael Kahn), a composer (John Williams), a production designer (Tom Sanders), five art directors, a costume designer (Joanna Johnston) and her 39-member crew, a set decorator (Lisa Dean Kavanaugh), sixteen makeup artists, ten assistant directors, and over six hundred other people, from sound recordists and Foley artists to electricians and best boys and grips to nurses, prosthetics specialists, drivers, negative cutters, accountants, caterers, and stuntmen. In practical terms, how can we consider this film to be "Steven Spielberg's *Saving Private Ryan*" without losing sight of the fact that it took a thousand people to make it? And what is a *best boy*, anyway?

AUTHORSHIP

Although there is continuing disagreement on the point, film scholars tend to credit the director as the chief creator of a given film. Directors—those whose works we study in most film classes, at least—are therefore the authors of the films in much the same way that a book's author is its writer, despite the fact that many other people are involved in a book's creation: an editor, a proofreader, a designer, a typesetter, and those who physically put the book together out of paper, ink, and adhesives. Every book is shaped in some manner by a team of people, but the writer generally gets the credit for its creation. So it is with film directors, though the cinema's technological nature is such that the amount of artistic input by others is much greater in filmmaking than in publishing.

There are both practical and theoretical reasons for treating a given film's director as its author. First, and certainly not least of all, it simplifies matters. Film historians are rarely present during the writing, production, and POSTPRODUCTION of the films we study, and without doing a great deal of archival research and interviews, it is impossible to know exactly who made every artistic decision in the creation of a motion picture. Even after doing detailed research, we find that many decisions remain unattributable. How do we know who exactly is responsible for what? Did Steven Spielberg tell Tom Hanks to play a given scene in *Saving Private Ryan* in a certain way, or did Hanks improvise his gestures and facial expressions? Was Spielberg even present on the set or location every single day? Could it have been an assistant director who suggested a particular gesture to Hanks? Perhaps the gesture was specified in Robert Rodat's screenplay. Or maybe Hanks performed it spontaneously and unconsciously without anyone directing him to do it, including himself. To make it possible to discuss *Saving Private Ryan*'s meaning in any detail and clarity, film studies make things frankly easier by assuming that because Steven Spielberg exerts an enormous amount of creative control over his films, he is the author of those films even though he did not write the screenplays and may not even have directed every single scene himself.

This holds true for all of the world's great directors, from Charles Chaplin and D. W. Griffith to John Ford and Howard Hawks to Jean Renoir, Kenji Mizoguchi, Federico Fellini, Rainer Werner Fassbinder, Satyajit Ray, and on and on. These directors generally did not compose every word of the scripts of their films, and in fact they may not have written any screenplays at all. But they undoubtedly oversaw all the important aspects of their films' creation, and so we consider them the films' creators.

A more defensible reason for treating a film's director as its author is that it is the director, not the screenwriter or the producer or any other member of the creative team, who generally decides where the camera goes, what it shoots, and where it moves. In fact, it is usually the director who is present through most of the stages of a film's creation, from casting through postproduction. Although it is the editor and his or her staff who literally piece the shots together to form the whole film, it's the director who provides the raw material. Some directors—like Billy Wilder and Alfred Hitchcock, for instance—were known for maintaining artistic control by doing what is called *editing in the camera*; in other words, they only shot precisely what they wanted to be included in the FINAL CUT. (A *final cut* is the last version of a film—the one that is released to the public. A ROUGH CUT is a preliminary version of a film, one that includes all the major sequences in their approximate length, but without finely tuned editing or the musical score. The term DIRECTOR'S CUT refers to the version of the film that the director deems to be finished, without the interference of producers, studios, censors, or distributors.) Lesser directors shot scenes that could be edited in various ways, but with Wilder, Hitchcock, and others, studio executives found it difficult to tamper with their films because they simply didn't have alternate footage to tamper with. There was not much celluloid left on the proverbial cutting-room floor in a Wilder or Hitchcock editing room.

One of the most famous cases of disputed authorship in the cinema is *Citizen Kane*, the screenplay of which was cowritten by Orson Welles and Herman Mankiewicz. Mankiewicz and his supporters resented the fact that Welles took the lion's share of the credit for the film's creation. While it is fair to say that Mankiewicz drafted *the screenplay*, the fact is that Orson Welles made *the film*. Readers of the script may legitimately attribute the script to Herman Mankiewicz, but *Citizen Kane*'s audiences see the work of Orson Welles.

THE AUTEUR THEORY

In 1948 the French film critic and theorist Alexandre Astruc coined the term *caméra-stylo*, or camera-pen, to describe the way a film director uses his or her camera—and sound recorders, lighting equipment, and so on—as a sort of writing instrument, a means of self-expression. For Astruc, the creation of a film was like the writing of a novel or a poem: it was not only a creative act, but a deeply personal one. He rejected the idea that a film director simply took a preexisting screenplay and filmed it according to its specifications. Instead, Astruc argued, the best directors created an entirely new and intensely personal work of art, with the screenplay being only a blueprint for story, plot, dialogue, and characters. Film art, he argued, was onscreen, not on the typed or printed page.

Astruc's followers, most notably the critic François Truffaut (who went on to become a director in his own right, as did Astruc himself), took this idea further by developing what they called the *politique des auteurs*, the assumption being that directors were in fact *auteurs*, or authors. For Truffaut and his circle, who wrote for the journal *Cahiers du cinéma*, it wasn't just that the director was the creator of his or her films, but that some directors were better at it than others. Not only did certain directors express themselves with their films, but what they expressed was especially worth expressing. Truffaut didn't call it the *politique des auteurs* for nothing. His championing of certain directors (Howard Hawks and Alfred Hitchcock at the top of the list) over others (Billy Wilder, most notoriously) expressed a kind of artistic politics that was based not only on judgments about a director's visual style but also in large measure on the perceived moral quality of his or her worldview. Wilder, for example, was both too cynical for Truffaut's taste and too invested in his own screenplays, which he always cowrote; since the *auteurists* tended to disregard screenwriters, a writer-director such as Wilder presented a cause for suspicion and consequent devaluation.

AUTEURISM was popularized in the United States by the critic Andrew Sarris, whose groundbreaking 1968 volume *American Cinema* ranked about two hundred Hollywood directors according to their ability to create a worldview over the course of their careers and the quality of that worldview. By *worldview*, Sarris and the other auteurists meant an overall vision of the way the world worked socially and philosophically, the way men and women dealt with each other and themselves, and the ethical and moral questions the directors grappled with over the course of their careers.

Given the way most of these films were made, it was surprising for Sarris to see the articulation of individual worldviews in them. Under the STUDIO SYSTEM, the mode of production that dominated American filmmaking from the 1920s to the late 1940s, each movie company signed most of its directors to long-term contracts, along with actors and other creative personnel. (Paramount, Metro-Goldwyn-Mayer, 20th Century-Fox, Warner Bros., RKO, Columbia, United Artists, and Universal were the eight dominant companies. Of these, Paramount, MGM, Fox, Warners, and RKO were considered the *major studios*, and the other three—Columbia, UA, and Universal—were the *minor studios*.) There was a writing department with a staff of screenwriters whose job it was to crank out filmable screenplays for commercial films; there were costume and props departments to provide and warehouse the required items, many of which were used over and over again; there were actors who were under contract and appeared in film after film . . . The studio system operated under a mass-production model in which films were made and distributed like sausages or boxes of cereal, and there was not a lot of room for individual directors to put their personal stamp on the films they made. It was all the more remarkable, then, for Sarris and others to discern elements of personal style in the work of two hundred Hollywood directors, many of whom worked in a variety of GENRES over the course of twenty or thirty years. (A *genre* is a category of film, such as the western, the horror film, the costume drama, the melodrama, and so on, with recognizable conventions and character types. This topic is covered in detail in chapter 10.)

Howard Hawks, for example, made screwball comedies (*Bringing Up Baby*, 1938; *Ball of Fire*, 1941, I *Was a Male War Bride*, 1948), westerns (*Red River*, 1948; *Rio Bravo*, 1959), musicals (*A Song Is Born*, 1948, *Gentlemen Prefer Blondes*, 1953), a film noir (*The Big Sleep*, 1946), combat films (*The Dawn Patrol*, 1930; *Sergeant York*, 1941), and a horror film (*The Thing from Another World*, 1951), and yet his worldview is remarkably consistent from genre to genre, film to film. Hawks's male characters demonstrate a more or less coherent code of ethical and emotional behavior—a certain stoicism in the face of adversity, for example—that runs from Cary Grant's exasperated paleontologist in the comedy *Bringing Up Baby* through John Wayne's obsessive cattleman in the western *Red River*. Truffaut, Sarris, and other auteurists appreciated the consistency of Hawks's moral universe as well as his understated and precise formal style.

Before Truffaut, Sarris, and the auteurists, critics tended to treat the films of Alfred Hitchcock as being merely highly polished entertainments. *Rebecca, Notorious, Strangers on a Train, Rear Window, Vertigo, Psycho* . . . Hitchcock's talent for creating suspense was widely appreciated by film reviewers and audiences, but his underlying worldview was largely ignored. The auteurists, however, perceived that Hitchcock was asking moral questions with his films: What is the nature of guilt, and is anyone ever truly innocent? Film scholars now understand that one can trace broad themes from *The Pleasure Garden*, Hitchcock's first film, to *Family Plot*, his last—that Hitchcock created a complex and coherent worldview with his body of work regardless of who wrote the scripts. His screenwriters varied; he worked with many producers and cinematographers; and his films were released under a variety of studio banners. But his visual style and thematic interests form a body of work that film scholars analyze for meaning in exactly the same way as literary scholars study the work of writers like Shakespeare, Faulkner, and Proust. Writers write with words; filmmakers write with images and sounds.

THE PRODUCER'S ROLE

If the director chooses camera angles, designs camera movements, and supervises the actors' performances, what does the producer do? Under the studio system, producers (or production supervisors, as they were sometimes called) were in charge of making sure their films stayed on schedule, or as close to schedule as possible. Producers (along with directors and some stars) looked at DAILIES or RUSHES, the developed footage just back from the processing lab, and either approved them or asked the director to film retakes. Because the studio system was more or less factory-like in its mode of production, the financing of individual motion pictures was not at issue in those days; the studios generally had the necessary capital to make their movies, so a film's producer didn't have to double as a fundraiser. But in today's filmmaking world, producers (like directors) are much more independent, and they must often arrange for the financing of each picture they make.

Several producers in the studio era exerted a profound influence over the films under their control. Irving Thalberg at MGM and Hal B. Wallis at Warner Bros., for instance, were more exacting in their tastes and authoritative in their artistic influence than many of the directors who actually shot the films. These producers monitored every step of their films' production, and they continued exerting control over the films during postproduction, long after the directors had moved on to other projects.

David O. Selznick was another powerful producer who began as a studio employee but, having outgrown the role of underling to the legendary studio boss Louis B. Mayer of MGM, Selznick became an independent producer. His greatest film, *Gone with the Wind*, had a total of three different directors (Victor Fleming is the credited director, but George Cukor and Sam Wood also worked on the film at the beginning of its production), so one could argue that Selznick is that film's real auteur. It was Selznick who supervised the screenplay's construction, Selznick who made all the important casting decisions, and Selznick who controlled the editing process. Unlike the auteur directors, however, even a powerful producer like David O. Selznick did not have a personal filmmaking style in the way Hitchcock or Hawks did. (As an example of an interesting clash between an auteur and a major producer, Hitchcock always maintained that his film *Rebecca* (1940) was not actually a Hitchcock picture, but rather a Selznick picture, because Selznick had insisted on lavishing his own trademark production values on the film.) If, as Alexandre Astruc proposed, filmmaking at its best is a kind of personal writing, then it might be said that producers like Selznick, Thalberg, and Wallis produced highly polished but relatively impersonal films.

Today, most producers are more like Selznick than the average studio-era producer in that they are often the ones who come up with the idea of making a film out of a given novel, story, play, or original screenplay, after which they put together a package—director, screenwriter, stars—and attempt to find financing. It is usually the producer, not the director, who buys the **option** (or the rights to make the film) on a given literary property. Producers may or may not be affiliated with one of the major studios, and even when they are under contract to a studio, they function more independently than producers did when the studio system was in effect. The studio era effectively ended in 1948 when the Supreme Court ruled in the antitrust case *United States v. Paramount Pictures et. al.* that the studios had to divest themselves of the movie theaters they owned, thus breaking the VERTICAL INTEGRATION model that enabled the movie companies to own not only production facilities but also distribution networks and exhibition houses.

How does the current scenario work? Well, two of the studios of old, 20th Century-Fox and Columbia Pictures, are now essentially film distributors that are owned by much larger media conglomerates—News Corp. and Sony, respectively—which either bankroll films by smaller production houses (Imagine Entertainment or Amblin, for example) or buy the distribution rights to films that are independently produced and financed; these transactions often take place at film festivals. By changing their original business model, Fox and Columbia are able to distribute films through their own outlets and still comply with antitrust laws. (In Fox's case, it's television stations; in Columbia's case, it's the Loews theater chain, which is a separate company owned by Sony.) Another way of maintaining the benefits of vertical integration while abiding by antitrust regulations is to control both an independent production company and a theater chain—for instance, Walden Media and Regal Cinemas, which are both owned by Philip Anschutz. Walden produces its films, and then Anschutz strikes deals with distributors (such as Disney) to put his Walden films on his own Regal screens.

TEAMWORK

CINEMATOGRAPHY is the province of the DP, otherwise known as the cinematographer. The DP is responsible for selecting the cameras, lenses, and film stocks, and also for overseeing the lighting design and the operation of the camera. On a big-budget film, a dedicated CAMERA OPERATOR usually has the job of running the camera itself. The chief electrician, who actually sets up the lighting equipment, is called a **gaffer**. The gaffer's assistant is the **best boy**. **Grips** perform various functions, not only for the cinematographer and gaffer but for the camera and props departments as well; *grips* are the cinematic equivalent of stage hands in the theater. The **first assistant camera operator**—called a **focus puller** in Europe—makes sure the image remains in focus during camera movements, not to mention being responsible for there being film in the **magazine** (the removable container of film that fits onto the camera). The **second assistant camera operator** (called a **clapper** in Europe), operates the **clapboard**, the device with a slate and a hinged arm that claps down onto the slate to signal the beginning of a take; when, in the editing room, the *clap* sound on the soundtrack is matched with the frame in which the arm hits the slate, the soundtrack and the image track are necessarily synchronized.

The **screenwriter** (how to phrase it?) writes the script. He or she may adapt an already-existing novel or play or compose an original screenplay.

The **production designer**, or **art director**, is in charge of designing and executing the *look* of a film—its sets and locations, primarily. In consultation with the director, the production designer designs the architecture and general decoration of the sets and supervises the choice of locations based on the requirements of the period in which the film is set and the mood the director wishes to create. Working under the production designer's guidance are **set decorators**, the **props master** and his or her staff, a construction crew with carpenters and painters and plasterers, and so on.

Since sound is the subject of chapter 5, you are already aware of the complexity of a soundtrack's creation, but in brief, a large sound crew is responsible not only for recording the dialogue and ambient sounds on the set or on location and creating all the sound effects but also for making sure that the enormous number of people present during filming do not create their own disruptive sounds that would ruin a take. Members of the sound crew include the **sound mixer** (usually the supervisor), the **sound recordist** (who is in charge of the recording apparatus and crew), **boom operators** (who hold the long arms from which microphones hang over the performers just above the camera's field of vision), FOLEY ARTISTS (who create aural effects that sound more realistic than the actual noises that were recorded), and others. Here's an example of what a Foley artist might do: upon playback, the filmmakers discover that the sound of a character walking on snow doesn't sound right, so a Foley artist creates a sound effect by pressing two pieces of Styrofoam together, the Styrofoam sounding more like shoes trampling in the snow than the actual sound of footsteps that was recorded when the scene was shot.

Thanks to the digital revolution, many of the original filmmaking jobs have changed. The first assistant camera operator, for example, is now responsible for making sure that memory cards are removed from the camera and the information on them is properly uploaded to a hard drive. And the clapper is now a digital slate attached to a **Digital Audio Recorder** (DAR); the DAR contains a time code generator, and the timing is recorded continuously on the tape. The time code is also displayed constantly on a large LED on a digital slate, which is shown to the camera before the action starts so the editor knows exactly what the tape's time code is and can synchronize it with the film. Sometimes a digital slate contains a clapboard, but it's not essential the way it once was.

Since special effects is the subject of chapter 11, here is a preview of coming attractions: **CG (computer graphics) artists, matte artists, model makers, rotoscope artists,** and COMPUTER GEEKS all work to create effects that would be impossible to film using only what material reality provides. These effects, as expensive as they may be, may nonetheless provide budgetary savings as well. Consider how much money it would have cost the director Peter Jackson and the studio New Line Cinema to pay, feed, house, and costume 10,000 orcs for the *Lord of the Rings* trilogy (2001, 2002, and 2003).

STUDY GUIDE: THE PROBLEM OF ATTRIBUTION

The goal of good writing is clarity. Whether you are writing a lab report in biology, a paper on the Iraq War for a history class, or an analysis of *The Matrix Reloaded* or *Ratatouille* for a film class, you should always try to present your ideas as lucidly and directly as possible. But film studies presents students with a particular problem: how can you ascribe artistic intention without specific evidence to back up the claim? As described in this chapter, film scholars tend to attribute even minor cinematic details to directors even though we recognize that the decisions may actually have been made by other people.

For example, in chapter 1 you read about the musical number in *Gentlemen Prefer Blondes* in which an extra kicked the film's star, Jane Russell, into a swimming pool during a take, but the director, Howard Hawks, used the mistake anyway. In fact, it was the film's choreographer, Jack Cole, who actually directed that particular scene; Hawks himself may or may not have been on the set when the accident happened as well as when the retakes were filmed. Nevertheless, it is appropriate to describe the film as a whole as Howard Hawks's *Gentlemen Prefer Blondes*, as well as to describe the decision to use the supposed mistake in the final cut as having been Hawks's. On a practical level, it was Hawks who had the final say in what take was used. And on a critical and theoretical level, film scholars like Robin Wood and others have demonstrated that throughout his films Hawks is interested in the conflict between the sexes. One can draw parallels between, say, Katharine Hepburn's character's abuse of Cary Grant's in *Bringing Up Baby* and the violent ending of the "Ain't There Anyone Here for Love?" number in *Gentlemen Prefer Blondes* without worrying about where Hawks was on the day Jane Russell got knocked into the pool. As loathe as some film scholars may be to acknowledge it, the fact is that film studies is an art, not a science, and it is not subject to the same concrete rules of provability that apply in chemistry or physics departments.

That said, there is a key question that every student and scholar must ask when writing a paper: *Do I know it for a fact?*

Here's an example of what not to write: "Howard Hawks personally directed an extra to kick Jane Russell into the swimming pool in *Gentlemen Prefer Blondes*." It is simply not a valid claim. Without careful and detailed research into the production of the films you write about, you cannot legitimately state what happened on the set. Instead, you may—in fact, you *should*—assert what you think a sequence *means*: "The strange way Hawks ends the number expresses his distrust of romance."

In most college film courses, particularly introductory level courses, you will not be asked to do primary research into a film's production history. Moreover, the films your professor is showing you are probably made by directors with strong authorial voices. So your best bet is to assume for now that the director not only made most if not all of the important artistic decisions in the film's creation but also that these decisions express ideas and emotions worth analyzing in detail.

WRITING ABOUT DIRECTORS

Unless the course you are taking is a study of one or two particular directors, you will not have the opportunity to put the auteur theory to extensive practice. Why not? Because auteurism discerns a director's personal style from his or her entire body of work. You would have to see a fairly large number of films by Hitchcock, or Hawks, or Ford, or Spielberg, or *any single director* in order to be able to make any substantial claims about his or her worldview.

What you *can* do, however, is to learn biographical and filmographical details about the men and women whose films you are seeing and to begin to see elements of personal style in an individual film. (A **filmography** is a simple list or more detailed catalog of the films made by an individual; directors, producers, screenwriters, actors, and so on all have filmographies.)

To start your study of whomever you or your professor chooses, go online to the Internet Movie Database (www.imdb.com) and do a simple search for the filmmaker or film in question. Like the *American Film Institute Catalog of Motion Pictures Produced in the United States*, both print and online editions, imdb.com is a very useful primary resource for film scholars who are researching the names-and-dates facts of a given film's production. Unlike the *AFI Catalog*, imdb.com has the virtue of being accessible from any computer in the world. The *AFI Catalog* print edition can be found in many college and university libraries, while the online edition is available only to subscribing individuals and institutions. (Check your library's catalog to see whether you are able to access it.) However, one should be aware that imdb.com—like Wikipedia and other online resources—may contain factual errors despite the best intentions of those who contribute information to the site. Some professors are therefore adamant that such sites not be used for academic research; ask your professor for the guidelines for your particular course.

Let's use as an example the pioneering female director Dorothy Arzner. Go to www .imdb.com, type the name "Dorothy Arzner" in the search box, and hit enter. The page that will appear contains her birth and death dates, the locations of her birth and death, the first lines of her IMDB biography, a few important details of her life—details that are erroneously labeled "trivia," which actually means "insignificant matters." (How "insignificant" is it that Arzner was the first woman to join the Directors Guild of America?) Then scroll down and find her filmography, which is itself broken down into several categories. We learn from this set of filmographies, for instance, that Arzner worked as an editor on six films and a writer on five. She worked as a director on a total of twenty films, several times in an uncredited capacity.

This page, and others like it, is only the beginning. There is a wealth of information available on imdb.com—information that would have taken previous generations of students a great deal of time, effort, and organizational skill to gather. Click, for example, on any of the links on the page to find out more about Dorothy Arzner: one leads to a thorough and informative biography, others to detailed pages on the films Arzner made. Click, for example, on the title *Christopher Strong* and you will be taken to a page devoted to that unusual film, one of the earliest in the star Katharine Hepburn's long career. On the left side of the screen on the *Christopher Strong* page is a list of links that yield particular information such as the film's release date, its technical specifications (the film's length in reels, its aspect ratio, and so on), and other data.

Now pick your own filmmaker and start researching.

CHAPTER 9
PERFORMANCE

PERFORMANCE AS AN ELEMENT OF MISE-EN-SCENE

How does film studies deal with acting? Movie reviewers tell us that certain performances are good while others are terrible. The Academy of Motion Picture Arts and Sciences gives awards every year in tribute to the quality of individual performances. And we all come away from the movies we see with opinions of whether the stars have done a good job creating their characters or not. But it should be clear by now that as an academic discipline, film studies is less interested in issuing judgments than in analyzing aspects and components of meaning. How, then, do we distinguish quantitative expressive meanings from qualitative opinions as far as acting is concerned?

In key ways, acting is actually an element of mise-en-scene—a human element, but an element nonetheless. Think back to the initial definition of MISE-EN-SCENE: *all of the elements placed in front of the camera to be photographed: settings, props, lighting, costumes, makeup, and figure behavior—actors, their gestures, and their facial expressions.* "Figure behavior" may seem like a cold, impersonal way of describing talented human beings, especially when they are as larger-than-life as movie stars appear to be. But the term does help both to demystify and to quantify film acting—to take the discussion of performance out of the realm of "Is it Oscar-worthy?" and put it into a less judgmental, more analytical category of discussion. One doesn't have to go as far as Alfred Hitchcock, who once compared actors to livestock, to see that for all their glamour and fame, film performers are just part of the overall production of meaning in a narrative film. (Hitchcock once clarified the point he was trying to make: "I didn't say actors are cattle. What I said was, actors should be *treated* like cattle.") From this perspective, actors' gestures and expressions are no different from the props they use and the costumes they wear.

Hitchcock's insulting joke aside, this is certainly not to say that actors are interchangeable, that talent doesn't matter, and that it isn't excruciatingly hard work to perform on film, let alone build and sustain a career as a movie star. On the contrary. But as you will see, film studies deals with actors analytically. Instead of applauding them, we study them, though these two activities are not mutually exclusive.

ACTING STYLES

Acting styles change over time. What one generation regards as a realistic and believable performance may be viewed by a later generation as highly stylized. To cite one famous family as an example, John Barrymore (1882–1942) was considered one of the greatest (if not *the* greatest) actor of his time. He appeared in such classic films as *Dinner at Eight* (1933) and *Twentieth Century* (1934), and he was known for his resonant, theatrical voice. Barrymore didn't talk onscreen the way ordinary people talk offscreen; he *projected* his voice and enunciated each word the way a trained theater actor did, and audiences admired him for it. He used his voice as a kind of musical instrument with great range and depth. But if Barrymore's granddaughter, Drew Barrymore (1975–), spoke onscreen today the way her grandfather did in the 1930s, audiences would likely find her performances unacceptably stylized—too self-conscious and theatrically over the top.

Because of this sort of change in public perceptions of what is realistic and what is not, it's better to avoid the concept of *realism* in favor of a related but more functional term: NATURALISM. *Naturalism* in acting is *an attempt by a performer to appear not to be performing*. Gestures that look spontaneous and unplanned, speech that doesn't call attention to itself—these are some of the tools of naturalistic actors. Classical stars who were naturalistic performers include Henry Fonda, James Stewart, and Joanne Woodward; current naturalistic stars include Denzel Washington, Julia Roberts, and George Clooney.

One star who was *not* especially naturalistic was Bette Davis, who once told an interviewer, "You still run into directors today who tell you [to] 'do less in a close-up than you do in a long shot. Don't, for God's sake, give any suggestion that you're *acting*. Just be natural.' No, no, no, no, no, *no!*" Davis wanted her performances to be seen as such: as noticeably crafted showpieces. A relatively recent, non-naturalistic performance, or set of performances, is Johnny Depp's in the *Pirates of the Caribbean* series (2003, 2006, and 2007); Depp's flamboyant gestures and exaggerated manner of speaking in those films are meant to be seen, heard, and appreciated specifically *as acting devices*.

But notions of what constitutes naturalism change, too. In the 1950s, an acting technique called THE METHOD drew national attention with the rapid rise of such stars as Marlon Brando and James Dean—actors who were trained to use their own emotions and backgrounds to inform the characters they played. At the time, Brando's performances in such films as *A Streetcar Named Desire* (1951) and *On the Waterfront* (1954) were perceived as being electrifyingly naturalistic and straight from the heart; more than fifty years later, these performances are still electrifying, but they seem much more stylized and less naturalistic than they did originally.

STARS AND CHARACTER ACTORS

Everybody knows what a movie star is, but outside of film studies textbooks and dictionaries, there are few clear and concise definitions. Here is one offered by Ira Konigsberg in his excellent reference book, *The Complete Film Dictionary*: A STAR is "*a performer with a national or international reputation who appears in major roles and has great box-office appeal.*"

This definition of *star* contains three key elements: widespread public knowledge of the performer, sizeable roles played by the performer, and the performer's ability to generate ticket sales on his or her own. Nobody can be a star without being well known on a very broad scale, and while stars may periodically make what is known as CAMEO APPEARANCES (that is, they appear in tiny roles specifically to be noticed by audiences as big stars in tiny roles—Brad Pitt's momentary flash onscreen in *Being*

John Malkovich, 1999, is just such a cameo)—they must appear mostly in leading roles, not supporting roles. The last element, *box-office appeal*, is particularly important to appreciate. Audiences have been willing to spend money to see the latest Charles Chaplin film, or the latest Julia Roberts film, not because of the subject of the film, but because that particular star appears in it. In such cases, it isn't the story that sells the film, nor is it the director or the producer. It's the star—hence his or her astronomical salary.

One common misperception about film acting involves stars who appear in relatively the same role in film after film—John Wayne, for instance. Because of the similarity of many of his characters, Wayne is sometimes called a *character actor*, but that term means something else entirely. CHARACTER ACTORS are not stars, but rather *secondary performers who specialize in playing similar, recognizable character types.* Under the studio system, character actors working at a given studio would turn up regularly onscreen in familiar but relatively small roles—the same performer would be seen often as a fast-talking salesman or a mug-faced gangster, the heroine's best friend or a kindly old lady. Now that the studio system and its long-term contracts have disappeared, character actors are much less common, though they still exist. Steve Buscemi, for instance, has become a familiar character actor through his appearances in a number of crime dramas, such as Quentin Tarantino's *Reservoir Dogs* (1992) and *Pulp Fiction* (1994) and David Chase's HBO series *The Sopranos* (1999–2007).

TYPE AND STEREOTYPE

Although movie stars are usually better looking than the average person, and we take the fact that they are idealized images for granted, one feature of most stars is their *representativeness*—their ability to personify a type of person. There is an important distinction to be made between the words *type* and *stereotype*. Whereas a **type** (as the film historian Richard Dyer puts it in his book *Stars*) is "*a shared, recognizable, easily-grasped image of how people are in society (with collective approval or disapproval built into it),*" a **stereotype** is not only conventional but formulaic. In short, *a stereotype is an oversimplified and sometimes demeaning type.*

An actor can represent a type without representing a stereotype. The stars who have played the character James Bond, for instance, are all of a certain type: Audiences perceive Sean Connery, Roger Moore, Pierce Brosnan, Daniel Craig, and others as being—like Bond himself—sophisticated, polished, clever, and sexually appealing in a ruggedly masculine way. One would not describe James Bond and the men who have played him as being a stereotype; they are, however, a particular *type*. The roles played by the Academy Award–winning, African American actress Hattie McDaniel, however, were largely *stereotypes*, because—despite her great talent—she was generally relegated to playing somebody's servant, albeit one who often spoke her mind. (McDaniel won her Oscar for playing Mammy, Scarlett O'Hara's slave, in *Gone with the Wind*, 1939.)

Both stars and the characters played by stars can be described as *types*. (The same cannot be said of the word *stereotype*, which is limited to characters.) One very popular type in Hollywood filmmaking is, to put it very plainly, *the Good Guy*. We are so familiar with this type of character that we take him totally for granted, but this character and star type is worth pursuing precisely because of his conventionality. By *the Good Guy*, we mean more than simply that the character or star conveys a positive image. We mean a particular *type* of positive image, with a specific set of traits. What are some of the characteristics of this *type*?

THE GOOD GUY

Friendly, but not aggressively so; he never glad-hands

Masculine; he is never effeminate

Easygoing, but not lazy

Smart enough, but not overly brainy—he doesn't use big words

Good looking—handsome, but not pretty

Honorable, especially in the end

Able to display a sense of humor—he can be funny but is rarely ridiculous

Some examples of stars who have been known as Good Guys, and who became known as Good Guys because they repeatedly *played* Good Guys, are William Holden, Denzel Washington, and perhaps most famously, John Wayne. When someone like Washington or Wayne plays a Bad Guy (Washington as a murderous drug lord in *American Gangster*, 2007; Wayne as Genghis Khan in *The Conqueror*, 1956), it's known as **casting against type**: the knowledge of the star's type that the audience brings into the filmgoing experience is deliberately challenged by casting against type.

WOMEN AS TYPES

The line that distinguishes type from stereotype can become disturbingly thin when it comes to women's characters in film. Take the example of Hattie McDaniel, the African American actress who won a Best Supporting Actress Oscar for playing Mammy in *Gone with the Wind*. Mc-Daniel brought great intelligence to her characters along with a sense of sassy independence, and yet in film after film she was consigned to the background as somebody's maid. There is nothing either comical or shameful about working as a housekeeper, but McDaniel's characters were often the brunt of jokes precisely because of her race and her characters' occupation.

Race is not the only factor that can blur the distinction between type and stereotype. An even more overarching constraint comes through the dual categories of sex and gender. In short, sex is biological; gender is cultural. Sex is the physiology we are each born with; gender is how we learn to understand the sexes—how we hold our books or look at our nails, and how we walk and talk, all of which communicates information about masculinity and/or femininity.

For example, one of the most notable and consistently popular female character types in cinema is *the Blonde Bombshell*, the curvaceous beauty with radiantly light-colored hair and, often, a certain lack of normal intelligence. Is she a type or a stereotype? Marilyn Monroe is the best-known star who embodied the Blonde Bombshell type. Other Blonde Bombshells include Mamie Van Doren and Jayne Mansfield, both of whom were designed to be competitors to Monroe in the 1950s; Jean Harlow in the 1930s (Harlow actually starred in a 1933 film called *Bombshell*); Brigitte Bardot in the 1960s; and others. The popular 2001 Reese Witherspoon comedy *Legally Blonde* (together with the hit Broadway musical that followed) plays on this character type. (Or is she a stereotype?)

Another popular female character type is the Femme Fatale, or Killer Dame; one often sees such murderous women in crime dramas. Some notable embodiments of the Killer Dame are Barbara Stanwyck in *Double Indemnity* (1944), Kathleen Turner in *Body Heat* (1981), and Glenn Close in *Fatal Attraction* (1987).

ACTING IN—AND ON—FILM

What distinguishes film acting from stage acting?

For one thing, theater is live, while film is recorded. This has important consequences for each category of performance. Theater actors must interact directly with audiences. As a result, they receive constant indications of how their audiences are responding, and they can pause for laughter to die down, speed up slightly if they sense boredom, emphasize certain lines and gestures depending on the particular audience they are playing to that day, and so on. And if they make a mistake such as flubbing a line, they must go on with the show as though nothing had happened. If a stage actor drops a plate by mistake and it breaks, he or she must either ignore the mistake or incorporate it into the action. Stage actors' performances are continuous; they run from beginning to end for the duration of the scene or the act.

Film actors, on the other hand, play their scenes before any number of people, but those people are the crew, not an audience, and the crew is not supposed to react. If, say, Ben Stiller does something funny during a take and a grip laughs audibly, the take might be ruined. Movie actors' performances are also discontinuous; depending on the director's preference and style, their performances may be given in short bursts lasting only for the duration of a single shot. If they are filming a close-up that occurs in the midst of a dialogue, for example, the other actor may not even be present. And because of this kind of discontinuity, film actors (with the aid of the continuity crewmember assigned to the task) must recall precisely where they were, what direction their heads were turned, and what expressions were on their faces from one shot to the next to make it possible for editors to match them in the editing room.

Whereas stage actors must, in both voice and gesture, express emotions clearly to audience members seated in the back of the balcony as well as in the front row, film actors must play to the camera and the microphone, both of which may be extremely close to them. What would be unnoticeable onstage—the slight raising of an eyebrow, or the delivery of a line in a bare whisper—will register much more definitely and expressively when blown up to the size of a cinema screen and projected through an extensive system of speakers. Film actors' images are large, but elements of their performances may be quite small.

One important aspect of any kind of acting is simply the way an actor looks on a blunt, physical level. It's an issue that's even more basic than the well-reported cases of a given actor gaining or losing a lot of weight in preparation for a particular role. (For his role as the boxer Jake LaMotta in Martin Scorsese's *Raging Bull*, 1980, for instance, Robert De Niro first trimmed down to fighting weight for the early scenes then gained a total of sixty pounds to play the aging, out-of-shape LaMotta in the final scenes.) Audiences make immediate judgments about a character based on the actor's face, or PHYSIOGNOMY. For better or worse, we make these judgments in real life as well, but we are only concerned with the cinematic consequences here. Again using Robert De Niro as an example, it's clear that he was chosen for the role of Jake LaMotta not only because he is a talented actor but because his face looks like it could be that of a champion Italian American boxer, and he has the physical dynamism of a boxer as well. From Scorsese's perspective, it was more important that audiences judged De Niro's physiognomy as appropriate than it was that De Niro bore a passing resemblance to the real Jake LaMotta. Similarly, Matt Damon was cast as Jason Bourne in the highly successful *Bourne* series (2002, 2004, 2007) because audiences respond positively to his strikingly handsome facial features. Sacha Baron Cohen would not cut quite the same figure as Jason Bourne, nor would Steve Buscemi—not because they aren't talented actors, but simply because of their quirkier physiognomies.

PUBLICITY: EXTRA-FILMIC MEANING

One aspect of film studies that has no counterpart in literary analysis is that film audiences know quite a bit of information about the stars they follow, and they bring that information to the films they see. When students and scholars read a novel, they may bring prior knowledge of the author or the genre to their initial experience of the book in question, but there are no real-life stories behind the characters, who are entirely fictional. (There are many exceptions, of course; Truman Capote's book *In Cold Blood* is known as a *nonfiction novel.*) But when we see a movie for the first time, we may know something not only about the director and the genre; we may also know information about the star's personal as well as professional life—the state of his or her current marriage, whether he or she has had a drug or alcohol addiction in the past, what designer made the gown she wore at the last Oscars ceremony, which political party the star supports, and so on. All of this information comes to us under the general heading of PUBLICITY. *Publicity* is defined as *the management of the public's perception of a person*; *publicity* can also be defined as the *creation and maintenance of a star's persona by extra-filmic means*—not the roles in which they appear onscreen, but the magazines and television shows and websites in which they appear offscreen.

What, then, is a PERSONA? A *persona is the role one consistently displays in public*, as opposed to the inner self known only to us as individuals. We each have a persona. Consider for a moment the persona that you project to others, and the difference, if any, between the persona you now have in college and the persona you used to have in high school. Now consider the difference between movie stars and the rest of us. Movie stars develop their personas on a national and even international scale, largely through the aid of publicity. Imagine the effect of having (and seeing) photos of yourself leaving a late-night party plastered in the pages of *Us* magazine, for instance. What might be a minor embarrassment for the rest of us is international news for a movie star.

FIGURE 9.1 Brad Pitt in *The Assassination of Jesse James by the Coward Robert Ford* (2007) (frame enlargement).

When the director Andrew Dominik's *The Assassination of Jesse James by the Coward Robert Ford* was released in 2007, Brad Pitt's fans went to the movie already knowing a great deal about Pitt and his persona. They were familiar with details of his romantic relationships with Gwyneth Paltrow, Jennifer Aniston, and Angelina Jolie; they knew that he has taken an active role in humanitarian causes like the rebuilding of New Orleans after Hurricane Katrina as well as having a longtime interest in architecture and design. They may have seen unauthorized paparazzi photos of him in celebrity magazines, and they may even find themselves speculating on aspects of his private life. These fans feel as though they know quite a bit about Brad Pitt even though they almost certainly have never met him themselves. Pitt's publicists attempt to control the flow and content of information about him by negotiating with magazines for cover stories and scheduling his appearances on talk shows, but they cannot control it all; paparazzi photos, being unauthorized, remain outside of publicists' power. But *all* of it contributes to the public's knowledge of Brad Pitt as a star, and all of it can be the object of analytical study in this academic discipline.

The question here is not whether Brad Pitt is a good actor or a bad actor, or whether or not he is a good mate for Angelina. Instead, legitimate questions in film studies are: What are the elements of Brad Pitt's persona? How did these elements become established? Have they changed over time, and if so, in what ways? Answering them requires research as well as analytical thinking; film scholarship in this case requires investigating popular magazines from the beginning of Pitt's career and other biographical research.

STUDY GUIDE: ANALYZING ACTING

A good way to begin learning how to put your new knowledge about film acting into practice is to take a fresh look at a familiar subject—your favorite star. It doesn't matter who you particularly admire—Cary Grant, Ving Rhames, Meryl Streep, Lucy Liu, Bette Davis, Ashton Kutcher . . . The field of possibilities is very wide. Your task instead is to translate your admiration, which exists on the level of qualitative opinion, into a more quantifiable, analytical set of observations. The goal is to be as descriptively precise as possible. (The next section, "Writing about Acting," will help you turn descriptive details into analytical observations about meaning.)

Here's a basic outline to guide you.

1. THE STAR'S PHYSICAL APPEARANCE

   A. Estimated age
   B. Facial features
      i. Most distinctive aspects
      ii. Eyes—color and shape
      iii. Mouth—shape and size
      iv. Hair—color and cut
   C. Body type
      i. Height—is he or she taller than average, shorter than average, or average?
      ii. Shape—slim, athletic/muscular, or heavy; have you seen photographs of the star unclothed, and if so, what did you notice?
   D. Real life or character? In other words, are the observations above based on the star as seen in magazines or as made up for a particular role?
   E. Ethnicity and race—what do you know, and what can you see, about the star's ethnic and racial background?

2. THE STAR'S VOICE

   A. Vocal quality—does the star have a high voice, or a low voice, or something in between?
   B. Volume—is the star known for speaking loudly (Bette Midler, for instance) or for speaking quietly (Clint Eastwood)?
   C. Distinctive elements of the voice
      i. National accent—is American English not the star's first language?
      ii. Regional accent—the differences, say, between Dolly Parton (Tennessee) and Mark Wahlberg (Boston)
      iii. Eccentric vocal style—can the star's voice be impersonated easily, and if so, what are the elements of the impersonation? (Stars who fall into this category include Bette Davis, Katharine Hepburn, James Cagney, and Jack Nicholson.)

3. THE STAR'S *TYPE*

    A. Is the star associated with a particular genre or two? For example, Joan Crawford appeared in several musicals but is mainly associated with the melodrama.

    B. Does the star have a definable persona throughout his or her career? Is he a Good Guy or a Bad Guy? Is she a Blonde Bombshell or a Career Girl?

4. PUBLICITY ABOUT THE STAR—list everything that you already know about the star's life, including marriages and affairs, awards , addictions, legal troubles, well-known hobbies, political activities, and so on.

WRITING ABOUT ACTING

Describing a star clearly and precisely is only half the game. Now you must expand your descriptions into assertions about the star's meaning. It is difficult enough for most introductory film students to ascribe meanings to a given scene's mise-en-scene or a certain sequence's editing, but at least whatever claims students make about these things have the virtue of being about fiction, where the consequences of being wrong are immaterial. (I say *The Wizard of Oz* is conservative or even reactionary, and you disagree. It's a lively discussion, but neither of us is making any claims about reality, let alone real people who have real feelings.)

Analyzing stars presents a problem that may at first inhibit you from opening your mind fully: You are being asked to build an argument, point by point, about a real human being and the meanings he or she generates as a star. However unconsciously, you may hesitate to describe a real person in unflattering terms. You may resist reaching an insulting conclusion. You may feel somehow that you have no right to judge other people, and thus you may be reluctant to include negative observations.

You must get over these hesitations and inhibitions. For our purposes, stars are simply human elements of mise-en-scene, and we should analyze their personae and performances for meaning as unemotionally as we do a camera movement or a cut.

Take the outline you prepared in the Study Guide, above, and push your descriptions into a series of analytical details. Look for any patterns that emerge, and formulate tentative arguments as you go along.

Let's use Clint Eastwood as an example—specifically the Clint Eastwood of *Unforgiven* (1992):

NOTES ON CLINT EASTWOOD

1. EASTWOOD'S PHYSICAL APPEARANCE

    A. Estimated age: *late 50s.* (In point of fact, Eastwood was 62 when *Unforgiven* was shot. You can look up such details online, but rely first on your own powers of observation.)

    B. Eastwood's facial features

FIGURE 9.2 A publicity still of Clint Eastwood in *Unforgiven* (1992). (Photofest)

    i. Most distinctive aspects: *craggy, weatherbeaten face*

    ii. Eyes—color and shape: *blue eyes that are often squinting, giving him the appearance of being at best skeptical and at worst hostile*

    iii. Mouth—shape and size: *thin lips often formed into a sneer*

    iv. Hair—color and cut: *gray, thinning hair*

c. Eastwood's body type

    i. Height—*he comes across as being tall*. (In fact, he is 6'2".)

    ii. Shape—*he is slim and in good physical condition despite his age; early publicity photos of Eastwood often included shirtless, beefcake shots that revealed a smooth, athletic physique. He no longer has the muscle tone of a 20- or 30-year-old, but his body still reflects vigorous masculinity.*

D. Real life or character? In other words, are the observations above based on the star as seen in magazines or as made up for a particular role? *The role of William Munny in* Unforgiven *required no aging makeup, dramatic weight gain or loss. It's incorrect to say Eastwood plays himself in* Unforgiven, *but he does play a* character tailored to his own familiar persona, which involves not only rugged masculinity but a strict sense of right and wrong and a tendency to exact violent revenge for what he perceives as infractions of his personal moral code.

E. Ethnicity, sexuality, religiosity, and race—*Eastwood is a white heterosexual who is not known for being especially religious.*

2. THE STAR'S VOICE

A. Vocal quality—*Eastwood's voice is low and distinctively raspy; it has a dusty quality, as though he and his characters have spent so much time outdoors in the West that his mouth, lungs, and vocal chords have absorbed the dirt of the landscape.*

B. Volume—*Eastwood speaks in a characteristically low volume; he rarely if ever yells.*

C. Distinctive elements of the voice

   i. National accent—*he speaks American English with no foreign accent, which contributes to his persona's conservative American values.*

   ii. Regional accent—*he has no regional accent; he could be from any state or region in the country.*

   iii. Eccentric vocal style—can the star's voice be impersonated easily, and if so, what are the elements of the impersonation? *Eastwood's low, raspy voice and laconic line delivery, together with his squinty eyes, form the foundation not only of Eastwood's personal style but of a larger, more overriding image of hard, unyielding American masculinity.*

3. THE STAR'S TYPE

A. Is the star associated with a particular genre or two? *Although Eastwood has appeared in many films, he is associated with the western and action genres.*

B. Does the star have a definable persona throughout his or her career? Is he a Good Guy or a Bad Guy? Is she a Blonde Bombshell or a Career Girl? *Eastwood's persona was formed early in his career and has been burnished over time. Because he has played a number of outlaws as well as a rogue cop or two, we might define his particular persona as a Bad Good Guy/Good Bad Guy.*

4. PUBLICITY ABOUT THE STAR—list everything that you already know about the star's life, including marriages and affairs, awards, addictions, legal troubles, well-known hobbies, political activities, and so on.

A. *Became a successful film director*

B. *Politically conservative but socially liberal; served as the Republican mayor of Carmel, California at one time*

c. *Married several times*

d. *Not known for particularly hard living—not seen as a druggie or alcoholic, doesn't get into public fights, has no well-known scrapes with the law*

e. Has won a number of prestigious awards, including several Oscars and the American Film Institute's Life Achievement Award

CHAPTER 10
GENRE

WHAT IS A GENRE?

GENRE (zhon'-ruh): *a type or category of film—such as the western, the horror film, the comedy, or the musical—that has its own recognizable conventions and character types.*

To return to a point raised while defining the term CONVENTION (chapter 7), we sometimes assume that art is about pure creativity—that great films (or novels, or paintings, or musical works) are a matter of complete originality. But genres belie that idea. Genres rely on repetition and variation rather than uniqueness—familiar, recognizable *conventions* rather than raw, pure *inventions*. It's true that a filmmaker may take an especially fresh approach to a genre by emphasizing an unexpected element, spinning a seemingly predictable story in a new and unusual direction, or having a central character behave in an unconventional way. But these are *variations*, not radical innovations. In a way, a film genre is rather like a language we all understand. One could make up an entirely new word, but nobody else would know what it means. It's the repetitive nature of language that enables it to have meaning and make communication possible. The same holds true for film genres.

The word *genre* comes from French, where it simply means *kind* or *type*. You may be familiar with the word *generic*, which is used to describe medicines and other products that are sold without a brand name. Tylenol is an individual brand name, for instance, but Tylenol's active ingredient, acetaminophen—a kind or type of pain reliever—is also sold in unbranded, *generic* form. You may also know the word *genus* in biology. A *genus* is a category of organism that falls on the taxonomic (or classificational) scale between *family* and *species*. (*Homo* is our genus, *sapiens* our species.) All of these terms—genre, generic, and genus—refer to ways of categorizing things according to their resemblance to each other. It's sometimes said that it is our differences that define us as individuals, but in genre criticism it's really quite the opposite: genres are defined by the similarities among a large number of films.

Critics have identified innumerable genres and subgenres over the years, from the action film (*Captain Blood*, 1934; *Indiana Jones and the Temple of Doom*, 1984; *Lara Croft: Tomb Raider*, 2001) and the baseball picture (*Bull Durham*, 1988; *The Natural*, 1984; *The Jackie Robinson Story*, 1950, which is also a biographical picture, or *biopic*) to the thriller (Alfred Hitchcock's *North by Northwest*, 1959; *Phone Booth*, 2003; *Angels and Demons*, 2009) and the women's prison picture (*Caged*, 1950; *Women's Prison*, 1955; *Caged Heat*, 1974). There are martial arts films, chick flicks, beach party pictures, costume dramas, sci-fi films, and slapstick comedies. There is a genre called the *blaxploitation film*, which began with Melvin Van Peebles' *Sweet Sweetback's Baadasssss Song* (1971) and continued with such films as Gordon Parks's *Shaft* (1971) and Quentin Tarantino's *Jackie Brown* (1997), though one might very well question the genre's name on the grounds that seeking African American audiences for films featuring African American action heroes is scarcely more exploitive than any other attempt to target a particular audience.

Many of the best films ever made are genre pictures. John Ford's *Stagecoach* (1939) is a western; Alfred Hitchcock's *Psycho* (1960) is a horror film; George Cukor's *A Star is Born* (1954) is a musical; Martin Scorsese's *Goodfellas* (1990) is a gangster picture. Each of these films has something original about it, but all of them depend on genre conventions to provide meaning and structure. Not all films fall readily into specific genres. *Citizen Kane* (1941) is a *drama*, one of the broadest possible genre categories, but as many scholars have noted, it contains elements of both the *mystery* and the *film noir* genres.

A **convention** is *a widely used and accepted device in an art form*. Film reviewers often use the term *conventional* as a put-down, a way of saying that they are tired of seeing the same technique, story element, or character type over and over onscreen. But film studies uses *conventional* in a nonjudgmental way. We see conventions not as exhausted clichés but as essential and valuable parts of a communication system, meaningful components in a wide network of shared ideas. In short, conventions are basic to culture, particularly popular culture. To repeat the definition provided earlier in this book, a convention is *an artistic practice or process or device that is commonly accepted and understood within a given culture*. Conventions are meaningful precisely because they are repetitive; if an artistic device was truly new and utterly unique, chances are we wouldn't understand it at all.

If the same character type appeared in the same costume and performed the same physical actions in the same general setting in film after film after film, some people might grow bored. But other people would remain interested—hence the profusion of similar westerns in the 1930s. The pleasure of reexperiencing the same basic genre elements in film over and over again—in this case, a cowboy, a horse, some sagebrush, an outlaw and/or some Indians—is not solely the province of the distant past. Think about the many commercially successful incarnations of the psychotic Michael Meyers in the *Halloween* horror series and the like (subgenre: the SLASHER FILM), or his equally crazed kin in the related but even more gruesome subgenre known as the SPLATTER MOVIE. Middlebrow critics may have yawned (and published their yawns as movie reviews), but audiences kept buying tickets to slasher and splatter movies, knowing more or less exactly what they were going to see and hear before they actually saw or heard it. That familiarity was part of their pleasure.

A **subgenre** is simply a smaller category within a genre category. The horror film has subgenres including the slasher movie, the splatter movie, and the monster movie (*Godzilla vs. Mothra*, 1964). Comedies can be categorized into subgenres such as the screwball comedy (*Bringing Up Baby*, 1938), the gross-out comedy (*Dumb and Dumber*, 1994), the black comedy (*Dr. Strangelove: or How I Learned to Stop Worrying and Love the Bomb*, 1964), and other subgenres.

Repetition: the repetition of genre conventions from film to film provides a built-in structure, a recognizable framework in which not only the filmmakers but audiences operate. Seen from this perspective, genre conventions support rather than challenge social, cultural, and artistic assumptions. When we see a western, for example, we are not surprised to meet a protagonist onscreen who embodies a certain kind of idealized man: strong, tough, individualistic, taciturn ... The classical western hero is reassuring in his familiarity. This character has appeared in film after film for almost a century, even though he has been played by such diverse figures as John Wayne (*Fort Apache*, 1948), Clint Eastwood (*Unforgiven*, 1992), and Heath Ledger (*Brokeback Mountain*, 2005). Each of these stars, and each of these films, reinforces social and cultural expectations about masculinity, for example, by way of physiognomy and performance style. The repetition of this character type is so basic to the western genre that it is impossible to imagine a western featuring as its hero, say, a very sweet, extremely short singing sheriff who rides around a frontier town on an adorable little Shetland pony. (Impossible perhaps for first-time film students, but not for those seasoned veterans who have seen the 1938 all-midget western *The Terror of Tiny Town*.)

Variation: at the same time, repetition is never purely so. Every new western, or screwball comedy, or splatter movie, brings *variation*. Each particular story (or plot, or location, or actor, or line of dialogue) constitutes a dissimilarity from other films in the genre or subgenre. Each iteration is unique. In *Fort Apache*, for instance, John Wayne's character, Capt. Kirby York, closes the film by upholding a moral and ethical position—the value of traditional leadership—that the film has severely questioned until that point; York thus defends certain conservative ideas about masculinity. In *Unforgiven*, Clint Eastwood's character, Bill Munny, ends up going on a murderous, bloody rampage, unleashing all his pent-up energy by slaughtering a number of other men in a spectacular, climactic shoot-out; this, too, is a statement about masculinity, but it's clearly quite different than that of *Fort Apache*. And finally, although Health Ledger's character in *Brokeback Mountain*, Ennis Del Mar, may look and talk like a classical American film cowboy (Ennis is technically a ranch hand, not a cowboy), his love for another man sets him distinctly apart from conservative notions of western heroism, not to mention conventional masculinity. All three films are westerns, all three begin with similar characters, and yet each has something quite different to say about what it means to be a man: repetition and variation.

A BRIEF TAXONOMY OF TWO FILM GENRES— THE WESTERN AND THE HORROR FILM

Here is a partial breakdown of two popular genres, the western and the horror film, and some of the subgenres into which they can be divided. The list is certainly not comprehensive, and the specific films listed in each subgenre are by no means the only examples available. They're offered simply to give you a sense of what repetition and variation means in specific cinematic instances:

THE WESTERN

In general, the western is a film that takes place in the nineteenth-century American West.[1]

Subgenre: Cowboys-and-Indians movie—racial and imperial conflict on the frontier
  Broken Arrow (1950)
  Drums Across the River (1954)
  Cheyenne Autumn (1964)
Subgenre: Vengeance western—a loner, sometimes an outlaw, seeks revenge
  Stagecoach (1939)
  One-Eyed Jacks (1961)
  The Outlaw Josey Wales (1976)
Subgenre: Spaghetti western—a western made by an Italian director and characterized by a certain pastiche quality, meaning that it seems to be quoting or even parodying classical American westerns
  The Good, the Bad, and the Ugly (1966)
  Django (1966)
  Compañeros (1970)
  Django and Sartana are Coming: It's the End! (1970)
Subgenre: Science-fiction western—the future meets the past in the American West
  Westworld (1973)
  Back to the Future III (1990)
  Oblivion (1994)

1. This is a clear and simple definition of the western, and it is problematic for that very reason. See below for a discussion of what makes it a problem.

THE HORROR FILM

The horror film induces fright or terror in an audience.[2]

Subgenre: Monster movie—a creature wrecks havoc
  Bride of Frankenstein (1935)
  Bride of the Monster (1955)
  Bride of Chucky (1998)

2. This, too, is a problematically simple definition. Can *any* genre be defined accurately and thoroughly in just a few words? Why not?

Subgenre: Monster-as-psychotic-human movie—the creature is one of us
  Psycho (1960)
  Halloween (1978)
  The Silence of the Lambs (1991)
Subgenre: Splatter movie—a horror movie that centerpieces blood and guts
  Night of the Living Dead (1968)
  The Evil Dead (1981)
  Dead Alive (1990)
Subgenre: J-HORROR—a gruesome Japanese horror movie with a perverse psychological bent
  Blind Beast (1969)
  Cure (1997)
  Audition (1999)
Subgenre: horror-comedy
  Young Frankenstein (1974)
  Attack of the Killer Tomatoes (1978)
  Shaun of the Dead (2004)
  Night of the Day of the Dawn of the Son of the Bride of the Return of the Revenge of the Terror of the Attack of the Evil, Mutant, Hellbound, Flesh-Eating Subhumanoid Zombified Living Dead, Part 3 (2005)

GENRE: THE SEMANTIC/SYNTACTIC APPROACH

What role does history play in the formation, development, and possible decline of certain genres? How do we describe the way that genres change over time and still remain consistent enough to be, in fact, genres? And what about variations that appear to defy genre definitions—westerns that don't take place in the American West, for instance? These are thorny questions.

The film scholar and theorist Rick Altman has proposed a model he calls the "**semantic/syntactic approach**" as a way of resolving these theoretical issues.[3] The terms *semantic* and *syntactic* come from the field of linguistics, the study of language and its component parts. *Semantic* refers to *meaning*; *syntactic* has to do with *structuring and ordering*. Consider the word *horse*. Semantically, *horse* refers to a large four-legged, hoofed mammal. Syntactically, *horse* is a noun that may appear at any of a number of appropriate places in a sentence as long as its usage conforms to the rules of grammar. (The cowboy rode his *horse*. The *horse* had no saddle. On a *horse*, a person may travel more quickly than on foot. Et-

3. Rick Altman, *Film/Genre* (London: British Film Institute, 1999).

cetera.) Syntactically, the word *horse* may change positions in a sentence; its placement is variable, and a given sentence makes sense by virtue of where the word *horse* falls in it. Semantically, however, the word *horse* remains more or less constant in terms of its meaning, and it does not even have to be used in a sentence at all to have meaning. Think about it: *horse*. You know what the word means on its own.

According to Rick Altman, there have been two schools of critical thought and practice in genre studies: the semantic model on the one hand and the syntactic model on the other. Critics who study film genres *semantically* have concentrated on the similarities of characters, locations, lighting styles, and so on within a given genre—in other words, each genre has a set of relatively fixed meanings. Just as *horse* has a given meaning, so the western, or the horror film, or any genre or subgenre has a given meaning. *Syntactically* oriented scholars, in contrast, describe genres in terms of variable relationships between structured, ordered elements. Instead of stressing what remains constant within a genre, syntactic critics find a much more fluid and changeable set of films as constituting a consequently more fluid and changeable genre. Just as the word *horse* appears variably in sentences, the western, the comedy, or any genre or subgenre appears variably over time and changes according to historical shifts, commercial decisions and economic trends, a specific director's individual concerns and visual style, and so on.

Altman uses as an example a semantic definition of the western offered by the French critic Jean Mitry: a western, for Mitry, is "a film whose action, situated in the American West, is consistent with the atmosphere, the values, and the conditions of existence in the Far West between 1840 and 1900." This is a fine example of a fixed, constant definition. For Mitry, it doesn't matter whether a film was made in 1909, 1959, or 2009: any film that is situated in the American West and has the values and atmosphere of the late nineteenth century is a western. There is something concrete about Mitry's definition—it's more or less stable and unchanging.

To provide a contrast, Altman cites the work of Jim Kitses as an example of a syntactic approach to the western. For Kitses, the western as a genre results from several overlapping thematic clashes: the West as desert versus the West as garden / nature versus culture / the individual versus the community. The fact that almost all westerns take place in the American West is actually of less interest to Kitses and other syntactic critics than the dialectics, or oppositional conflicts, that generate these films' narratives. For Kitses and others, the western is variable—it generates and regenerates all the time. Such constant regeneration crosses cultures as well as decades: Terrence Malick's *Badlands* (1973) can be considered a western, and even more flexibly, so can Ang Lee's *Crouching*

Tiger, Hidden Dragon (2000), thanks to its use of western (and Western) conventions (like riding off into the sunset) and its theme of money and civilization encroaching on the old ways of the frontier.

The semantic definition is, frankly, easier to grasp than the syntactic, which depends on the abstract philosophical concept of dialectics, but the syntactic approach yields a more dynamic vision of what constitutes the growth, sustenance, and variation within genres. Moreover, as Altman notes, while the semantic definition has the virtue of being able to clearly describe and unify large numbers of films, the syntactic definition makes it possible for us to isolate underlying themes and conflicts even though such isolated thematic clashes may not ultimately have broad applicability to every single film in a genre or subgenre. How do we resolve this apparent contradiction?

For Altman, and for the many film scholars he has influenced, these two schools of thought and practice are not opposites at all. Instead, they complement each other. Just as *horse* has both a semantic and a syntactic aspect, so genre criticism may point out both the relatively constant meaning of a given genre and its dynamic variability—similarities and differences, repetitions and variations.

One final note: what about those odd westerns that don't take place in the West? A 1939 film called *Allegheny Uprising*, starring John Wayne, contains a number of elements common to westerns—an outlaw/hero, Indians, a fort, a vision of life on the American frontier—but the film is set in colonial times in Pennsylvania's Allegheny Valley, well east of the Mississippi River (the conventional divide between East and West). Under Jean Mitry's semantic definition, *Allegheny Uprising* cannot be a western; it takes place in the East during the eighteenth century. But as Rick Altman points out, under the complementary semantic/syntactic model, films like *Allegheny Uprising* (and John Ford's *Drums Along the Mohawk*, 1939; Cecil B. DeMille's *Unconquered*, 1947; and others) are accounted for as westerns. These films, though located in the East, are nevertheless set on the American frontier, and they all provide variations of Kitses' dialectical clashes between desert and garden (though the conflict is actually between *forest* and garden), individual and community, and nature and culture, all in the overarching context of American history. These films thus form a subgenre with a paradoxical name: the *eastern western*.

FILM NOIR: A CASE STUDY

One of the most intriguing genres in film history is the **film noir**. *Film Studies* focuses on this genre for several reasons: film noir has readily identifiable themes, visual conventions, character conventions, and story conventions; it's a particularly homegrown American genre that says some surprising things about our culture; it raises some fascinating historical and theoretical questions; and classic film noirs often serve as key screenings in introductory film courses.

Film noir developed—and critics began to perceive it as a genre—at a specific point in history: the 1940s. After the end of World War II (1939–1945), American films—which had been banned under the Nazi occupation of France—cascaded back into French movie theaters. Thanks to the critical distance afforded to them by differences in language and culture, French critics noticed what Americans hadn't yet perceived, not consciously anyway: that during the previous few years, Hollywood had been producing a cycle of especially dark-tempered and morbid films. American audiences had been seeing and presumably enjoying these films for a year or two during the later years of the war, but it took some highly perceptive French critics *after* the war to see the repetition and variation of formal elements and narrative themes among a group of films, and on that basis they classified a new genre: *film noir*, or "black film."

These films have an unusual emotional goal: they induce a sense of tension and *malaise* in their audiences. They're feel-bad movies. The male protagonists are usually troubled, and women are often deadly, vicious, alluring temptresses. The films often take place at night, in bad parts of town, with shadowy, low-key lighting and a lot of tough talk. It's an ugly world—a paranoid world. Urban and dirty. Full of greed, lust, and corruption. In short, film noir explores the dark side of American culture.

World War II certainly played a role in the genesis of film noir's gritty, grim moodiness, but it wasn't just the war's tensions and devastation that provoked and sustained the genre; film noir continued for many years after the war ended. In 1952, for instance, just when everybody was supposed to be happily building houses in the happy suburbs, the director Fritz Lang made a film noir called *The Big Heat* in which Lee Marvin's character throws a pot of scalding coffee right in Gloria Grahame's character's face in the middle of the film. (Fortunately, she hurls another pot of equally hot coffee in Marvin's face later in the film, so she gets even.) A poster for *The Big Heat* featured the tag line, "Somebody's going to pay—because they forgot to kill me!" That's the perverse basis on which this particular film noir was sold to the public as mass entertainment in 1952: the protagonist (Glenn Ford) seeks vengeance for someone's failure to kill him.

FIGURE 10.1 A still from the classic film noir *Murder, My Sweet* (1944)—Mike Mazurki (*left*), Dick Powell (*right*).
(Photofest)

FILM NOIR: A BRIEF HISTORY

Billy Wilder's *Double Indemnity* (1944) and Otto Preminger's *Laura* (1944) are widely considered to be not only two of the first film noirs but also two of the greatest and most definitive. (In the former, an insurance salesman plans the murder of one of his own clients with the aid of the client's killer-dame wife; in the latter, a detective investigating a murder finds himself falling disturbingly in love with the victim.) But film scholars have noted that John Huston's *The Maltese Falcon* and Orson Welles's *Citizen Kane*, both released three years earlier, in 1941, also contain elements of film noir, though scholars rarely classify them simply (or, better, solely) as film noirs.

Other notable film noirs from the mid-to-late 1940s are Howard Hawks's *The Big Sleep* and Fritz Lang's *Scarlet Street* (both 1945), Jacques Tourneur's *Out of the Past* (1947), and Jules Dassin's *The Naked City* (1948). In 1950 alone, the following noirs were released: *D.O.A.*, *Dark City*, *In a Lonely Place*, *No Way Out*, *Panic in the Streets*, *Where Danger Lives*, and *Where the Sidewalk Ends*. Their titles alone convey a sense of the genre's bleak emotional tenor. The fifties went on to feature many more downers: Lang's *Clash by Night* (1952), Samuel Fuller's *Pickup on South Street* (1953), Robert Aldrich's *Kiss Me Deadly* (1955), Alfred Hitchcock's *The Wrong Man* (1956), and Orson Welles's *Touch of Evil* (1958), to name only a few.

There is widespread disagreement about what happened to (or with) film noir as a genre from about 1960 to the present day. Some people think that film noir adapted over the years and still continues as an active genre today; they call these later films **neo-noirs** to distinguish them from those of the classic period. Still others see the genre as ending in the late 1950s and early 1960s and refuse to classify as film noir any film made thereafter. A few of the best-known films that fall into this disputed territory are Robert Altman's *The Long Goodbye* (1973), Roman Polanski's *Chinatown* (1974), Quentin Tarantino's *Reservoir Dogs* (1992), and Curtis Hanson's *L.A. Confidential* (1997). And what of Joel and Ethan Coen's *No Country for Old Men* (2007)? Could it be a *neo-noir western*?

FILM NOIR'S CONVENTIONS

Film noir's conventions are both thematic and formal. That is, there are great similarities among the stories and plots of these films, their central and secondary characters' occupations and personalities, what the films are about on a philosophical level, and the ways the films look and sound. These likenesses, after all, are what makes film noir a genre.

Many (though not all) film noirs feature a murder or multiple murders; on this basis alone, one can safely say that questions about violence, mortality, and death lie at the heart of the genre. Because a killing so often motivates the narratives of these films, many film noir protagonists are detectives who are hired to solve the case and nab the killer. There is thus an epistemological quest at the heart of the genre—a search for knowledge. (*Epistemology* is a branch of philosophy concerned with questions of *knowing*—as opposed to *ontology*, which is about *being*.)

One odd way the genre formalizes this epistemological quest is to feature especially convoluted stories with plotting that does not serve to clarify events but instead overcomplicates them. The detective/protagonist often serves as the audience's onscreen surrogate, trying to make sense not only of an apparently senseless murder but, by extension, a whole moral universe of confusion and meaninglessness. There is a *nihilistic* quality to these films—a sense of cold, cosmic hostility, a feeling that life is empty and nothing matters. The most illustrative example of noir's theme of uncertainty and disorder is Hawks's *The Big Sleep*, a film so convoluted and bewildering in its story and structure that halfway through the production Hawks reportedly sent a telegram to Raymond Chandler, the author of the novel on which the film is based, asking him to clarify something: who killed one of the characters? Chandler wired back that he had no idea.

Low-key lighting that creates ominous shadows, the striped effect of bright light shining into a dim room through Venetian blinds, and striking black-and-white cinematography—sometimes gritty, sometimes polished—are three of the most significant formal conventions of film noir. In fact, the presence or absence of black and white instead of color can be used to define what is and what is not a film noir. Since all the original film noirs were made in black and white, later directors' use of color—Altman in *The Long Goodbye*, Polanski in *Chinatown*, Tarantino in *Reservoir Dogs*—may be seen as constituting so significant a variation from one of the genre's essential conventions that no color film can be, strictly speaking, a film noir. This is, of course, debatable, as all good points must be.

STUDY GUIDE: GENRE ANALYSIS FOR THE INTRODUCTORY STUDENT

Studying genre presents a particular challenge for the beginning film student. While one can learn to describe mise-en-scene elements in detail by watching a five-minute clip from any film, for instance, studying a genre demands that one be familiar with at least several films within a particular genre, if not more. In fact, to fully appreciate what genre means from both historical and formal perspectives—to see the macro-picture of how films are classified by way of similarities—one needs to be familiar with a very large number of films. Apparently simple questions turn out to be surprisingly dependent on advanced knowledge:

- How does one genre differ from another?
- What role does history play in generating, sustaining, changing, and even eliminating genres and subgenres?

First-time film studies students must learn to ask these questions, but they can rarely answer them accurately on their own. Just as you cannot legitimately make claims about a director's worldview based on only one example of his or her work, so you must rein in any generalizations you might try to make about genres. Unless you bring extensive prior viewing experience to the table, you need a study guide that teaches you to learn independently about a subject that, by its nature, requires familiarity with large numbers of films.

So, start small. Deal with genre on a micro level.

Note the title of a movie you have seen recently (outside of class, that is), and attempt to classify it as a genre and/or subgenre. Don't simply name a genre right away, even if you think you know the answer. (And it's cheating to simply look it up online and accept someone else's genre classification.) Instead, take a more methodical approach by creating a taxonomic outline. Collect and enumerate facts, and use reason to deduce an answer. In simpler terms, identify the film's most noteworthy traits, and see if the results suggest that the film belongs to a particular genre and/or subgenre or whether the film is a mix of genres.

Here's an example:

THE DARK KNIGHT (Christopher Nolan, 2008)

1. **MISE-EN-SCENE ELEMENTS**
   A. Color—does any color or tone predominate?
   B. Lighting—high key, low key, or a mix of both?
   C. Urban location
   D. Similarities with other art forms
      i. Art form A
      ii. Art form B

E. Costumes
   i. Bruce Wayne's costumes
   ii. Batman's costume
   iii. Other characters' costumes
F. Makeup
   i. Bruce Wayne's makeup
   ii. The Joker's makeup
   iii. Other characters' makeup

2. CHARACTER TYPES
   A. Bruce Wayne (Christian Bale)
   B. Batman (Christian Bale)
   C. The Joker (Heath Ledger)
   D. Rachel Dawes (Maggie Gyllenhaal)
   E. Harvey Dent/Two Face (Aaron Eckhart)
   F. Other characters

3. STORY AND PLOT ELEMENTS
   A. Central story events
   B. Daytime scenes vs. nighttime scenes
   C. Presence or absence of explicit violence (For instance, could *The Dark Knight* be a splatter film?)
   D. Plot structure
      i. Presence or absence of flashbacks
      ii. Plot twists / revelations

4. THEMES
   A. Dualities and secret identities
   B. Double crosses

Conclusion: *The Dark Knight* is a _____.

WRITING ABOUT GENRE

The key challenges when writing about genre are to confine your discussion to what you can prove you know and to avoid making claims you cannot support. You *can* write about *The Dark Knight*'s visual and aural style, its roots in another art form, and the moral questions the film raises. You can also analyze the Joker's makeup and costuming as particular expressions of the film's thematic concerns. You can write about any formal aspect of *The Dark Knight* that interests you—as long as you have seen *The Dark Knight*, that is.

What you should not attempt to do is tackle the too-broad topic of the superhero film by using *The Dark Knight* as an example. Why not? Well, for one thing, you will have to have seen a number of superhero films in order to make any legitimate claims about the genre. *Fair enough*, you may counter; *I have seen* Superman *(1978)*, Batman *(1989)*, Darkman *(1990)*, Spider-Man *(2002)*, Ultraman *(2004)*, Mercury Man *(2006)*, and The Adventures of Sharkboy and Lavagirl 3-D *(2005), so why can't I write about them?*

The answer is, *you can try*. And you may succeed—but only if you deal with these films in specific, concrete detail. Do you remember them so well that you can describe and analyze their mise-en-scenes effectively? If so, great! To do it well, you would end up with at least a 10- to 12-page paper, if not a much longer one. A better idea is to tailor your genre paper's topic. It's always better to write a shorter, tighter paper that proves you know what you're talking about than a longer, flabbier paper full of generalizations and vague descriptions.

When writing a paper about genre—unless your professor gives you a specific assignment that differs, of course—use these three guidelines to form your topic and shape the paper:

1. **Construct a provable thesis**. The thesis of your paper is its argument—what you are setting out to prove. For example, you will not be able to prove anything about all superhero movies in an average-length college paper. You don't have enough space, let alone knowledge. You *can* prove, however, that *The Dark Knight*, a single superhero movie, is about moral relativism, or that its protagonist has something in common with its villain, or that particular aspects of its mise-en-scene visually express the gloom suggested by its title. Your best bet is to particularize your thesis as much as possible to an individual film, and leave broader arguments about entire genres to upper-level film classes.

2. **Stay focused on the film in question**. Having constructed a provable thesis that confines itself to a particular aspect of a single movie, stick to it. If you find yourself beginning a sentence with the phrase "Most superhero movies" or anything like it, delete it immediately and start again. You are not writing about most superhero movies. You are writing about *The Dark Knight*.

3. **If you can't help yourself and are compelled to mention something about an entire genre or subgenre, cite an expert**. Let's face it: professors are looking for things to object to in your papers. (That's what we do. It's in our contract.) It is much more difficult for professors to object to any broad claim you make about a genre (or any subject) if you can find a film scholar to say it for you. For example:

- *Unacceptable*: "Most superhero movies feature protagonists who have a single superpower and a one-dimensional personality to match."—Timothy Burton, freshman, Middlebury College
- *Acceptable*: "According to the critic and film scholar Vicki Vale in the journal *Annals of Cinematicity*, 'Most superhero movies feature protagonists who have a single superpower and a one-dimensional personality to match' (Vale, p. 373).—Jim Gordon, sophomore, Haverford College

CHAPTER 11
SPECIAL EFFECTS

BEYOND THE ORDINARY

A train pulls into a station in Louis Lumière's 50-second 1895 film, *The Arrival of a Train at La Ciotat*. A train wrecks when the high bridge it is crossing collapses in Buster Keaton's 1927 comedy, *The General*. A circus train jumps the tracks and wrecks in Cecil B. DeMille's 1952 drama, *The Greatest Show on Earth*. The first two films used real locomotives, while the third used a small model. But even the real train in *The General* had to be wrecked by way of SPECIAL EFFECTS.

The term *special effects* is broadly defined as *any image or element within the image that has been produced by extraordinary technical means*. By *extraordinary*, we mean exactly that—*in excess of the ordinary technology necessary for the production of motion pictures*. When Louis Lumière set out to film the train arriving at a station in southern France, he needed only the basic technological elements of filmmaking: a camera, some film,

FIGURE 11.1 A real train wrecks in Buster Keaton's *The General* (1927) (frame enlargement).

FIGURE 11.2 A toy train wrecks in Cecil B. DeMille's *The Greatest Show on Earth* (1952) (frame enlargement).

FIGURE 11.3 *L'arroseur arrosé* (*The Sprinkler Sprinkled*, 1895) by Louis Lumière (frame enlargement). (Photofest)

FIGURE 11.4 *Un homme de têtes* (*The Four Troublesome Heads*, 1898) by Georges Méliès (frame enlargement).

enough light, and an event to photograph. Buster Keaton required the same elements to film *The General*, but because he insisted for the sake of veracity on destroying a real bridge and sending a real train crashing onto a valley floor, there was considerably more technology involved. The bridge, after all, was not going to collapse on its own. Technicians had to go beyond the normal filmmaking apparatus; they had to use explosives. By the same token, unless Cecil B. DeMille's purpose was to make his scene look like the wreck of a toy train full of miniature circus animals, unusual technical effects had to be employed. For DeMille's train wreck to look even slightly plausible, a team of specialized technicians was employed to create the effect—hence the term *special effects*. (It must be noted that *The Greatest Show on Earth*'s special effects appear rather primitive by today's standards, to the point that the sequence does indeed look like the wreck of a toy train.)

There are three broad categories of visual special effects: **optical effects, mechanical effects,** and COMPUTER-GENERATED IMAGERY (**CGI**). Each is described in depth below. But before plunging into the details, consider for a moment—in the hopefully bright light of what you have learned in this book—the issues raised in the introductory chapter: questions of reality and representation. If motion pictures are—at least to some extent—an attempt to represent the real world artistically, what does it mean when filmmakers deliberately construct something artificial to film? Or purposely tamper with the photographic process specifically in order to create something that looks unreal? Once again, we find that what we like to call "reality" or "realism" is neither a useful nor a reliable measure of cinematic goals and results.

The tension between the real and the unreal has existed in cinema since its earliest days. While Louis Lumière and his brother Auguste were developing a documentary cinema by filming a real train arriving at a real train station, another filmmaker, Georges Méliès, was heading in quite the opposite direction. Whereas the Lumières saw films as a way to represent the real world in art, Méliès saw the potential for film art to represent things and events that did not *and could not* exist in reality. The titles of some of his most important films tell the story on their own: *A Trip to the Moon* (1902), *The Man with the Rubber Head* (1902), *The Mermaid* (1904), *The Impossible Voyage* (1904), *20,000 Leagues Under the Sea* (1907). Méliès was a pioneer in science fiction and fantasy films—two genres that depend on special effects for their very existence.

OPTICAL AND MECHANICAL SPECIAL EFFECTS

Two of the transitional devices you have already learned about are in fact optical special effects: DISSOLVES and SUPERIMPOSITIONS. They, along with other effects, are called **process shots** because they are created in the processing lab. A *superimposition* occurs when two or more images are visible onscreen at the same time; a *dissolve* is a transition from one shot to another in which the first shot fades out while the second shot fades in, creating a superimposition at the midway point. These special effects are created by filming two shots separately and combining them optically onto a single strip of film during processing.

More technically complex is a special effect called **rear projection**, which is achieved on a soundstage by filming actors against the background of a film screen, onto which is projected, from behind it, an already filmed shot. The benefit of rear projection is that the actors can be lit and miked in the carefully controlled conditions of the soundstage while placing them against a dramatic exterior background. Cary Grant's character in Hitchcock's *North by Northwest* (1959) can thus appear to be driving dangerously and erratically on a winding coastal highway without Grant actually having to put himself in danger. **Front projection** achieves the same effect but in a more visually lifelike way; the projected images are both clearer and brighter than with rear projection. Here, a semireflecting (or two-way) mirror bounces the projected background around the actors onto a screen that has been set up behind them.

Another way of combining two separately shot images into one is called MATTE WORK. To create a matte, one area of the image is filmed—either by shooting a real background directly or by painting one and shooting the painting—while the remaining area is left blank by blocking a corresponding area of the lens. The blank area is then filled by filming, with the opposite area being blocked, after which the two areas are combined in processing. Let's say a director is making a film set in a fantastically ornate castle. Instead of having to build the exteriors of a real castle or find an appropriate real one, she has a team of matte artists paint a variety of views of the castle. Her characters are thereby given a background in the lab when these shots are matted with shots of the actors—shots that are filmed separately. These static mattes are called **matte paintings**.

Mattes may also be moving images; these are called TRAVELING MATTES. A common way of achieving a traveling matte is the use of a so-called BLUESCREEN. In this process, which is also known as CHROMA KEY, a specific color is rendered invisible, unable to register on film (or video). When actors are placed before a screen that has been painted uniformly in that particular color, usually blue, their images are recorded against a blank background; later, that background is filled in with separately shot images.

Not all special effects are created by processing. Some are made by constructing models or otherwise replicating objects or events that would not exist or occur naturally. Must a director, actors, and the whole crew stand around and wait for it to rain before filming a storm scene? Hardly. A special effects team creates the effect by using a machine to simulate rain and another machine to simulate wind. These, and others like them, are called *mechanical effects*.

Other kinds of mechanical effects include *pyrotechnics*, the creation of fiery explosions; *model building*; and elaborate *makeup*. Steven Spielberg's *Jaws* (1975), for example, employed a famously mechanical shark that ends up chomping Robert Shaw's character. (There were actually three separate mechanical sharks used to make *Jaws*, and no actors were eaten during the production of the motion picture.) As for makeup, perhaps needless to say, the splatter film subgenre would not exist without special effects makeup. The plausible recreation of moist, freshly exposed human guts and decomposing zombie flesh is key to both the critical and commercial success of George Romero's *Dawn of the Dead* (1979), to cite only one well-known example.

COMPUTER-GENERATED IMAGERY (CGI)

CGI is defined as *any image that has been created by or manipulated by the use of a computer and software*. According to Terrence Masson in his compendium *CG 101*, **computer graphics (CG)** began as a visualization tool for researchers at such companies as Boeing and Bell Labs in the 1950s, though a decade earlier mathematicians at the Massachusetts Institute of Technology had developed models that created highly accurate depictions of lighting setups. (Lacking an output device, the MIT mathematicians had to cut out pieces of colored paper by hand to match their calculated patterns.)

The term *computer graphics* (CG) was coined in 1960 by a Boeing engineer, William Fetter, to describe his drawings of pilots experiencing various specific cockpit conditions. As computers developed in the 1950s and 1960s, so did CG and CGI. The first short film made on a digital computer was John Whitney Sr.'s 1968 *Permutations*; Whitney was an animator who had worked on the opening credits sequence for Hitchcock's *Vertigo* (1958), among other films. CG made its first appearance in a feature film in Michael Crichton's 1973 *Westworld* (subgenre: science fiction western); the sequence represented an android's point of view by using PIXILATION—the averaging together of blocks of individual pixels to create a kind of mosaic effect. (The word *pixel* means *picture element*.) A few years later, the algorithmic artist Larry Cuba created a spectacular CGI effect for George Lucas's *Star Wars* (1977): the simulated fly-through of the Death Star's trench, a narrow rectangular chasm in an enormous globelike space station.

There are too many CGI milestones to mention more than a few here, but some notable ones are *Star Trek II: The Wrath of Khan* (1982)—the first entirely digital CGI sequence in a feature film; *Howard the Duck* (1986)—the first digital WIRE REMOVAL in a feature film, wherein the rigging cables that support actors who are suspended in the air are digitally removed from the image, thus making it appear that the characters are flying; and *Willow* (1988)—the first use of digital MORPHING technology in a feature film. *Morphing* is the technique in which images of two or more distinct objects, animals, or characters are blended together to form a new, interpolated result.

ANIMATION, itself an important form of special effects, has come to rely on CGI for detailing that would be too expensive and time-

FIGURE 11.5 Gollum, a major character created by CGI, in *The Lord of the Rings: The Return of the King* (2003) (frame enlargement).

consuming to create by hand. Animation is *any process that simulates movement by filming a series of individual drawings, objects (such as clay figures or dolls), or computer images; tiny shifts in the positions and shapes of these drawings, things, or images create the sense of motion.* While much animation has been created entirely by hand from scratch, the process of ROTOSCOPING was developed as early as the 1910s to assist the animator; *rotoscoping* means *projecting live-action footage, frame by frame, onto an animator's drawing table so that he or she can trace the figures with great precision.* The director Richard Linklater has in fact made two films entirely using rotoscoping, *Waking Life* (2001) and *A Scanner Darkly* (2006).

STUDY GUIDE: EFFECTS AND MEANING

With all of these new technical terms, you might assume that the goal of studying special effects is to learn to identify them on sight—to determine when filmmakers used special effects in a given film, and to classify the effects taxonomically as optical or mechanical or CGI and then pinpoint the precise special effect used in each case. That assumption is off base.

If *Film Studies* has taught you anything, it is that the search for expressive meaning is the most important aspect of your work. Upper-level undergraduate film classes and graduate programs expand this fundamental principle considerably to include the detailed study of film history and theory as well as technology. But for the time being, the question of locating and describing a film's meaning remains your central focus.

In terms of special effects, this means concentrating on the *effects* of what you see and hear rather than on their special nature. Just as you learned to notice, describe, and analyze the expressive effect of a bare brick wall or a lone sheep bolting from its herd in long shot or low-key lighting in a film noir or any of the other topics covered in this book, your objective here is to describe and analyze special effects not with an eye toward categorizing the specialized technologies that created them but rather toward articulating their *effective meaning*. The rest of this chapter serves as a practical example of how to go about achieving this goal.

For key scenes in his suspense film *Vertigo* (1958), Alfred Hitchcock employed a real location that he and his team then embellished with special effects. The old Spanish mission at San Juan Bautista had low exteriors that met Hitchcock's vision of how certain scenes in the film should look, but *Vertigo*'s central story events required a tall bell tower, and this particular mission had no tower. (There was once a relatively small steeple, but it had been demolished.) Conceivably, Hitchcock could simply have found another location—an old Spanish mission that had a tower. But he didn't have to. He knew he could get exactly what he wanted by using a mix of exterior location shooting, interior set construction, and special effects to augment both the existing location and the constructed set.

Building the tower's narrow interior, including a steep staircase, required skilled design work and carpentry—the ordinary technology of filmmaking. Hitchcock went so far as to create an unusual and innovative mobile framing device to express the particular mental and emotional crisis the protagonist faces in the tower, but even this device is the result of one ordinary camera operation—a reverse tracking shot—combined simultaneously with another ordinary camera operation—a zoom forward. As striking as the effect may be—and it's very striking indeed—it isn't a *special* effect.

Film scholars know from doing research—examining production records, conducting interviews with people who worked on the film, or even simply reading those printed interviews—that the bell tower exterior is in fact a matte painting, or more accurately, a series of matte paintings. And while the simultaneous zoom forward/track back is not itself a special effect as far as the camera is concerned, research reveals that the shot was taken not from the top of the studio-constructed staircase, the set, but rather from

FIGURE 11.6 A bird's-eye shot—expressing a God's-eye view—in one of the bell tower sequences in Alfred Hitchcock's *Vertigo* (1958) (frame enlargement).

the side of a miniature staircase—a model—which was placed on its side in front of the camera. That model is therefore a special effect even though the means of taking the shot is not.

Unless you are asked to research a film's production—in this case, *Vertigo*'s—you cannot be expected to know and describe what is and is not a special effect. What you *can* do—in fact, what you *must* do—is analyze the film's *meaning*. In this case, you could begin with the film's title and learn what it means. You could then relate what you learned about the medical condition called *vertigo* to the film's story, plot, and central themes. You might describe in great detail the complex visual effect of the famous simultaneous zoom-tracking shots and relate it to what you have learned about the title, story, plot, and themes of the film. And as you will see in the following section, you could drive your points home by analyzing in detail a single shot. The example below describes a shot taken from near the top of the mission tower approximately one hour and twenty minutes into the film.

WRITING ABOUT SPECIAL EFFECTS

Although we know from having researched the production of *Vertigo* that (a) the tower section of the image is a matte painting and everything else is live action, and (b) these two separately filmed portions of the image were combined in a film-processing lab to create the composite shot, it's still the shot's expressive effect that really matters. With this in mind, you will find that writing about special effects is no different than writing about any other aspect of a film. Keep it simple:

- Describe the shot in detail
- Offer suggestions about the expressive effects of the shot
- Venture an educated guess or two about what the shot means

For example: figure 11.6 is a reproduction of one frame in a shot that runs for about twenty seconds. What cannot be reproduced here, but is vital to appreciate about the shot, is the motion that occurs in two areas of the image: there are people climbing onto the tile roof just to the left of the tower's base, and to the right of the tower a man is walking out of the archway and slinking around the corner of the building. (You can see him, and the shadow he casts, in the left branch of the cross-shaped sidewalk in the lower right corner of the image.) The following three paragraphs begin with a detailed description of the shot, move through suggestions about its expressive effects, and arrive at a statement not only of what the shot means but what the film may mean as a whole:

There is a remarkable crispness of focus to all the depth planes in this shot. The very top of the tower is cut out of the image by the top edge of the frame, but the bulk of the tower is visible in what is effectively the foreground and middleground, and it's all in sharp focus. Also in the middleground but extending to both edges of the image is the tile roof of the mission's sanctuary (on the left) and entryway (on the right), and the whole expanse of roof is in equally sharp focus. While the trees in the top left corner of the image are not quite as sharp as the tower and tile roof, they remain more or less in focus, but in any case Hitchcock draws the viewer's attention away from them to the opposite corner by way of movement—the man's emergence from the archway, his sneaking away next to the building, and his disappearance around the corner. He, too, remains in crisp, sharp focus. This is a deep-focus exterior shot.

The primary expressive effect of this shot is that the people in it look especially tiny. We see them in extreme long shot, and they're miniscule. The people climbing on top of the roof are certainly noticeable (although they are difficult to make out in the above reproduction), but the man's more distinct movement draws the eye toward him, and in fact it is he—the film's acrophobic protagonist—who is the central emotional subject of the shot. He has just experienced a crisis that has made him feel utterly ineffectual, a state of mind Hitchcock expresses by reducing him onscreen to the size of a flea.

The looming tower's size as well as its sharp focus enhances this effect by lending an unnatural quality to the image. It's as though Hitchcock's camera has the ability to see this man more clearly, and to assess him more coldly, than an ordinary human eye could. It's not a bird's-eye view as much as it is a God's-eye view—clear and distant, sharp and judgmental. The cross-like shape in the lower right corner of the shot only adds a touch of direct symbolism to the viewer's growing sense that Hitchcock is working with grand religious themes such as guilt, mortal sin, and damnation.

CHAPTER 12

PUTTING IT TOGETHER: A MODEL 8- TO 10-PAGE PAPER

HOW THIS CHAPTER WORKS

This chapter, the last one in the book, is a hands-on guide to writing an introductory-level film paper. Footnotes serve as a running commentary on the pros and cons of the paper's content, format, writing style, and so on. Every issue covered in these footnotes, even those that seem embarrassingly obvious, is based on an actual student paper received by, read by, and graded by the author of this textbook over the course of twenty-five years of teaching. They range from simple points of common sense and grammar to more substantive issues of content and style.

Introducing Tyler[2]
by Robert Paulson[3]
Colorado College

A film about male bonding through shared dissatisfaction and communal violence, David Fincher's *Fight Club* (1999) presents a disturbing vision of American society, a culture that is overdue for drastic change.[4] Based on the novel of the same name by Chuck Pahlaniuk, *Fight Club* suggests that the depressing conformity of modern corporate life—interchangeable hotel rooms, impersonal airports, dull business suits, heartless jobs—needs to be confronted, challenged, and ultimately destroyed. The catalyst of change in *Fight Club* is an underground network of men who work out their frustrations by clobbering each other. The instigator of these fights, Tyler Durden (Brad Pitt), inspires men around the country to become revolutionaries, apolitical terrorists who act out their contempt for traditional American values in increasingly violent ways.[5] **Fincher introduces this incendiary character with a subtle but profound tracking movement that reveals much more than it appears to at first; beginning as a shot of *Fight Club*'s unnamed narrator (Edward Norton), alone in profile, it proceeds to make Tyler seem to emerge out of the narrator—a crucial key to Tyler's real identity.**[6]

Foreshadowing the violence that follows, Fincher sets up his introduction of Tyler with a scene of chaos: consumed with anomie, the narrator morbidly livens things up by imagining himself in a crashing airplane.[7] "Every time the plane banked too sharply on take-off or landing, I prayed for a crash," he says in voice-over in a flat, affectless tone, as he holds a tiny cherry tomato impaled on a fork in front of him. He looks to his left, and Fincher cuts to a shot of the airplane window as lights from another small aircraft hurtle toward the plane. Fincher then cuts to a shot taken from the back of the plane for the moment of impact; the even rows of bland blue seats are suddenly shaken by an explosive blast on the left side of the image. Windows

1. Every page of your paper should be numbered, if for no other reason than the fact that it proves you have completed the assignment. If your professor has assigned a five-page paper, prove it by ending on page 5.

2. Every paper must have a title, and the title must be that of the paper itself, not the film you are writing about. If this student simply ripped off the title of the movie and called his paper "*Fight Club*," his professor would have no clue what the paper intended to discuss. Here, the title pertains to the sequence the student is writing about. It specifies the paper's topic without being overly pedantic, though more detailed titles—for instance, "Introducing Tyler: A Character Splits in Two in *Fight Club*"—are certainly acceptable. Unless your professor instructs you otherwise, you do not need to create a separate title page. If you do create a separate title page, that page must not be numbered; numbered pages begin on the first page of text.

3. This may seem ridiculous, but it bears stating directly: every paper must have the author's name on it. (Do you want your professor to be forced to identify your paper by process of elimination and grade your work with that pointless irritation in mind? I didn't think so.) Unless your professor gives you specific instructions about the format, you may give yourself a by-line, as this student has done, or simply put your name at the top of the first page. And by the way—do yourself and your professor a favor: staple the pages of your paper together. Staples prevent pages from coming loose and getting lost. Paperclips are far riskier for everyone concerned, and under no circumstances should you ever just fold the tips of the corners down. That's just stupid.

4. (A) Unless you are instructed otherwise, your paper should be double-spaced with 1-inch or 1.5-inch margins on the sides and 1-inch margins on the top and bottom of each page. Professors react badly to dumb tricks like widening the margins to an absurd degree and triple-spacing the text to make a paper seem longer than it really is.

(B) Film titles should be italicized or underlined; do not place them within quotation marks. The film's date (the date of its release) should appear in parentheses after the title the first time you refer to it.

5. It's better to refer to a character by the character's name rather than the name of the actor; if you want to identify the actor, place his or her name in parentheses after the character's name.

6. (A) This sentence, reproduced here in bold type for emphasis, is the paper's thesis statement. Every paper must have one. (You should not set your own thesis statement in bold type unless your professor tells you to do so.) An effective thesis statement defines the argument that the paper sets out to pursue, and it does so in as detailed a way as possible, given the limitations of an individual sentence. Here, the writer is arguing that a particular camera movement, a lateral track, reveals an important clue to a character's identity. The rest of the paper pursues this idea in concrete detail. A less effective thesis statement would attempt to say the same thing, only more vaguely. For example: "Fincher introduces Tyler Durden in an interesting way." True, yes; substantive, no. Even if the rest of the paper went on to cite the same details this paper does, its weak thesis statement would spell the difference between a very high grade and a lower one.

burst inward on both sides of the plane and newspapers fly in all directions as the once calm cabin turns instantly into every air traveler's nightmare—every traveler, that is, except our narrator, who has created this terrifying scene not as a nightmare but as a wish.

The camera pans slightly to the right before Fincher cuts to a close-up of the narrator, his eyes shutting reflexively as pieces of white debris fly past his face.[8] The camera tracks a bit to the left as sounds of screams mixed with rushing air are heard on the soundtrack.[9] Fincher cuts again, this time to a shot of the central part of the cabin. The camera pans to the right past mostly empty seats as a lone oxygen bag falls from the ceiling.[10] As the camera continues to pan, the entire side of the plane falls off, revealing the lights of a cityscape below. A passenger seated on that side of the plane disappears, apparently having fallen out of the gaping hole in the plane.[11] Another traveler, in medium shot on the right of the image, struggles in his seat against the rush of air.[12]

Fincher cuts to another close-up of the narrator, this time taken from behind his seat. He has turned around in his seat and is looking behind him with his eyes half-shut against the rushing air and his mouth open in an expression of shock. Debris continues to fly past him from right to left across the screen.

"Life insurance pays off triple if you die on a business trip," the narrator dryly notes in voice-over. It's an ironic observation coming from him, given that he has no friends or family to act as the beneficiaries of any insurance policies he might be holding. Aside from the connections he makes at his various support group meetings—connections that are fundamentally false, based as they are on his nonexistent medical conditions—this man is entirely alone in the world.

The *ping* of the seat belt sign accompanies the next shot—of the sign itself—and the sound brings the narrator back to reality, a state of mind Fincher wryly expresses with a front-and-center close-up of the narrator jerking his exhausted-looking head forward in his seat. The plane is once again calm; the crash was all in the

(B) Counterintuitively, this paragraph was the last one the writer wrote. He waited until he composed not only the body of his paper but also his conclusion before he wrote the introduction. Why? As it happens, he is the kind of writer who doesn't know exactly what he's trying to say until he has actually said it. Having written the body of the paper first, he is in a much better, more knowledgeable position to compose an introduction, especially a thesis statement. He wasn't sure where the paper would lead him until he had written a first draft, at which point he could clearly define his thesis. This strategy may not work for everyone, but if you are having trouble getting started, try it and see if it works for you.

(C) Note that the writer confines his subject to *Fight Club*, the film at hand. Often, beginning writers feel a wrongheaded need to begin papers with grand statements about the way the world works, as though such claims give the paper weight it would not otherwise have. In fact, it creates the opposite effect. An example of this tendency is as follows: "American men are dissatisfied with the corporate culture in which they are stuck." This claim may or may not be true, but it is irrelevant to the subject of the paper. That subject is David Fincher's *Fight Club*, not American men in general. Remember: you are only setting out to prove that you know something specific about a given film—not that you have confronted and answered the big questions of life.

7. *Anomie* means a feeling of depressed, bored, and even suicidal alienation from society caused by the absence of beneficially supporting social structures.

8. For the sake of clarity, the writer has chosen to describe the sequence shot by shot in the order in which it plays out in the film itself. This is probably the safest strategy for the beginner to adopt, since the sequence's own order provides a ready-made structure that (presumably) already makes sense. Still, keep in mind that other structures are possible. For example, a paper may jump around from shot to shot within a sequence, as long as this structure (a) makes sense to the writer, and (b) the writer successfully conveys that sense to the reader.

9. Whatever structure you choose for your paper, try to vary your descriptions of editing and camera movements from sentence to sentence. Here, the writer has chosen a variety of sentence structures to break up what would otherwise be a series of sentences beginning with "Then Fincher cuts to a shot of . . ." There's nothing *wrong* with that. It's just boring.

10. Is it a tracking shot or a pan? The writer wasn't certain. But he decided to take the risk of being wrong rather than hedging his bets and being noncommittal.

11. This detail—the disappearance of the passenger from the image—only became evident to the writer after multiple viewings of the sequence, the final one in slow motion. Remember that your experience as a film scholar is in certain ways more like that of an editor than an audience member. Don't hesitate to run the sequence in slow motion or even frame by frame in order to collect data about its contents. Use the tools that DVD technology gives you.

12. A handy rule of thumb for any writer is this: if you find yourself using the same word in two back-to-back sentences, use a thesaurus to find a synonym. Here, the writer noticed in his first draft that the word *passenger* appeared twice in a row, so he used his word-processing application's built-in thesaurus to find the word *traveler*.

narrator's perverse mind, expressing a deep-seated desire for excitement—*any* excitement, even it results in his own violent death. But to paraphrase the narrator's much-repeated expression, this is "Jack's reality," and for the narrator, Jack's reality is worse than death.

Take a close look at him. He is a handsome if bland-looking man who appears to be about thirty years old. He has dark hair with a conservative, businessman-type haircut. We can see the shoulders of his gray, conservative suit jacket and the white collar of his dress shirt. He is centered on the screen; the very top part of his head is cut out by the frame. He is in crisp focus, but the background is out of focus. Still, we can clearly see some blue curtains in the center-left of the image, with some bright curved airplane windows on the far right in the background. The curtains match the blue of the seat; the windows, appearing white, match the headrest. It's all terribly tasteful—and dull.[13] And, to the narrator, meaningless.[14]

The aspect ratio is that of a fairly wide rectangle, which creates the effect in this shot of isolating the narrator against an empty-seeming background. There is another man in the image—he is seated in the row behind the man in close-up—but he is the only other person in the image, and he is indistinct. The narrator, in contrast, has a bright light shining on his forehead and nose, but his eyes are notably in shadow, although we can clearly see dark circles under his eyes, indicating tiredness and a sense of profound boredom. Everything about this man is conventional, from his face and suit and haircut to his surroundings on this utterly ordinary airplane. But this man's life is about to change radically. And although he does not yet know it, he is the actual author of that change, a fact expressed by one of Fincher's most subtle but meaningful camera movements.[15]

The narrator blinks twice, rapidly, as though to wake himself up, but Fincher accomplishes that task more profoundly by cutting to a shot taken from the narrator's side. Seen now in profile, the narrator blinks again and remains staring blankly forward as Fincher tracks his camera to the right. Whereas the beginning of the shot suggested that

13.   With this paragraph and the one that follows, the writer uses the notes he took and the writing exercise he performed for the first chapter of this book. It may seem at first glance to be a simple description of the contents of the image, but it is actually the foundation of his argument about Tyler's introduction. The contrasts Fincher creates between the narrator and Tyler would not have been quite as noticeable to the writer, and therefore to the reader, if he hadn't described the narrator's mise-en-scene in specific detail.

14.   This is a sentence fragment. Technically, it's faulty syntax. But the writer has employed it as a stylistic device with which to end the paragraph. It's okay to break the rules once in a while. Just make sure that you're breaking them on purpose, and not because you don't know how to construct a proper sentence. If your professor calls you on it, just say you did it for stylistic reasons.

15.   This is called *foreshadowing*. The writer is alluding here to an idea he will introduce and develop in the next paragraph and beyond. Foreshadowing is an effective device to employ because it piques readers' interest without giving away too much too soon.

the narrator was either alone in a new scene or else still sitting next to the African American woman he'd been speaking with before imagining the plane crash, the tracking camera reveals that he is in fact seated next to a new character—a man both surprisingly different and oddly familiar.

This new guy is noticeably unlike the narrator. He is strikingly handsome, with chiseled features and a flashy, spiky haircut. He is wearing sunglasses—on an airplane at night. The window beside him has its shade up, but no light is coming in, which suggests that the sunglasses are purely a matter of style rather than practicality. Most notable of all, though, is the new character's red jacket with its wide lapels with two thin white stripes running vertically down their edges. The narrator's shirt collar remains tucked neatly inside his dull gray jacket; this hipster's wide white shirt collar, on the other hand, lands flamboyantly over the collar of his jacket.

It's the jacket's color that stands out most against the blues, whites, and grays of the airplane interior. Aside from the narrator's single-serving cherry tomato at the beginning of the imaginary crash sequence, and the flashing red light on the wing of the plane just before impact, this is the first appearance of the color red in *Fight Club* in a rather long time.

Red is a strongly suggestive and evocative color, especially in the context of its standing out against a field of blues and whites. As the expression "seeing red" serves to prove, the color expresses great anger, even out-of-control rage. Indeed, the rest of *Fight Club* will explore the narrator's desperate desire to be violent—not simply to imagine violence being committed against him, as with the imaginary plane crash in which he is a passive victim, but to engage in violence as an active instigator. He blows up his own apartment, engages in underground no-holds-barred fights with an army of equally violent coconspirators, and ultimately blows half his face off with a gun.[16] In short, there's a lot of anger there, and his seatmate's flaming red jacket is the first indication of it.[17]

16.   Although this paper is about Tyler's introductory scene in *Fight Club*, the writer finds support for his point by referring to other scenes in the film. These other scenes do not require the level of descriptive and analytical detail of the scene under discussion, and in fact such minute details would distract from the argument at hand. But referring to other scenes lends weight to the writer's observations by demonstrating his command of the whole film.

17.   Is this character's red jacket really "the *first* indication" of the narrator's rage in *Fight Club*? Maybe, maybe not. It doesn't matter. For the purposes of this paper, what's important here is that the writer *asserts* that it is so. He's trying to convince his professor that his larger argument about the meaning of the sequence is valid, and he makes this claim with breezy confidence and keeps pressing forward. The worst thing that can happen is that his professor may challenge him. He can live with that, as can his professor.

Although this scene serves as Tyler's introduction, we have actually seen him several times before. Fincher has inserted a few frames of him, in miniature medium shot, superimposed on Marla Singer's body as she walks away from a support group meeting after enraging the narrator by her very presence. The narrator detests Marla Singer (Helena Bonham Carter) because, as he puts it, her lie threatens to expose *his* lie—namely, that he has none of the illnesses for which he attends support groups. Neither does Marla, and he hates her for it. His rage at Marla incarnates itself, if only for a few frames, as an alter ego—one whose stylistic flare matches that of the flashy Marla.

Fincher provides a more lingering look at Tyler several scenes later. As the narrator is traveling up an escalator at yet another airport, Fincher suddenly pans to the left—the shot is taken from a few steps lower on the escalator—to center on another traveler heading down the escalator next to him. The narrator doesn't notice this other traveler, but the camera does—and we do, too. He's wearing over-sized sunglasses and a white sports jacket over a yellow shirt. In this instance, Tyler appears not in the context of rage but of boredom. Like the narrator, he, too, looks as though he has seen a few too many interchangeable air-port interiors; his expression is blank as he heads down the escalator. But unlike the narrator, he is not wearing a bland corporate uniform. At least he counters his boredom with fashion.

When Fincher finally introduces him to the narrator on the plane, Tyler is reading aloud from the airline's passen-ger safety card in the seat in front of him. "An exit door pro-cedure at 30,000 feet. Mm-hmm," he says sarcastically.[18] As he continues to explain the pointlessness of evacua-tion plans with a knowledgeable air, Fincher records the conversation in a series of shot/reverse shots of the two men, thereby both contrasting and linking them. One is not seen without the other as they begin their relationship. Ultimately, Fincher reveals that Tyler Durden is a figment of the narrator's imagination, but for the moment his use of a

18.   To keep things moving, and also to keep them simple, the writer has chosen in this paragraph to quote only one or two lines of dialogue to convey the subject and tone of the conversation. Unless you are closely analyzing each line of dialogue, there is no need to provide extensive quotations from the film. It's better to summarize what the characters are saying by paraphrasing.

shot/reverse-shot pattern seems to suggest the beginning of a friendship between two strangers.[19]

"Blank faces," says the man in the sunglasses as Fincher cuts to a rendering of cartoon passengers bracing for a collision—"calm as Hindu cows." Tyler is pointing out that the oxygen masks that are supposed to fall from the plane's overhead units in case of an emergency are actually designed to narcotize passengers before they die violent deaths. The narrator smiles; he's pleased and amazed by his new friend's logic.

"What do you do?" the narrator asks.

"What do you mean?" the man in sunglasses replies.

The narrator, of course, means to ask what profession the man has, but the question has a deeper, more philosophical meaning—one the narrator appears not to have considered before meeting the man in the flaming red jacket. By asking for clarification, Tyler is calling into question more than simply the narrator's need for chit-chat. He is striking at the very heart of the system under which men like the narrator—American men, businessmen, young and middle-aged men, *average* men—go through the motions of their empty lives. If the question "what do you do?" refers only to what job one has, then *doing* something in and with one's life is reduced simply to being a meaningless, mindless drone in the service of a world that doesn't care.

The narrator, surprised at his seatmate's cut-through-it frankness, laughs nervously, only to be told that his laughter has "a kind of sick desperation" to it. As the man in sunglasses begins to stand up, Fincher cuts on the action to a shot of his hand reaching for one of two identical briefcases on the floor of the plane. The narrator looks down in the next shot and, with a tone of wonder in his voice, observes that he and his seatmate "have the exact same briefcase," a further clue to the man's real identity. What seems at this point like mere coincidence is in fact key to the narrator's own split personality. "And this is how I met . . . " the narrator says in voice-over, "Tyler Durden," he reads from Tyler's business card.

19. Notice the writer's use of the words "seems to" in this sentence. Why has he used them? In this case, the writer is making the point that what appears to be a new friendship between two strangers is in fact something else: the creation of a split personality. Student writers often insert the expressions "seems to" and "appears to" as a way of hedging their bets on the points they are making. There is no reason to do this. Simply make the assertion you want to make, and save "seems to" and "appears to" for situations in which you are discussing the difference between appearance and reality.

Tyler's response is hilarious: "Did you know if you mix equal parts of gasoline and frozen orange juice concentrate you can make napalm?" The creation of incendiary substances is, for Tyler, as matter of fact as a conversation with one's seatmate on an ordinary airplane ride.

Tyler soon insults the narrator, who has told him that he is "by far the most interesting single-serving friend" he has ever met. It's a good line, and the narrator knows it, but he tips his hand by going on to explain it to Tyler, as though its meaning was not already clear. "Oh, I get it," Tyler responds. "Very clever. How's that working out for you?" Tyler then gets up from his seat. "Now a question of etiquette as I pass: do I give you the ass or the crotch?" Fincher pans to the right as Tyler moves in front of the narrator—giving him the ass—and cutting the narrator out of the image. Tyler walks away from the camera and the narrator, presumably heading to the restroom.

Tyler's attitude is worth describing in more detail, especially in light of the fact that the narrator's next line reveals that the two men come to live with each other. If Tyler represents the narrator's unfulfilled desires, what is it that remains unfulfilled in the narrator? As a corporate cog, the narrator has mastered the art of airplane small talk, but as Tyler points out, such cleverness has been of little real use. It's a way of passing the time, nothing more. Tyler, on the other hand, doesn't hesitate to be rude. He delivers the line "How's that working out for you?" with a smirk, suggesting that he knows the score better than the narrator—that he doesn't buy into the need for meaningless pleasantries exchanged between strangers, but instead cuts through them to something more genuine underneath.[20]

He proves it with the "ass or the crotch" line. Every airplane traveler has experienced the awkwardness of this decision—which part of one's intimate anatomy to confront a stranger with when squeezing out of a seat—but it's a social interaction that always goes unremarked. Except by Tyler Durden, who not only flouts social conventions but trumpets their destruction. Tyler is right: whether to present one's back or one's front to a complete stranger

20.   This paragraph and the one that follows do not set out to provide revolutionary ideas, but simply to explore the meaning of a few lines of dialogue. Remember: you are not expected to write the last word on the subject. If inspiration strikes you and you come up with a truly brilliant observation, so much the better. Your real task, though, is to explore the sequence and its meanings to the best of *your* ability, and to get the job done by the deadline. Everything else is icing on the cake.

is an etiquette decision, but conventional etiquette demands that the decision remain completely unspoken. Tyler speaks it. From the destruction of superficial politeness to the creation of napalm with household chemicals, Tyler is an incendiary personality.

Ultimately, Fincher reveals that Tyler Durden and the unnamed narrator are the same man—that the narrator has created Tyler as an alter ego who acts out all of his unfulfilled desires. From the simple if brutal fights between them to the destruction of skyscrapers, the narrator's anger finds satisfaction in acts of increasing violence. Only by blowing half his own face off with a gun near the end of the film can the narrator reclaim his integrity as an individual, an act that suggests futility by way of its own impossibility. After all, no one could survive such a gaping wound.

The revelation that Tyler is actually an aspect of the narrator himself may come as a surprise. But in looking back on Tyler's introductory scene, it's clear that the secret has been suggested all along, if not explicitly revealed. With the first shot of Tyler in that scene, David Fincher has provided a subtle indication that Tyler is an outgrowth of the narrator and his barely suppressed rage. By tracking the camera to the side when introducing this seemingly new character, Fincher effectively makes Tyler appear to emerge from the narrator's own body. When the camera tracks to the right, the narrator visually splits in two. To use psychological language, out of a troubled ego, an ego ideal emerges.[21]

21. (A) The concluding paragraph of a paper should do more than just summarize what the writer has already written. If the paper has succeeded to any extent, a routine summary is worse than no conclusion at all. Why? Because the reader already knows what he or she has read and does not need to have it repeated in even shorter and simpler terms. Instead, the conclusion should go beyond repetition by broadening the topic—by demonstrating that the writer not only has command of the sequence but of the film as a whole. The writer may also go one step further, as this student has done. (See the following section.)

(B) The word ego means the self as a distinct individual, and the term ego ideal refers to the part of the ego that maintains an overly romanticized, impossibly perfect vision of one's self. The student who wrote this paper happens to be a junior psychology major, and he saw no reason not to put his knowledge of another field to use in his film paper. It's not only acceptable but even advisable to demonstrate the breadth of your general knowledge when writing a paper, as long as your point is germane and you don't get sidetracked by secondary topics. In this student's case, he assumed that his professor would be familiar with the terms ego and ego ideal. That can be both a fair assumption and a risky one. It's fair in this case because, throughout the semester, his professor often used psychological language in his lectures, and the student saw no need to define the terms for him. It would have been a bit riskier if psychology had played no role in class. When in doubt, just remember the cardinal rule of good writing: be clear. If you bring in material from other disciplines, you may provide a brief explanation if you think it's necessary, but don't go off on tangents.

GLOSSARY

180° SYSTEM: A convention of narrative filmmaking in which the director establishes an imaginary line running across the set; the director then keeps the camera on one side of this line for every shot taken so as to avoid making characters and objects appear to flip suddenly from one side of the screen to the other when the sequence is edited together and eventually projected on a screen.

ACADEMY RATIO *or* **ACADEMY APERTURE:** The standard aspect ratio established in 1932 by the Academy of Motion Picture Arts and Sciences; it's often said to be 1.33:1, but in fact it's 1.37:1—a rectangle that is about a third again as wide as it is tall.

AMBIENT SOUND: The appropriate sounds of daily life that accompany the image, whether the scene is set inside (a restaurant scene may include the clatter of dishes and flatware hitting tables, distant conversations, and so on) or outside (a scene set in a farmer's field may be accompanied by the sounds of chickens cackling or the rustle of leaves).

AMPLITUDE: The loudness or softness of sound; its *volume*.

ANAMORPHIC LENS: A lens in the camera that squeezes a widescreen image onto a normally shaped frame of film, and/or a lens in the projector that unsqueezes the image back out to widescreen width.

ANIMATION: any process that simulates movement by filming a series of individual drawings, objects (such as clay figures or dolls), or computer images; tiny shifts in the positions and shapes of these drawings, things, or images create the sense of motion.

ANIMATION CEL: a clear sheet of plastic on which artists draw individual elements of an image; when aligned with one another, cels form an impression of depth; the stacks of cels are then photographed onto motion picture film, and the slight variations of position from one stack of cels to another create the impression of movement.

ASPECT RATIO: The ratio of the film image's width to its height. See *Academy ratio*, *Cinema-Scope*, *Panavision*, *VistaVision*, and *widescreen*.

ASYNCHRONOUS SOUND: See *offscreen sound*.

AUTEURISM: A critical theory developed originally in France in the 1950s by critics affiliated with the French film journal *Cahiers du cinéma*, and later popularized in the United States by Andrew Sarris, that views the director as a film's chief creator, values a director's personal style over whatever literary merit a screenplay may have, and ranks directors according to the perceived morality of their worldviews.

AVANT-GARDE FILM: any experimental and noncommercial film; from the French, meaning *advanced guard*.

BIRD'S-EYE SHOT: A shot taken from an extremely high angle.

BLUESCREEN: a type of traveling matte in which a specific color is rendered invisible, unable to register on film or video; actors are then placed before a screen that has been painted uniformly in that particular color, usually blue, and their images are recorded against a blank background; later, that background is filled in with separately shot images; also known as *chroma key*.

BOOM: A long, broomstick-like arm onto which a microphone is attached before being held out over the heads of actors just out of camera range.

CAMEO: an appearance by a recognizable star in a very small or even tiny role.

CAMERA OPERATOR: the member of the cinematographer's crew who is chiefly responsible for running the camera and setting the camera in place with the aid of a viewfinder; other crew members involved include the *first assistant camera operator* (called a *focus puller* in Europe), who is in charge of keeping the image in focus during camera movements, and the *second assistant camera operator* (called a *clapper* in Europe), who marks the slate and operates the *clapboard*, the device with a hinged arm that snaps shut at the beginning of each take so that the editor can match the soundtrack with the image track (the frame in which the arm hits the slate on the image track matches the *clap* sound on the soundtrack).

CELLULOID: The transparent plastic material, technically *cellulose nitrate*, that was originally used in motion picture photography; because cellulose nitrate is extraordinarily flammable and prone to rapid deterioration, its use was discontinued in favor of *cellulose acetate*; the term *celluloid* continues to be used to describe both film stock and processed film in general.

CGI, OR COMPUTER-GENERATED IMAGERY: The creation of 3-D computer graphics in cinema and television instead of real physical objects and people; the benefits of CGI include decreased cost (it's cheaper to create a crowd of 100,000 alien warriors amassing on a computer screen than it would be to hire, costume, feed, and pay 100,000 people to gather on a real field) and fewer personnel (one CGI artist versus all the filmmaking crew plus 100,000 extras); drawbacks include the tendency of modern audiences to assume that every visual effect has been faked, a trend the director Werner Herzog challenged when he forced Christian Bale, the star of his film *Rescue Dawn* (2007), to eat a bowl of real, live maggots onscreen in order (as Herzog put it) to "get people to start believing their own eyes again."

CHARACTER ACTOR: a secondary performer who specializes in playing a similar, recognizable character type from film to film.

CHROMA KEY: see *bluescreen*.

CINEMASCOPE: the anamorphic process for widescreen films introduced by 20th Century-Fox in 1953; its aspect ratio was originally 2.35:1 but was adjusted later to be 2.40:1; some particularly great CinemaScope films are Otto Preminger's *River of No Return* (1954), Max Ophüls' *Lola Montes* (1955), and Nicholas Ray's *Rebel without a Cause* (1955) and *Bigger than Life* (1956).

CINEMATOGRAPHER: also known as the Director of Photography or DP; the person in charge of selecting the cameras, lenses, film stocks, and overall lighting design in the making of a motion picture and overseeing the work of the camera operator if he or she is not operating the camera him- or herself.

CINEMATOGRAPHY: the photography of motion pictures.

CINERAMA: a lush but cumbersome widescreen process that used three interlocked cameras to record three separate images which, when projected across a specially curved screen, yielded a single continuous widescreen image with an aspect ratio of 2.77:1; examples include *This Is Cinerama* (1952), *How the West Was Won* (1962), and many travelogues.

CLOSE-UP: a shot that isolates an object in the image, making it appear relatively large.

COMPOSITION: The formal arrangements of shapes within the image, including people, sets, props, and landscape elements.

COMPUTER GEEK: A person who spends too much time in front of a computer screen, especially playing games or making picky corrections to Wikipedia entries; the word *geek* was originally used in the world of circuses and carnivals to describe a sideshow freak.

COMPUTER-GENERATED IMAGERY (CGI): see *CGI, or computer-generated imagery.*

CONTINUITY EDITING: a set of editing practices that establish spatial and/or temporal continuity between shots; the various techniques that filmmakers employ to keep their narratives moving forward logically and smoothly, without jarring disruptions in space or time despite hundreds or even thousands of the discrete bits of celluloid called shots, and without making the audience aware that they are in fact watching a work of art. See *eye-line match*, *glance-object match*, *graphic match*, and *matching on action*.

CONVENTION: an artistic practice or process or device that is widely used and commonly accepted and understood within a given culture; for example, the so-called "happy ending" is a convention of the romantic comedy film, and the knife-wielding homicidal maniac is a convention of the splatter film. See *romantic comedy* and *splatter film*.

CRANE: a camera movement in which the camera moves up and down through space; the camera is mounted on a kind of cherry-picker, which enables it to ascend from ground level into the sky or descend from the sky to ground level.

CRAWL: a series of words that appears at the bottom of the screen and moves upward; the end credits of a film often take the form of a crawl.

CROSSCUTTING: editing that alternates two or more lines of action occurring in different places or times, thereby connecting them; for example, a director crosscuts from a shot of a woman tied to railroad tracks to a speeding train to a man on horseback to the woman to the train to the woman to the man on horseback and so on until either the man saves the woman or she gets turned into bloody pulp by the train.

CUT: the simplest form of transition from one shot to another; in filmmaking (as opposed to video), the first shot is literally cut with a blade and taped to the second shot, which has been similarly trimmed; in video, the process happens electronically.

CUTTING: the process of splicing one shot to another; synonymous with editing; see *montage*.

DAILIES: a day's worth of processed but unedited footage freshly back from the lab; also called *rushes*.

DIEGESIS: the world of the film; all the story elements presented by the narrative, no matter whether they are actually seen or heard onscreen or not; music broadcast from an onscreen radio is diegetic, whereas the film's musical score is nondiegetic.

DIEGETIC SOUND: Sounds (including most dialogue and sound effects and some music) that are sourced in the world of the film's story; see *nondiegetic sound* for its opposite.

DIGITAL AUDIO WORKSTATION (DAW): a computer and accompanying software used to edit motion picture sound digitally.

DIRECTOR OF PHOTOGRAPHY (DP): see *cinematographer*.

DIRECTOR'S CUT: the version of the film the director considers to be finished, without interference from the studio or the producers.

DISSOLVE: a transition from one shot to another in which the first shot fades out while the second shot fades in, creating a *superimposition* at the midway point.

DOCUMENTARY: a film about facts rather than fiction; an account of real events. Documentaries often take a particular point of view toward their subject(s), and they are always a matter of selectively presenting the facts they chronicle. They may or may not tell stories, but they are always nonfiction.

DOLBY: The noise-reduction system invented by Ray Dolby in 1965; Dolby reduces background noises, cuts down on the noise created by the process of recording itself, and enhances the clarity of dialogue, music, and sound effects.

DOLLY: see *tracking shot*.

DUTCH TILT SHOT: a shot that tilts, often drastically, off the standard horizontal and/or vertical axes; Dutch angles are commonly used to express abnormal states of mind; also called a *canted angle shot*.

EDITING: the process of splicing one shot to another; synonymous with *cutting*.

END CREDITS, OR END TITLES: the list of personnel involved in making the film, from the actors to the caterers, that appears at the end of the film, often in the form of a *crawl*.

EXTRA: a performer who has no dialogue in a crowd scene and receives no credit for appearing in the film.

EYE-LEVEL SHOT: a shot taken from the height of an average human being, so the camera appears to be looking straight at the characters and/or objects being filmed.

EYE-LINE MATCH: a type of continuity editing that relies on the direction of one or more characters' glances to maintain spatial relationships from shot to shot; for instance, a character looking offscreen right in the first shot is followed in the second shot by another character looking offscreen left, the two characters appearing to look at each other even though they are in separate shots.

FABULA: the events of the narrative in chronological order, along with the personal associations brought to the narrative by each audience member; more or less synonymous with *story*, but in addition to the story the film tells us, it includes the individual stories we each tell ourselves.

FADE-IN AND FADE-OUT: the gradual increase (fade-in) or decrease (fade-out) in the strength and clarity of the filmed image or recorded sound; fade-ins generally begin with a pure white or pure black screen in the case of the image track and silence in the case of the soundtrack, while fade-outs usually begin with a clear image or sound, which then disappears to white or black or diminishes to silence; fade-ins and fade-outs are often used as transitional devices between scenes.

FILM STOCK: Raw, unexposed footage.

FINAL CUT: the last version of a film as it is being produced—the one that is released to the public; see *rough cut* and *director's cut*.

FLASHBACK: a shot, sequence, or scene that takes place in the past, before the present-day time frame established by the film.

FLASHFORWARD: a shot, sequence, or scene that takes place in the future, after the present-day time frame established by the film.

FOLEY ARTIST: A member of the sound team who specializes in duplicating sound effects that, for whatever reason, don't sound accurate when recorded directly at the time of shooting.

FORM: in art, the shape and structure of the artwork; in film, all the specific techniques used by filmmakers to create expressive meaning.

FRAME: (a) the individual rectangular photographs on a strip of motion picture film which, when run through a projector, yield the impression of movement owing to slight variations in the position of the objects being photographed; (b) the four borders of the projected image.

FULL SHOT: a shot that includes the entire human body from head to toe, with little space above the head and below the feet.

GENRE: a category of film, such as the western, the horror film, the costume drama, the melodrama, and so on, with recognizable conventions and character types.

GLANCE-OBJECT MATCH: an eye-line match that occurs between a human being and the object he or she is supposed to be looking at; for example: a woman looks offscreen left in the first shot, and the second shot is of a ringing telephone.

GRAPHIC MATCHING: a type of continuity editing that relies on the similarity of compositional shapes from one shot to the next to bridge the cut smoothly; for instance, a shot of a doorway is followed by a shot of another doorway, the two shots being matched by the similar positions the two doorways occupy onscreen.

HAND-HELD SHOT: a shot taken from a camera that is small and lightweight enough to be carried by the camera operator, unlike cameras that are mounted on devices such as tripods or dollies or cranes, hand-held cameras record the bodily movements of the camera operators, lending a somewhat jerky quality to hand-held shots.

HIGH-ANGLE SHOT: a shot taken from a camera that is positioned much higher than the subject being filmed, so that the effect is that of looking down on the subject.

IMAGE TRACK: that portion of the cinematic medium that contains the picture, as opposed to the *soundtrack*.

INVISIBLE EDITING: see *continuity editing*.

IRIS-IN AND IRIS-OUT: transitional devices between shots and/or scenes in which the image appears first as a small circle in the center of the screen (iris-in) and expands outward until it fills the screen, or the reverse (iris-out).

J-HORROR FILM: a gruesome Japanese horror subgenre with a perverse psychological bent.

LETTERBOXING: preserving the original widescreen aspect ratio when transferring the film onto video.

LEXICONNING: a process by which films are shortened for broadcasting on television; the standard 24 frames per second speed is increased by a matter of hundredths of a frame per second, the cumulative effect of which may shorten the film by as much as 6 or 7 percent of its total running time.

LOCATION: a real place used by filmmakers as the setting of a given scene, as opposed to a set that is specifically designed and constructed for a film; outdoor scenes in westerns are usually shot on location, for example, because not even the most expansive outdoor set can convey either the natural beauty or the desolation of the American West.

LONG SHOT: a shot in which the camera appears to be fairly far away from the subject being filmed, though special lenses can create the impression of great distance where much less distance exists.

LONG TAKE: a single shot of an unusually long duration; a detailed description of the complex long take that begins *Boogie Nights* (1997) can be found in the "Editing within the Shot" section of chapter 2.

LOW-ANGLE SHOT: a shot taken from a camera that is positioned much lower than the subject being filmed, so that the effect is that of looking up at the subject.

MASKING: Covering the top and/or bottom of the image with an aperture plate to create a widescreen effect.

MASTER SHOT: a shot taken from a long distance that includes as much of the set or location as possible and all the characters in the scene; for example, a master shot of a scene set in a dining room would capture the whole dining table, at least two of the four walls, all of the people sitting around the table, and perhaps the bottom of a chandelier hanging over the table; a director might run the entire scene from beginning to end in a master shot and, later, intercut close-ups, two-shots, and three-shots for visual and dramatic interest.

MATCHING: any of three ways of diminishing the jarring effect of splicing one shot to another; see *matching on action*, *eye-line matching*, and *graphic matching*.

MATCHING ON ACTION: an editing technique that uses an action begun in the first shot to bridge the cut to the second shot; for example: a baseball thrown across the screen from left to right in the first shot enters the second shot from screen left and travels across the image in a rightward direction.

MATTE: a type of special effect in which one area of the image is filmed, either by shooting a real background directly or by painting one and shooting the painting, while the remaining area is left blank by blocking a corresponding area of the lens; the blank area is then filled by filming, with the opposite area being blocked, after which the two areas are combined in processing.

MEDIUM SHOT: a shot taken from a medium distance from a person or object; with a person, a medium shot is from the waist up.

METHOD, THE: an acting technique derived from the teachings of Konstantin Stanislavsky and popularized by Lee Strasberg and his New York drama school, the Actors Studio, through which performers explore their own feelings and memories in an attempt to create more naturalistic characters onstage and onscreen.

MISE-EN-SCENE (*also*** MISE-EN-SCÈNE):** all of the elements placed in front of the camera to be photographed: settings, props, lighting, costumes, makeup, and figure behavior (meaning actors, their gestures, and their facial expressions); from the French, meaning *that which has been put into the scene or onstage.*

MIXING: Combining dialogue, sound effects, and music (both diegetic and nondiegetic) onto a single soundtrack; adjusting and balancing volume, tone, and direction of sound.

MOBILE FRAMING: the general term that describes the camera's ability to move; whereas still photography is, in a word, *still*, cinema is about *motion*—the objects and characters in the image move, and so may the camera itself; see *crane, hand-held shot, moving shot, pan, Steadicam,* and *tilt.*

MONTAGE: (a) in the French definition, any type of editing; (b) in the American definition, a rapidly cut, rather kaleidoscopic series of images that often condenses (but sometimes expands) time and space, such as a travel montage showing a character's progression across the United States in a matter of 20 seconds; (c) in the Soviet definition, a dynamic, expressly political type of film editing that uses the dialectics, or conflicts, of a given situation (a thesis and its antithesis) to produce a revolutionary synthesis in the mind of the spectator.

MORPHING: a CGI technique in which images of two or more distinct objects, animals, or humans are blended together to form a new, interpolated result.

MOTIVATED AND UNMOTIVATED CAMERA MOVEMENTS: Motivated camera movements are those that are prompted by the characters and events in the film; unmotivated camera movements are those that pertain to the filmmakers' commentary on characters and events. (Please note: unmotivated camera movements are something of a misnomer; they, too, are motivated—but by the director, not the characters or events in the film.)

MOVING SHOT: a camera movement that results from the camera shooting from a moving object, such as a shot taken out of a train window as the train speeds along, or a shot of the ocean taken from the deck of an oceanliner as it sails.

NARRATIVE: another word for storytelling.

NATURALISM: In acting, an attempt by a performer to appear not to be performing; because of changing ideas about what constitutes a realistic performance, the term *naturalistic* is more flexible and useful than *realistic.*

NONDIEGETIC SOUND: Sounds, including some sound effects and the film's score, that are not sourced in the world of the film's story; see *diegetic sound* for its opposite.

NONSYNCHRONOUS SOUND: Sounds that do not occur at the same time that their sources appear onscreen; see *sound bridge.*

OFFSCREEN SOUND: Sounds that occur at the same time that the event occurs in the image, but without the event appearing onscreen; for example, a shot of a writer holding his head in his hands inside his apartment is accompanied by the sound of a car horn being held down, presumably outside his window—the car cannot be seen, but its sound can be heard.

OVERCRANKING: a special effect created by speeding up the film as it moves through the camera from its usual 24 frames per second; when overcranked footage is run through a projector—which still operates at the normal 24 frames per second—the effect created is slow motion; see *undercranking*.

PAN: a camera movement achieved by pivoting the camera on its horizontal axis, or from side to side; for example, a pan might begin with the left field bleachers at a baseball park and move horizontally to the left, taking in the cheering crowd, until it gets to the press box to the right of home plate; to describe this shot, one would simply say or write, "The camera pans left from the bleachers to the press box."

PANAVISION: though the term can be used to describe any film made with cameras and lenses patented by the company named Panavision, it also specifically describes the company's widescreen processes; with a current aspect ratio of 2.40:1, Panavision is the most widely used anamorphic process today; some particularly notable Panavision films are Billy Wilder's *The Apartment* (1960), George Sidney's *Bye Bye Birdie* (1963), Robert Mulligan's *Inside Daisy Clover* (1965), and Sergio Leone's *Once upon a Time in America* (1984); see *anamorphic lens*.

PERSONA: the role a person consistently displays in public, as opposed to the inner self; in the case of a film star, the general character he or she represents to the public, based on the roles he or she plays and the content of his or her publicity.

PHYSIOGNOMY: the characteristics of a human face, especially as they reveal—or *seem* to reveal—the character of a person.

PITCH: The relatively high, medium, or low quality of a sound that depends on the frequency of sound waves created by the sound's source.

PIXILATION: a computer-generated special effect that consists of the averaging together of blocks of individual pixels to create a mosaic effect.

PLOT: the ordering or structuring of story events as they are presented in the film.

POINT-OF-VIEW SHOT (POV): a particular type of shot that suggests that the camera is recording exactly what a character is seeing at that moment; POV shots are not approximations of a character's position—they aren't taken from the general vicinity of a character, but rather from the precise position of that character's eyes; POV shots are therefore intensely subjective, since they effectively put the audience inside the character's head.

POSTPRODUCTION: The period of filmmaking after shooting has been completed.

PUBLICITY: the management of the public's perception of a person; the creation and maintenance of a star's *persona* by extra-filmic means—not the roles in which they appear on-screen, but the newspapers, magazines, television talk shows, and websites in which they appear offscreen.

RADIO MICROPHONE: A wireless mike that is affixed to a sound source, usually an actor.

REFRAMING: any camera movement, including even the most minute readjustment—for instance, the camera pans ever so slightly to the left to keep a character's head centered in the image when she shifts a little in close-up.

REPRESENTATION: a sign or symbol that communicates meaning with a combination of content and form; a horse is real, whereas a sculpture of a horse is an artist's representation. All films and photographs are representations, no matter how realistic they may seem.

RETAKE: A second, third, tenth, or even hundredth attempt to film a given shot; the term *retake* sometimes implies that the shooting occurs on a day subsequent to the original takes; actors are often brought back to the studio at the end of production to shoot retakes of shots and scenes the director finds to be problematic for one reason or another.

ROMANTIC COMEDY: a subgenre of the comedy genre in which two people fall in love with each other by going through a series of mishaps and confusions; some notable romantic comedies are *Bringing Up Baby* (1938), *Pillow Talk* (1959), *When Harry Met Sally* (1989), and *Knocked Up* (2007).

ROOM TONE: The faint, barely audible sounds of the particular room in which dialogue has been recorded; room tone is recorded separately from dialogue.

ROTOSCOPING: the projection of live-action footage, frame by frame, onto an animator's drawing table so that he or she can trace the figures with great precision.

ROUGH CUT: a preliminary, edited version of a film that includes all the major story elements, but without any fine-tuning of the visual and audio tracks.

RUSHES: see *dailies*.

SCENE: a unit of dramatic action that takes place in one location during a single time period; see *sequence*.

SCORE: The music, usually nondiegetic, that accompanies the images.

SEGMENTATION: a formal, written breakdown of a film's narrative into its component parts; see chapter 7 for a detailed discussion of segmentation and some examples.

SEQUENCE: a component of film narrative that maintains a unity of time, place, or dramatic action but introduces a discontinuity; for example, a single dramatic action (a man goes shopping) continues throughout a sequence but the locations change (a large department store, a jewelry shop, a florist, a sporting goods store) and time is speeded up (shots of clocks on the wall reveal the passing of an entire afternoon); see *scene*.

SEQUENCE SHOT: a single shot that serves, seemingly paradoxically, as its own sequence or scene; a particular type of long take that covers an entire sequence or scene from beginning to end; an example of the sequence shot that begins *Scarface* (1931) can be found in the "Editing within the Shot" section of chapter 2.

SHOT/REVERSE-SHOT PATTERN: an editing technique that records the interaction between two characters, usually a conversation, who are facing one another with one series of shots often taken over the shoulder of one character and another series of shots taken over the shoulder of the other character; note that the so-called reverse shot is not actually taken from the truly opposite angle, because such an angle would violate the 180° system.

SHOT: the basic element of filmmaking—a piece of film run through the camera, exposed, and developed; an uninterrupted run of the camera; or an uninterrupted image on film.

SHOTGUN MICROPHONE: A specialized mike that must be pointed directly at a sound source but that can pick up sound at a great distance.

SLASHER FILM: a subgenre of the horror film characterized by the menacing presence of a psychotic who wields a butcher knife, meat cleaver, machete, straight razor, box cutter, pigsticker, or X-acto knife to bloody and fatal effect; classic examples of the subgenre are *Halloween* (1978) and *Friday the 13th* (1980).

SOUND BRIDGE: An aural transition from one scene to the next in which the sound of the second scene is heard at the tail end of the image track of the first; for instance, the last few seconds of an exterior street scene are accompanied by the sound of a telephone ringing, after which the director cuts to a shot of a bedroom interior with a ringing telephone on the night table.

SOUND ON DISC: An early method of synchronizing sound to motion picture images in which sound was recorded on phonograph discs (records) and played back when the film was screened; see *sound on film*.

SOUND ON FILM: The dominant method of synchronizing sound to motion picture images in which sound is converted to optical signals and placed on a soundtrack on the film itself; the projector reads the signals and converts them back into sound; see *sound on disc*.

SOUNDTRACK: that portion of the cinematic medium that contains aural information—dialogue, music, and sound effects; on celluloid, it's the squiggly line on the side of the image frames; see figure 1.14 for a simple illustration; see figure 5.1 for a more complicated—and contemporary—illustration.

SPECIAL EFFECTS: any image or element within the image that has been produced by extraordinary technical means—that is, beyond the ordinary technology required to make a film.

SPLATTER FILM: a subgenre of the horror film that features as its main convention the liberal use of stage blood; critics cite the shower montage in Alfred Hitchcock's *Psycho* (1960) as the most important precursor of the splatter film, which began in earnest with George Romero's *Night of the Living Dead* (1968).

STAR: a film performer who has a national or international reputation and sizeable box office appeal and who consistently appears in major roles.

STEADICAM: an apparatus that fits onto a camera operator's body (via a vest) in such a way that when he or she walks, the camera—which is small and lightweight enough to be carried—records a very smooth movement, as opposed to a hand-held camera that records every bump in every step.

STORY: all the events of the narrative as they occur in chronological order from beginning to end, including not only those that we see and hear, but those we infer.

STUDIO SYSTEM: the mode of production that dominated American filmmaking from the early 1920s to the late 1940s, a period during which the so-called Hollywood studios were actually vertically integrated distribution companies that produced and exhibited their own products—movies; see *vertical integration*.

SUPERIMPOSITION: a special effect in which there are two or more images visible onscreen at the same time; the midway point of a *dissolve* is a superimposition.

SYNCHRONIZED SOUND: dialogue, sound effects, and diegetic music that are heard at the same time that the source appears onscreen.

SYUZHET: more or less synonymous with *plot*: the ordering of story events within the film.

TAKE: a single attempt to record a shot; a shot may require many takes before a director is satisfied; see *retake*.

THREE-QUARTER SHOT: a shot taken from a distance that reveals the human body from the head to just below the knees.

TALKIES: Films with synchronized dialogue; short for *talking pictures*.

TELEPHOTO LENS: A lens that greatly magnifies distant objects, the way a telescope does; a telephoto lens has a shallow *depth of field*, meaning that only objects in the distance are in focus, with everything in front of them appearing blurry. See *wide-angle lens* and *zoom*.

THREE-POINT LIGHTING: A very commonly used lighting setup, consisting of three main light sources—a key light, a fill light, and a backlight; the effect is a centrally illuminated subject (by the key light) seen in an evenly lit setting (by the fill light) but separated visually from the background (by the backlight).

THREE-SHOT: a shot in which three people dominate the image—not three people surrounded by a crowd, but three people who are framed so as to constitute a distinct group, with little space between them and the frame.

TILT: a camera movement achieved by pivoting the camera on a vertical axis, or up and down, with the camera remaining stationary on the ground; for example, a tilt could begin with the ground floor of a skyscraper and end with the top of the building; to describe this shot, one would say or write, "The camera tilts from the ground floor to the top of the building."

TIMBRE: All the qualities of a sound that are not described by *volume* and *pitch*, such as its richness or tinniness, its fullness or hollowness, its nasalness if it's a human voice, and so on; synonymous with *tone quality*.

TITLE CARD: Words printed on a page or piece of cardboard, photographed, and edited into a film (usually a silent film), conveying bits of dialogue or information about location, time frame, or backstory.

TRACKING SHOT: a mobile framing shot in which the camera moves forward, backward, or laterally; also called a *dolly*.

TRANSITIONS: Any of a number of methods by which one shot is linked to the next; see *cut*, *dissolve*, *fade-in* and *fade-out*, *iris-in* and *iris-out*, and *wipe*.

TRAVELING MATTE: matte work that consists of two separately shot moving images that are combined in processing; see *bluescreen*.

TWO-SHOT: a shot in which two people appear, usually in medium distance or closer; two-shots are dominated spatially by two people, making them ideal for conversations.

UNDERCRANKING: a special effect created by slowing down the film as it moves through the camera from its usual 24 frames per second; when undercranked footage is run through a projector—which still operates at the normal 24 frames per second—the effect created is fast motion; see *overcranking*.

VERTICAL INTEGRATION: the system of production, distribution, and exhibition that characterized Hollywood's studio system; the so-called studios were essentially distribution and exhibition companies that provided their own product to distribute and exhibit, thereby integrating their operations in a three-tiered, or vertical, way.

VERTICAL PAN: see *tilt*.

VISTAVISION: a widescreen process developed by Paramount Pictures in 1953 and 1954 to compete with 20th Century-Fox's CinemaScope; while CinemaScope's frames ran vertically on the celluloid, VistaVision's frames ran horizontally, with the sprocket holes on the top and bottom of each frame; most VistaVision films used mattes or masking to produce aspect ratios that ranged from 1.66:1 and 1.85:1 to 2:1; a few notable VistaVision films are John Ford's *The Searchers* (1956), Stanley Donen's *Funny Face* (1957), and Alfred Hitchcock's *Vertigo* (1958) and *North by Northwest* (1959).

WIDE-ANGLE LENS: a lens with a wide horizontal field of view, the opposite of a telephoto lens; wide-angle lenses have great *depth of field*, meaning that objects at various degrees of distance from the camera can remain in focus, while only objects very close or very far away from the camera are blurry. See *telephoto lens* and *zoom*.

WIDESCREEN: a general term for any of the processes that yield an aspect ratio wider than the standard Academy ratio of 1.37:1; these include CinemaScope, Cinerama, Panavision, SuperPanavision 70, Techniscope, Technirama, Todd-AO, Tohoscope, VistaVision, and UltraPanavision 70; for a few notable examples, see *CinemaScope*, *Panavision*, and *VistaVision*; see also *Academy ratio*.

WIPE: a type of transition from one shot to another in which the second shot appears to push the first shot off the screen; wipes may take the form of a horizontal or vertical line moving across the screen, or they may take graphic shapes such as a *star wipe*, a *spiral wipe*, or an *iris wipe*.

WIRE REMOVAL: a CGI technique in which the rigging cables that support actors who are suspended in the air are digitally removed from the image, thus making it appear that the characters are flying.

ZOOM: a lens with a variable focal length, meaning that it shifts from wide-angle to telephoto and back; with a tracking shot, the whole camera moves, whereas with a zoom, only parts of the lens move but the camera itself remains in place. See *telephoto lens* and *wide-angle lens*.

ACKNOWLEDGMENTS

I am particularly grateful to John Belton, who has taught me, inspired me, guided me, and corrected my factual errors for thirty years. I also especially thank Juree Sondker, my first editor, for initiating this project at Columbia University Press, and the amazing Jennifer Crewe, associate director and editorial director, who saw it through to completion, as well as Martin Hinze, the book's designer; its illustrator, Vic Kulihin; Afua Adusei-Gontarz, executive editorial assistant; and my ace copyeditor Roy Thomas, senior manuscript editor.

There were times when I was stuck; Adam Orman and Dan Schackman helped me get unstuck. My students at Haverford and Colorado College taught me how to teach; thanks to all of them. I'm indebted to David Bordwell and Kristin Thompson, Timothy Corrigan and Patricia White, Ira Konigsberg, James Monaco, and their various illustrators. My gratitude also goes to Chris Bram, George Butte, Floyd Casey, Liz Hinlein, Gregor Meyer, Matthew Mirapaul, William Paul, John Simons, the many good people at the PLM PD forum, and Joe Smith, George Robinson, and the rest of the Ira guys. It wouldn't be an honest acknowledgments page if I didn't thank my mother, Betty Sikov. Special thanks to my agent, Edward Hibbert. Most of all, I thank Bruce Schackman for putting up with my, uh, creative temperament.

INDEX

Page numbers followed by *f* indicate figures and captions. Page numbers followed by *n* indicate notes.

Academy aperture. *See* Academy ratio

Academy of Motion Picture Arts and Sciences, 20, 129, 187

Academy ratio, 20, 39, 41*f*

acting, analyzing and writing about, 138–42

acting styles, 130–31

action films, 144

The Actors Studio, 193

The Adventures of Sharkboy and Lavagirl (2005), 157

Aldrich, Robert: *Kiss Me Deadly* (1955), 153

Alien (1979), 113

All About Eve (1950), 31, 32

Allegheny Uprising (1939), 150

Altman, Rick, 148–50

Altman, Robert: *The Long Goodbye* (1973), 153, 154

ambient sounds, 79

Amblin Entertainment, 123

American Cinema (Sarris), 120

American Film/American Culture (Belton), 111–15

American Film Institute Catalog of Motion Pictures Produced in the United States (AFI Catalog), 127

American Gangster (2007), 133

American montage, 58

American Optical Company, 40

amplitude, 81–83

analog recording and editing, 77

analysis in film studies: of acting, 138–42; of attribution, 126–28; of camera movement, 34–37; of cinematography, 53–54; discussed, 104; of genre, 155–57; of scene-to-scene editing, 101–102; of shots, 21–23; of shot-to-shot editing, 70–73; of sound, 84–88; of special effects, 166–68; of story, 113–15

anamorphic frames, 40*f*

anamorphic lens, 39

Anderson, Paul Thomas, 33; *Boogie Nights* (1997), 29, 30, 35–37, 192

Angels and Demons (2009), 144

animation, 164–65

animation cels, 2

Aniston, Jennifer, 137

Annie Hall (1977), 63

Anschutz, Philip, 123

The Apartment (1960), 194

A pictures, 96

Aristotle, 105, 106

The Arrival of a Train at La Ciotat (1895), 158

art, films as, 4

art director. *See* production designer

Arzner, Dorothy, 127; *Christopher Strong* (1933), 127–28

aspect ratio: depicted, 41*f*; discussed, 20, 39–42; form and meaning, 42–44. *See also* Academy ratio; CinemaScope; Panavision; VistaVision; widescreen processes

The Assassination of Jesse James by the Coward Robert Ford (2007), 137, 137*f*

Astruc, Alexandre, 119, 122

asynchronous sounds, 79. *See also* offscreen sound

Attack of the Killer Tomatoes (1978), 148

attribution, 126–28

Audition (1999), 148

Auntie Em (movie character), 100

aural space, 82

auteurism, 120, 127

auteur theory, 119–21

authorship in filmmaking, 117–19

avant-garde films, 90

backlight, 45, 46*f*

backstage musicals, 80

Back to the Future III (1990), 147

Bad Guy type, 133

Badlands (1973), 149

Bale, Christian, 188

Ball of Fire (1941), 120

Bardot, Brigitte, 134

Barrymore, Drew, 130

Barrymore, John, 130

base (motion picture film), 48

baseball films, 144

Batman (1989), 157

Battleship Potemkin (1925), 33, 59, 60*f*, 98

Bazin, André, 60

behind the camera space, 32

Being John Malkovich (1999), 131–32

Bell Labs, 164

Belton, John, 111–115

best boy, 123

Bigger Than Life (1956), 188

The Big Heat (1952), 151

The Big Sleep (1946), 120, 153, 154

biopics, 144

bird's-eye shots, 12, 13*f*, 167*f*

black-and-white cinematography, 50, 154

black-and-white negative film stock, 49

black-and-white print film stock, 49

black comedies, 145

The Blair Witch Project (1999), 26

blaxploitation films, 144

Blind Beast (1969), 148

blocking, 43–44

Blonde Bombshell type, 134

bluescreen, 163

B movies, 96

Body Heat (1981), 134

Boeing, 164

Bombshell (1933), 134

Bond, James (movie character), 132–33

Bong Joon-ho: *The Host* (2006), 82–83

Boogie Nights (1997), 29, 30, 35–37, 192

boom, 76

boom operators, 124

Bordwell, David, 91

Bourne, Jason (movie character), 136

Bourne series (2002, 2004, 2007), 136

Brando, Marlon, 131

Bride of Chucky (1998), 147

Bride of Frankenstein (1935), 147

Bride of the Monster (1955), 147

Bringing Up Baby (1938), 120, 121, 126, 145, 195

Brokeback Mountain (2005), 103, 146

Broken Arrow (1950), 147

Brosnan, Pierce, 132

Bull Durham (1988), 144

Burch, Noël, 31

Buscemi, Steve, 132, 136

B westerns, 96

Bye Bye Birdie (1963), 194

Caged (1950), 144

Caged Heat (1974), 144

Cagney, James, 138

Cahiers du cinéma (journal), 119, 187

cameo appearances, 131–32

camera angle, 12–16

camera movement: analyzing, 34–37; editing within the shot, 28–30; mobile framing, 24–25; space and movement, 30–33; types of, 25–28; writing about, 34–37

camera operators, 123

caméra-stylo, 119

canted angle shots. *See* Dutch tilt shots

Capote, Truman, 136

Captain Blood (1934), 144

Carrey, Jim, 116

Casablanca (1942), 19

Case, Arthur (movie character), 108, 109, 110, 111, 112, 113, 114

casting against type, 133

celluloid, 2, 17*f*

cellulose acetate, 188

cellulose nitrate, 188

CG. *See* computer graphics (CG); computer graphics (CG) artists

CG 101 (Masson), 164

CGI. *See* computer-generated imagery (CGI)

"Chaiyya, Chaiyya," 111, 114

Chandler, Raymond, 154

Channing, Margo (movie character), 32

Chaplin, Charles, 118, 132; *City Lights* (1931), 32, 71–73

character actors, 132

character in narrative, 97–98

Chase, David: *The Sopranos* (1999–2007), 132

Cheyenne Autumn (1964), 147

Chinatown (1974), 153, 154

Christopher Strong (1933), 127–28

chroma key. *See* bluescreen

CinemaScope, 39, 188, 198

cinematographers, 42, 123

cinematography, 53–54, 123; aspect ratio, 39–44; black, white, gray, and color, 49–50; defined,

38; film stocks, 48–49; lenses, 50–52; lighting, generally, 44–45; motion picture photography, 38; three-point lighting, 45–47

Cinerama: aspect ratio, 39, 41*f*; discussed, 39, 39*n*; examples of, 189; as widescreen process, 198

Citizen Kane (1941), 12, 14, 51, 52*f*, 97, 98, 119, 144, 153

City Lights (1931), 32, 71–73

clapboard, 123, 188

clapper. *See* second assistant camera operator

Clash by Night (1952), 153

classical Hollywood style, 61, 63, 95. *See also* continuity editing

classical unities, 106–107

A Clockwork Orange (1971), 75

Clooney, George, 131

Close, Glenn, 134

close-ups, 10, 11*f*

Clouseau, Jacques, Inspector (movie character), 80

Coen, Joel and Ethan: *No Country for Old Men* (2007), 153

Cohen, Sacha Baron, 136

Cole, Jack, 126

color cinematography, 49–50

color negative film stock, 49

color print film stock, 49

Columbia Pictures, 120, 123

combat films, 120

comedies: black comedies, 145; discussed, 145; horror-comedies, 148; romantic comedies, 195; screwball comedies, 120, 145

Compañeros (1970), 147

The Complete Film Dictionary (Konigsberg), 131

composers, 77

composition, 18–20, 44

computer geeks, 125

computer-generated imagery (CGI), 2, 164–65, 165*f*

computer graphics (CG), 164

computer graphics (CG) artists, 125

conflict in narrative, 98–100

Connery, Sean, 132

The Conqueror (1956), 133

continuity editing, 61–67. *See also* eye-line matching; glance-object matching; graphic matching; matching on action

contrast, 49

conventions: discussed, 104–105; in film noir, 153–54; in genres, 143, 145–46

Corrigan, Timothy, 80

cowboys-and-Indians movies, 147

Craig, Daniel, 132

crane shots, 26

Crawford, Joan, 139

crawl, 116

Crichton, Michael: *Westworld* (1973), 147, 164

crime dramas, 132

crosscutting, 95, 96–97

Crouching Tiger, Hidden Dragon (2000), 149–50

Cruise, Tom, 82

Cruz, Luis, 3, 4

Cuba, Larry, 164

Cukor, George: *Gone with the Wind* (1939), 122; *A Star is Born* (1954), 144

Cure (1997), 148

Curtiz, Michael: *Casablanca* (1942), 19

cut, defined, 57

cutting, 97. *See also* editing; montage

Dafoe, Willem, 109, 111, 114

dailies, 121

Damon, Matt, 136

DAR. *See* Digital Audio Recorder (DAR)

Darius, Captain (movie character), 109, 111, 114

Dark City (1950), 153

The Dark Knight (2008), 155–57

Darkman (1990), 157

Dassin, Jules: *The Naked City* (1948), 153

Davis, Bette, 31, 32, 131, 138

DAW. *See* digital audio workstation (DAW)

Dawn of the Dead (1979), 163–64

The Dawn Patrol (1930), 120

Dead Alive (1990), 148

Dean, James, 131

deep focus, 51, 52*f*

Del Mar, Ennis (movie character), 146

DeMille, Cecil B.: *The Greatest Show on Earth* (1952), 158, 159*f*, 161: *Unconquered* (1947), 150

De Niro, Robert, 135–36

Depp, Johnny, 131

depth of field, 51, 197, 198

desire in narrative, 97–98

dialogue (sound on film), 78

diegesis, 91

diegetic sound, 78, 80, 91. *See also* nondiegetic sound

diegetic space, 31. *See also* nondiegetic space

Digital Audio Recorder (DAR), 124

digital audio workstation (DAW), 77

digital recording and editing, 77

Dinner at Eight (1933), 130

director's cut, 118

directors of photography (DPs). *See*
cinematographers

direct sound, 83

Disney, Walt: *The Hunchback of Notre Dame*, 2

dissolves: discussed, 30, 96, 162; superimpositions
and, 190, 196

distance, 82

Django (1966), 147

Django and Sartana are Coming: It's the End! (1970),
147

D.O.A. (1950), 153

documentaries, 90

Dolby, Ray, 75, 189

Dolby Laboratories, 75

Dolby system, 75

dolly. *See* tracking shots

Dominik, Andrew: *The Assassination of Jesse James
by the Coward Robert Ford* (2007), 137, 137*f*

Donen, Stanley: *Funny Face* (1957), 198

Dorothy (movie character). *See* Gale, Dorothy

Do the Right Thing (1989), 19, 111

Double Indemnity (1944), 103, 134, 152–53

dramas, 144

dramatic unities, 106

Dreyer, Carl Theodor: *The Passion of Joan of Arc*
(1928), 12

*Dr. Strangelove: or How I Learned to Stop Worrying
and Love the Bomb* (1964), 145

Drums Across the River (1954), 147

Drums Along the Mohawk (1939), 150

Dumb and Dumber (1994), 145

Dutch tilt shots, 13, 13*f*

Dyer, Richard, 132

eastern westerns, 150

Eastman Color. *See* black-and-white
cinematography

Eastwood, Clint, 138, 139–42, 146; *Unforgiven* (1992),
139–42, 140*f*

editing: continuity editing, 61–67; depicted, 55*f*;
discussed, 19; Kuleshov experiment, 60–61,
96; montage, 57–60; 180° system, 67–68; shot/
reverse-shot pattern, 68–69; transitions, 55–57;
writing about, 71–73. *See also* cutting

editing in the camera, 118

editing matches, 63–67

editing within the shot, 28–30

Edwards, Blake: *A Shot in the Dark* (1964), 80

Eisenstein, Sergei, 59; *Battleship Potemkin* (1925), 33,
59, 60*f*, 98

emulsion, 48

end credits (end titles), 116

epistemological quests, in film noir, 154

Eternal Sunshine of the Spotless Mind (2004), 116

ethnicity issues in films, 111–12

The Evil Dead (1981), 148

Ewell, Tom, 80

exposure index of film stock, 48, 49

extras, 29, 116

extreme close-ups, 10

extreme long shots, 10

eye-level shots, 12, 13*f*

eye-line matching, 64–65

fabula, 91

fade-in, 95

fade-out, 95

Family Plot (1976), 121

fantasy films, 162

Fassbinder, Rainer Werner, 118

fast film, 49

Fatal Attraction (1987), 134

Fellini, Federico, 118

Femme Fatale (Killer Dame) type, 134

Fetter, William, 164

Fight Club (1999), 19, 21–23, 22*f*, 170–85

fill light, 45, 46*f*

film acting, 134–36

film directors as authors, 117–19

The Film Experience (Corrigan and White), 80

film magazines (containers), 56, 123

filmmakers: attribution, 126–28; auteur theory,
119–21; authorship, 117–19; discussed, 116–17;
producer's role, 121–23; teamwork, 123–25; writing about, 127–28

film noir: conventions, 153–54; depicted, 152*f*; discussed, 150–51; examples of, 120, 152–53; history
of, 152–53; role of dialogue, 103

filmography, 127

film sound. *See* sound on film

film speed. *See* exposure index of film stock

film stock, 48–49

final cut, 118

Fincher, David: *Fight Club* (1999), 19, 21–23, 22*f*,
170–85

first assistant camera operator, 123, 124, 188

flashbacks, 95

flashforwards, 95

Fleming, Victor: *Gone with the Wind* (1939), 122; *The Wizard of Oz* (1939), 97, 98–102, 99f, 104, 106–107

focus pull. *See* rack focus shots

focus puller. *See* first assistant camera operator

Foley artists, 77, 124

Foley walkers, 77

Fonda, Henry, 47–48f, 131

Ford, Glenn, 151

Ford, John, 12, 118: *Drums Along the Mohawk* (1939), 150; *The Fugitive* (1947), 47–48f; *The Searchers* (1956), 198; *Stagecoach* (1939), 144, 147

foreshadowing, 175n

form, 2–3

Fort Apache (1948), 146

Foster, Jodie, 108, 109

frame, 18, 20

Frazier, Detective Keith (movie character), 108, 109, 110, 111, 112, 114

French montage, 57

Friday the 13th (1980), 196

front projection, 163

The Fugitive (1947), 47–48f

Fuller, Samuel: *Pickup on South Street* (1953), 153

full shots, 10

Funny Face (1957), 198

gaffers, 123

Gale, Dorothy (movie character), 98, 99, 99f, 102, 107

Gandolfini, James, 85f

gangster films, 144

Garland, Judy, 99f, 101

gauge, of film stock, 48

gender issues in films, 134

The General (1927), 158, 159f, 161

Genghis Khan (movie character), 133

genres: analyzing, 155–57; conventions, repetitions, and variations, 145–46; defined, 120; discussed, 46–47, 143–44; examples of, 144; film noir (*see* film noir); horror films (*see* horror films); semantic/syntatic approach, 148–50; westerns (*see* westerns); writing about, 156–57

Gentlemen Prefer Blondes (1953), 9, 120, 126

Gewirtz, Russell, 108

The Girl Can't Help It (1956), 80

glance-object matching, 65

Godzilla vs. Mothra (1964), 145

Gollum (movie character), 165

Gondry, Michel: *Eternal Sunshine of the Spotless Mind* (2004), 116

Gone with the Wind (1939), 122, 133, 134

The Good, the Bad, and the Ugly (1966), 147

Goodfellas (1990), 144

Good Guy type, 133

Grahame, Gloria, 151

Grant, Cary, 121, 126, 138, 162–63

graphic matching, 65–67, 66f

The Greatest Show on Earth (1952), 158, 159f, 161

Griffith, D.W., 118

grips, 123

Gulch, Miss (movie character), 100, 107

Halloween (1978), 148, 196

Halloween series, 145

hand-held cameras, 26

hand-held shots, 26–27

Hanks, Tom, 116, 118

Hanson, Curtis: *L.A. Confidential* (1997), 153

Harlow, Jean, 134

Hawks, Howard, 12, 118, 119, 120–21, 126; *Ball of Fire* (1941), 120; *The Big Sleep* (1946), 120, 153, 154; *Bringing Up Baby* (1938), 120, 121, 126, 145, 195; *The Dawn Patrol* (1930), 120; *Gentlemen Prefer Blondes* (1953), 9, 120, 126; *I Was a Male War Bride* (1948), 120; *Red River* (1948), 120, 121; *Rio Bravo* (1959), 120; *Scarface* (1932), 29–30, 195; *Sergeant York* (1941), 120; *A Song Is Born* (1948), 120; *The Thing from Another World* (1951), 120

hearing sound, 84–88

Hepburn, Katharine, 126, 128, 138

Herzog, Werner, 188: *Rescue Dawn* (2007), 188

high-angle shots, 12, 13f

high key, 46n

high-key lighting, 45–47

Hitchcock, Alfred, 118, 119, 121, 122, 130; *Family Plot* (1976), 121; *North by Northwest* (1959), 144, 162–63, 198; *Notorious* (1946), 121; *The Pleasure Garden* (1925), 121; *Psycho* (1960), 8, 121, 144, 148, 196; *Rear Window* (1954), 19, 121; *Rebecca* (1940), 121, 122; *Rope* (1948), 56–57; *Strangers on a Train* (1951), 121; *Vertigo* (1958), 121, 164, 166–67, 167f, 198; *The Wrong Man* (1956), 153

Holden, William, 133

horror-comedies, 148

horror films: defined, 147, 147*n*; examples of, 120, 144, 147–48; subgenres, 147–48

The Host (2006), 82–83

Howard the Duck (1986), 164

How the West Was Won (1962), 39, 189

The Hunchback of Notre Dame, 2

Huston, John: *The Maltese Falcon* (1941), 153

images, writing about, 22–23

image track, 17

Imagine Entertainment, 123

IMAX Dome, 20*n*

The Impossible Voyage (1904), 162

In a Lonely Place (1950), 153

In Cold Blood (Capote), 136

Indiana Jones and the Temple of Doom (1984), 144

Inside Daisy Clover (1965), 194

Inside Man (2006), 108–111, 108*f*, 113–15

intermediate film stock, 49

Internet Movie Database (imdb.com), 127

interpositive film stock, 49

invisible editing. *See* continuity editing

irises, 95–96

iris-in, 95

iris-out, 95

I Was a Male War Bride (1948), 120

Jackie Brown (1997), 144

The Jackie Robinson Story (1950), 144

Jackson, Peter: *Lord of the Rings* trilogy (2001, 2002, 2003), 125, 165*f*

Jaws (1975), 163

The Jazz Singer, 75

J-horror films, 148

Johnston, Joanna, 117

Jolie, Angelina, 137

Jolson, Al, 75

Kahn, Michael, 117

Kaminski, Janusz, 117

Kane, Charles Foster (movie character), 12, 97, 98

Kaufman, Charlie, 116

Kavanaugh, Lisa Dean, 117

Keaton, Buster: *The General* (1927), 158, 159*f*, 161

key light, 45, 46*f*

Killer Dame (Femme Fatale) type, 134

Kiss Me Deadly (1955), 153

Kitses, Jim, 149, 150

Knocked Up (2007), 195

Konigsberg, Ira, 131

Kubrick, Stanley: *A Clockwork Orange* (1971), 75; *2001: A Space Odyssey* (1968), 39*n*, 66–67, 66*f*

Kuleshov, Lev, 61

Kuleshov experiment, 60–61, 62*f*, 96

Kutcher, Ashton, 138

L.A. Confidential (1997), 153

LaMotta, Jake, 136

LaMotta, Jake (movie character), 135

lamps, 47

Lang, Fritz: *The Big Heat* (1952), 151; *Clash by Night* (1952), 153; *Scarlet Street* (1945), 153

Lara Croft: Tomb Raider (2001), 144

L'arroseur arrosé (*The Sprinkler Sprinkled*, 1895), 160*f*

Laura (1944), 81, 152–53

Ledger, Heath, 146

Lee, Ang: *Brokeback Mountain* (2005), 103, 146; *Crouching Tiger, Hidden Dragon* (2000), 149–50

Lee, Spike, 33; *Do the Right Thing* (1989), 19, 111; *Inside Man* (2006), 108–111, 108*f*, 113–15; *Malcolm X* (1992), 17, 111

Legally Blonde (2001), 134

lenses, 50–52

Leone, Sergio: *Once upon a Time in America* (1984), 194

letterboxing, 42, 43*f*

lexiconning, 17–18

lighting, 44–45, 154

Linklater, Richard: *A Scanner Darkly* (2006), 165; *Waking Life* (2001), 165

Liu, Lucy, 138

location, 6

Lola Montes (1955), 188

The Long Goodbye (1973), 153, 154

long shots, 10, 11*f*

long takes, discussed, 29, 33

Lord of the Rings trilogy (2001, 2002, 2003), 125, 165*f*

low-angle shots, 12, 13*f*

Lowes theater chain, 123

low key, 46*n*

low-key lighting, 45–48*f*, 154

Lubitsch, Ernst: *The Merry Widow* (1934), 47*f*

Lucas, George: *Star Wars* (1977), 91, 164

Luhrman, Baz, 103: *Romeo + Juliet* (1996), 103

Lumière, Auguste, 162

Lumière, Louis, 162: *The Arrival of a Train at La Ciotat* (1895), 158; *L'arroseur arrosé* (*The Sprinkler Sprinkled*, 1895), 160f

magazines (film containers), 56, 123

major studios, American studio system, 120

makeup, for special effects, 163

Malcolm X (1992), 17, 111

Malick, Terrence: *Badlands* (1973), 149

The Maltese Falcon (1941), 153

Mammy (movie character), 133, 134

Mancini, Henry: "Theme from *A Shot in the Dark*," 80

Mankiewicz, Herman, 119

Mankiewicz, Joseph: *All About Eve* (1950), 31, 32

Mansfield, Jayne, 134

Man with a Movie Camera (1929), 59

The Man with the Rubber Head (1902), 162

Marvel, Professor (movie character), 100, 107

Marvin, Lee, 151

masking, 40, 42

Massachusetts Institute of Technology (MIT), 164

Masson, Terrence, 164

master shots, 14–15f, 16

matching. *See* eye-line matching; graphic matching; matching on action

matching on action, 63–64

The Matrix Reloaded (2003), 126

matte artists, 125

matte paintings, 163

mattes, 40

matte work, 163

Mayer, Louis B., 122

Mazurki, Mike, 152f

McDaniel, Hattie, 133–34

McDonald, Jeanette, 47f

mechanical special effects, 163–64

medium close-ups, 10

medium shots, 10, 11f

Méliès, Georges, 162: *The Impossible Voyage* (1904), 162; *The Man with the Rubber Head* (1902), 162; *The Mermaid* (1904), 162; *A Trip to the Moon* (1902), 162; *20,000 Leagues Under the Sea* (1907), 162; *Un homme de têtes* (*The Four Troublesome Heads*, 1898), 161f

Mercury Man (2006), 157

The Mermaid (1904), 162

The Merry Widow (1934), 47f

Method acting (the Method), 131

Metro-Goldwyn-Mayer (MGM), 120, 122

Meyers, Michael (movie character), 145

MGM. *See* Metro-Goldwyn-Mayer (MGM)

Midler, Bette, 138

minor studios, American studio system, 120

mise-en-scene (mise-en-scène): aspect ratios, 43; camera angle, 12–16; composition, 18–20; discussed, 5–7, 24; performance as element of, 129–30; the shot, 7–9; space and time on film, 16–18; subject-camera distance, 9–12

Mission: Impossible II (2000), 82

Mitry, Jean, 149, 150

mixing (sound), 77–78

Mizoguchi, Kenji, 118

mobile framing, 24–25. *See also* crane; hand-held shots; moving shots; pan; Steadicam; tilt

model building, 163

model makers, 125

model student paper, 169–85

monochromatic. *See* black-and-white cinematography

Monroe, Marilyn, 9, 134

monster-as-psychotic-human movies, 148

monster movies, 145, 147

montage, 57–60, 60f, 95

Moore, Roger, 132

morphing, 164

motion picture photography, 38

motivated camera movements, 28. *See also* unmotivated camera movements

movement and space on film, 30–33

moving shots, 26

Mozhukin, Ivan, 61

Mulligan, Robert: *Inside Daisy Clover* (1965), 194

Munny, Bill (movie character), 146

Murder, My Sweet (1944), 152f

Murnau, F. W., 33

music (sound on film), 78

musicals, 120

The Naked City (1948), 153

narrative: analyzing conflict, 98–100; character, desire, and conflict, 97–98; defined, 90; scenes and sequences, 91–95; story and plot, 90–91; transitions from scene to scene, 95–97

narrative structure, 89–90, 101–102, 103–104

The Natural (1984), 144
naturalism, 130–31
negative film, 49
neo-noirs, 153
News Corp., 123
Newton, Thandie, 82
Nicholson, Jack, 138
Nielsen, Leslie, 40*f*
Night of the Day of the Dawn of the Son of the Bride of the Return of the Revenge of the Terror of the Attack of the Evil, Mutant, Hellbound, Flesh-Eating Subhumanoid Zombified Living Dead, Part 3 (2005), 148
Night of the Living Dead (1968), 148, 196
No Country for Old Men (2007), 153
Nolan, Christopher: *The Dark Knight* (2008), 155–57
nondiegetic sound, 78, 80, 91. *See also* diegetic sound
nondiegetic space, 32. *See also* diegetic space
non-letterboxed images, 43*f*
nonsynchronized sound, 79
North by Northwest (1959), 144, 162–63, 198
Norton, Edward, 22*f*
Notorious (1946), 121
No Way Out (1950), 153

Oblivion (1994), 147
offscreen sound, 79
offscreen space, 31
OMNIMAX system, 20*n*
Once upon a Time in America (1984), 194
180° system, 67–68, 67*f*
One-Eyed Jacks (1961), 147
On the Waterfront (1954), 131
Ophüls, Max, 33: *Lola Montes* (1955), 188
optical special effects, 162–63
option, 122
The Outlaw Josey Wales (1976), 147
Out of the Past (1947), 153
overcranking, 17. *See also* undercranking
Owen, Clive, 108, 108*f*

Paltrow, Gwyneth, 137
pan, 25
Panavision, 39, 194, 198. *See also* anamorphic lens
Panic in the Streets (1950), 153
Paramount Pictures, 120, 198
Parks, Gordon: *Shaft* (1971), 144
Parton, Dolly, 138
The Passion of Joan of Arc (1928), 12

Pathé, 49
Pearce, Craig, 103
performance: acting styles, 130–31; as element of mise-en-scene, 129–30; film acting distinguished from stage acting, 134–36; publicity and, 136–37; stars and character actors, 131–32; type and stereotype, 132–33; women as types, 133–34
Permutations (1968), 164
persona, 136–37, 137*f*, 194
phase, 83
Phone Booth (2003), 144
physiognomy, 135–36
Pickup on South Street (1953), 153
Pillow Talk (1959), 195
Pirates of the Caribbean series (2003, 2006, 2007), 131
pitch, 83
Pitt, Brad, 131, 137, 137*f*
pixilation, 164
The Pleasure Garden (1925), 121
plot: discussed, 24; distinguished from story, 90–91, 105–106, 111
Plummer, Christopher, 109
Poetics (Aristotle), 105
Polanski, Roman: *Chinatown* (1974), 153, 154
politique des aueurs, 119
positive print, 49
postproduction, 77, 117
Powell, Dick, 152*f*
Preminger, Otto: *Laura* (1944), 81, 152–53; *River of No Return* (1954), 188
Procrustes, 18
producers' role in filmmaking, 121–23
production designer, 124
props master, 124
Psycho (1960), 8, 121, 144, 148, 196
publicity, 136–37
publicity still, 99*f*
Pudovkin, Vsevolod, 59
Pulp Fiction (1994), 132
pyrotechnics, 163

Quasimodo (movie character), 2

Rabinowitz, Jakie (Jack Robin) (movie character), 75
racial issues in films, 111–12, 134
rack focus shots, 52
radio microphones, 76

Raging Bull (1980), 135

Ratatouille (2007), 126

Ray, Nicholas: *Bigger Than Life* (1956), 188;
    Rebel without a Cause (1955), 188

Ray, Satyajit, 118

real time, 17

rear projection, 162–63

Rear Window (1954), 19, 121

Rebecca (1940), 121, 122

Rebel without a Cause (1955), 188

Red River (1948), 120, 121

reel time, 17

reflected sound, 83

reflectors, 47

reframing, 32–33

Regal Cinemas, 123

Renoir, Jean, 118

repetition, 145–46

representation, 1–2

Rescue Dawn (2007), 188

Reservoir Dogs (1992), 132, 153, 154

retakes, 19

reverse angle. *See* shot/reverse-shot pattern

Rhames, Ving, 138

Rio Bravo (1959), 120

River of No Return (1954), 188

RKO, 120

The Robe (1953), 39

Roberts, Julia, 131, 132

Robin, Jack (Jakie Rabinowitz) (movie
    character), 75

Rodat, Robert, 116, 118

Romance & Cigarettes (2005), 84–87, 85*f*

romantic comedies, 195

Romeo + Juliet (1996), 103

Romero, George: *Dawn of the Dead* (1979),
    163–64; *Night of the Living Dead* (1968),
    196

room tone, 80

Rope (1948), 56–57

rotoscope artists, 125

rotoscoping, 165

rough cut, 118

Rule, Ja, 40*f*

rushes. *See* dailies

Russell, Dalton (movie character), 108, 108*f*,
    109, 110, 111, 112, 113, 114

Russell, Jane, 9, 126

Russian Formalism, 91

Sanders, Tom, 117

Sarris, Andrew, 120, 121, 187

Saving Private Ryan (1998), 116, 117, 118

A Scanner Darkly (2006), 165

Scarface (1932), 29–30, 195

Scarlet Street (1945), 153

Scary Movie (2003), 40*f*

scenes, 91–95. *See also* sequences

scene-to-scene editing, 101–102

science fiction films, 162

science fiction westerns, 147, 164

score (musical accompaniments), 77

Scorsese, Martin, 33: *Goodfellas* (1990), 144;
    Raging Bull (1980), 135

screenplays: narrative structure, 103–104;
    samples, 92–94; screenwriting, 104–105;
    segmentation, 105–12

screenwriters, 103, 124

screenwriting, 104–105

screwball comedies, 120, 145

The Searchers (1956), 198

second assistant camera operator, 123, 124, 188

segmentation: defined, 105; depicted,
    108*f*; discussed, 98–100; examples,
    98–99, 108–110; form, 105–107; meaning,
    107–112; writing about, 113–15

Sellers, Peter, 80

Selznick, David O., 122: *Gone with the Wind*
    (1939), 122, 133, 134

semantic study of film genres, 148–50

sequences, 71, 91–95. *See also* scenes

sequence shots, 29

Sergeant York (1941), 120

set decorators, 124

sets, 2

sexual issues in films, 134

Shaft (1971), 144

Shaun of the Dead (2004), 148

Shaw, Robert, 163

shotgun microphones, 76

A Shot in the Dark (1964), 80

shot/reverse-shot pattern, 68–69, 68*f*

shots, 7–9, 21–23

shot-to-shot editing, 70–73

Sidney, George: *Bye Bye Birdie* (1963), 194

The Silence of the Lambs (1991), 148

silent films, 20, 39, 74–75

Skywalker, Luke (movie character), 91

slasher films, 145, 196

slow film, 49

A Song Is Born (1948), 120

Sony, 123

The Sopranos (1999–2007), 132

sound bridges, 79

sound crew, 124

sound effects, 78

sound mixers, 77–78, 124

The Sound of Music (1965), 113

sound on disc, 75

sound on film: analytical categories of, 78–81; analyzing, 84–88; history of, 74–75; recording, rerecording, editing, and mixing, 76–78; space and, 81–83; writing about, 84–88

sound on film system, 75

sound perspective, 83

sound recordist, 124

soundtracks, 17, 76–78, 76f. *See also* image track

Soviet cinema, 58–59

Kuleshov experiment, 60–61, 96

space on film, 16–18, 30–33, 81–83

spaghetti westerns, 147

special effects: analyzing, 166–68; computer-generated imagery (CGI), 164–65; defined, 158; depicted, 159f, 160f, 161f; discussed, 158–62; mechanical special effects, 163–64; optical special effects, 162–63; writing about, 167–68

Spider-Man (2002), 157

Spielberg, Steven, 117, 118: *Jaws* (1975), 163; *Saving Private Ryan* (1998), 116, 117, 118

splatter films: conventions in, 145; examples of, 148, 196; use of makeup for special effects, 163–64

stage acting, 134–36

Stagecoach (1939), 144, 147

Stanislavsky, Konstantin, 193

Stanwyck, Barbara, 134

A Star is Born (1954), 144

stars (actors), 131–32, 133

Stars (Dyer), 132

Star Trek II: The Wrath of Khan (1982), 164

Star Wars (1977), 91, 164

star wipe, 96

Steadicam, 27

stereotype, 132–33

Stewart, James, 17, 131

Stiller, Ben, 135

story: analyzing, 113–15; discussed, 24; distinguished from plot, 90–91, 105–106, 111; writing about, 113–15. *See also* fabula

Strangers on a Train (1951), 121

Strasberg, Lee, 193

Streep, Meryl, 138

A Streetcar Named Desire (1951), 131

studio system, 120–22, 132. *See also* vertical integration

subgenre, 145

subject-camera distance, 9–12

Sunset Boulevard (1950), 9

superimpositions: discussed, 96, 162; dissolves and, 190, 196

Superman (1978), 157

SuperPanavision 70, 198

suspense films, 121

Sweet Sweetback's Baadasssss Song (1971), 144

synchronized sound, 78–79

synchronized sound film, 17

syntatic study of film genres, 148–50

syuzhet, 91. *See also* plot

takes, 8–9. *See also* retakes

talkies (talking pictures), 75

Tarantino, Quentin: *Jackie Brown* (1997), 144; *Pulp Fiction* (1994), 132; *Reservoir Dogs* (1992), 132, 153, 154

Tashlin, Frank: *The Girl Can't Help It* (1956), 80

teamwork in filmmaking, 123–25

Technicolor, 50

Technirama, 198

Techniscope, 198

telephoto lens, 10, 52, 197. *See also* wide-angle lens; zoom

television, 18, 42

The Terror of Tiny Town (1938), 146

Thalberg, Irving, 122

The Thing from Another World (1951), 120

This Is Cinerama (1952), 39, 189

three-act structure, 105

three-point lighting, 45–47, 46f

three-quarter shots, 10

three-shots, 14–15f, 16

thrillers, 144

tilt, 25

timbre, 16, 83

time and space on film, 16–18

tinting, 49

title cards, 74–75

Todd, Mike, 40

Todd-AO, 40, 198

Tohoscope, 198

Toland, Gregg, 51

tone quality. *See* timbre

toning, 49

top lighting, 46

Toto (movie character), 99*f*, 107

Touch of Evil (1958), 29, 153

Tourneur, Jacques: *Out of the Past* (1947), 153

tracking shots, 26, 27

train wrecks (special effects), 158–61

transitions, 55–57, 95–97. *See also* cut; dissolves; fade-in; fade-out; iris-in; iris-out; wipe

traveling mattes, 163. *See also* bluescreen

A Trip to the Moon (1902), 162

Truffaut, François, 119, 121

Turner, Kathleen, 134

Turturro, John: *Romance & Cigarettes* (2005), 84–87, 85*f*

20th Century-Fox, 120, 123, 188

Twentieth Century (1934), 130

20,000 Leagues Under the Sea (1907), 162

2046 (2004), 116

2001: A Space Odyssey (1968), 39*n*, 66–67, 66*f*

two-shots, 14*f*, 16

type, 132–34

UA. *See* United Artists (UA)

Ultraman (2004), 157

UltraPanavision 70, 198

Unconquered (1947), 150

undercranking, 16–17. *See also* overcranking

Unforgiven (1992), 139–42, 140*f*, 146

Un homme de têtes (*The Four Troublesome Heads*, 1898), 161*f*

United Artists (UA), 120

United States v. Paramount Pictures et al., 122

Universal Studios, 120

unmotivated camera movements, 28. *See also* motivated camera movements

Van Doren, Mamie, 134

Van Peebles, Melvin: *Sweet Sweetback's Baadasssss Song* (1971), 144

variation in genres, 146

varifocal lenses, 27

vengence westerns, 147

vertical integration, 122–23

vertical pan. *See* tilt

Vertigo (1958), 121, 164, 166–67, 167*f*, 198

Vertov, Dziga, 59: *Man with a Movie Camera* (1929), 59

VistaVision: aspect ratio, 40, 41*f*; discussed, 39–40; examples of, 198; as widescreen process, 198

voice-over (VO), 81

volume. *See* amplitude

Wahlberg, Mark, 138

Waking Life (2001), 165

Walden Media, 123

Wallis, Hal B., 122

Warner Bros., 120, 122; *The Jazz Singer*, 75

Washington, Denzel, 108, 131, 133

Wayne, John, 121, 132, 133, 146, 150

Wayne's World (1992), 63

Wells, Orson, 119; *Citizen Kane* (1941), 12, 14, 51, 52*f*, 97, 98, 119, 144, 153; *Touch of Evil* (1958), 29, 153

westerns: conventions in, 145–46; defined, 147, 147*n*, 149; examples of, 120, 144, 146, 147, 149–50; role of dialogue, 103; subgenres, 147

Westworld (1973), 147, 164

When Harry Met Sally (1989), 195

Where Danger Lives (1950), 153

Where the Sidewalk Ends (1950), 153

White, Madeleine (movie character), 109, 110, 112, 114

White, Patricia, 80

White Christmas (1954), 39

Whitney, John Sr., 164: *Permutations* (1968), 164

Wicked Witch of the West (movie character), 98, 100, 107

wide-angle lens, 27, 51–52, 198. *See also* telephoto lens; zoom

widescreen processes, 39. *See also* Academy ratio; CinemaScope; Panavision; VistaVision

Wilder, Billy, 12, 118, 119; *The Apartment* (1960), 194; *Double Indemnity* (1944), 152–53; *Sunset Boulevard* (1950), 9

Williams, John, 117
Willow (1988), 164
wipe, 96
wire removal, 164
Witherspoon, Reese, 134
The Wizard of Oz (1939), 97, 98–102, 99*f*, 104, 106–107
Wizard of Oz (movie character), 100
women as types, 133–34
Women's Prison (1955), 144
women's prison movies, 144
The Wonderful World of the Brothers Grimm (1962), 39
Wong Kar-Wai: *2046* (2004), 116
Woo, John: *Mission: Impossible II* (2000), 82
Wood, Robin, 126
Wood, Sam: *Gone with the Wind* (1939), 122
Woodward, Joanne, 131

worldviews of directors, 120–21
writing tips: on acting, 139–42; on camera movement, 34–37; on cinematography, 53–54; on directors, 127–28; on editing, 71–73; on genre, 156–57; on images, 22–23; model student paper, 169–85; on narrative structure, 101–102; on sound and soundtracks, 87–88; on special effects, 167–68; on writing (story segmentation), 113–15
The Wrong Man (1956), 153

York, Kirby, Captain (movie character), 146
Young Frankenstein (1974), 148

zoom, 27. *See also* telephoto lens; wide-angle lens
zoom lens, 52

FILM AND CULTURE

A SERIES OF COLUMBIA UNIVERSITY PRESS

Edited by John Belton

What Made Pistachio Nuts? Early Sound Comedy and the Vaudeville Aesthetic

HENRY JENKINS

Showstoppers: Busby Berkeley and the Tradition of Spectacle

MARTIN RUBIN

Projections of War: Hollywood, American Culture, and World War II

THOMAS DOHERTY

Laughing Screaming: Modern Hollywood Horror and Comedy

WILLIAM PAUL

Laughing Hysterically: American Screen Comedy of the 1950s

ED SIKOV

Primitive Passions: Visuality, Sexuality, Ethnography, and Contemporary Chinese Cinema

REY CHOW

The Cinema of Max Ophuls: Magisterial Vision and the Figure of Woman

SUSAN M. WHITE

Black Women as Cultural Readers

JACQUELINE BOBO

Picturing Japaneseness: Monumental Style, National Identity, Japanese Film

DARRELL WILLIAM DAVIS

Attack of the Leading Ladies: Gender, Sexuality, and Spectatorship in Classic Horror Cinema

RHONA J. BERENSTEIN

This Mad Masquerade: Stardom and Masculinity in the Jazz Age

GAYLYN STUDLAR

Sexual Politics and Narrative Film: Hollywood and Beyond

ROBIN WOOD

The Sounds of Commerce: Marketing Popular Film Music
JEFF SMITH

Orson Welles, Shakespeare, and Popular Culture
MICHAEL ANDEREGG

Pre-Code Hollywood: Sex, Immorality, and Insurrection in American Cinema, 1930–1934
THOMAS DOHERTY

Sound Technology and the American Cinema: Perception, Representation, Modernity
JAMES LASTRA

Melodrama and Modernity: Early Sensational Cinema and Its Contexts
BEN SINGER

Wondrous Difference: Cinema, Anthropology, and Turn-of-the-Century Visual Culture
ALISON GRIFFITHS

Hearst Over Hollywood: Power, Passion, and Propaganda in the Movies
LOUIS PIZZITOLA

Masculine Interests: Homoerotics in Hollywood Film
ROBERT LANG

Special Effects: Still in Search of Wonder
MICHELE PIERSON

Designing Women: Cinema, Art Deco, and the Female Form
LUCY FISCHER

Cold War, Cool Medium: Television, McCarthyism, and American Culture
THOMAS DOHERTY

Katharine Hepburn: Star as Feminist
ANDREW BRITTON

Silent Film Sound
RICK ALTMAN

Home in Hollywood: The Imaginary Geography of Cinema
ELISABETH BRONFEN

Hollywood and the Culture Elite: How the Movies Became American
PETER DECHERNEY

Taiwan Film Directors: A Treasure Island
EMILIE YUEH-YU YEH AND DARRELL WILLIAM DAVIS

Shocking Representation: Historical Trauma, National Cinema, and the Modern Horror Film
ADAM LOWENSTEIN

China on Screen: Cinema and Nation
CHRIS BERRY AND MARY FARQUHAR

The New European Cinema: Redrawing the Map
ROSALIND GALT

George Gallup in Hollywood
SUSAN OHMER

Electric Sounds: Technological Change and the Rise of Corporate Mass Media
STEVE J. WURTZLER

The Impossible David Lynch
TODD MCGOWAN

Sentimental Fabulations, Contemporary Chinese Films: Attachment in the Age of Global Visibility
REY CHOW

Hitchcock's Romantic Irony
RICHARD ALLEN

Intelligence Work: The Politics of American Documentary
JONATHAN KAHANA

Eye of the Century: Film, Experience, Modernity
FRANCESCO CASETTI

Shivers Down Your Spine: Cinema, Museums, and the Immersive View
ALISON GRIFFITHS

Weimar Cinema: An Essential Guide to Classic Films of the Era
NOAH ISENBERG

African Film and Literature: Adapting Violence to the Screen
LINDIWE DOVEY

Film, A Sound Art
MICHEL CHION

Hollywood Lighting from the Silent Era to Film Noir
PATRICK KEATING

Levinas and the Cinema of Redemption: Time, Ethics, and the Feminine
SAM B. GIRGUS